JUN - 4 2008

CHILD POVERTY IN AMERICA TODAY

CHILD POVERTY IN AMERICA TODAY

Volume 4: Children and the State

Edited by Barbara A. Arrighi and David J. Maume

Praeger Perspectives

Westport, Connecticut
London

Library of Congress Cataloging-in-Publication Data

Child poverty in America today / edited by Barbara A. Arrighi and David J. Maume.
    p. cm.
    Includes bibliographical references and index.
    ISBN 978–0–275–98926–2 (set : alk. paper)—ISBN 978–0–275–98927–9 (v. 1 : alk. paper)—
ISBN 978–0–275–98928–6 (v. 2 : alk. paper)—ISBN 978–0–275–98929–3 (v. 3 : alk. paper)—
ISBN 978–0–275–98930–9 (v. 4 : alk. paper)
    1. Poor children—United States.   2. Poor families—United States.   3. Poverty—United States.
    4. Child welfare—United States.   5. Children—United States—Social conditions.
    6. Children—Government policy—United States.   I. Arrighi, Barbara A.   II. Maume, David J.
HV741.C4875   2007
362.7086′9420973–dc22   2007003046

British Library Cataloguing in Publication Data is available.

Library of Congress Catalog Card Number: 2007003046
ISBN-10: 0–275–98926–7 (set)   ISBN-13: 978–0–275–98926–2 (set)
          0–275–98927–5 (vol. 1)   978–0–275–98927–9 (vol. 1)
          0–275–98928–3 (vol. 2)   978–0–275–98928–6 (vol. 2)
          0–275–98929–1 (vol. 3)   978–0–275–98929–3 (vol. 3)
          0–275–98930–5 (vol. 4)   978–0–275–98930–9 (vol. 4)

First published in 2007

Praeger Publishers, 88 Post Road West, Westport, CT 06881
An imprint of Greenwood Publishing Group, Inc.
www.praeger.com

Printed in the United States of America

The paper used in this book complies with the
Permanent Paper Standard issued by the National
Information Standards Organization (Z39.48–1984).

10 9 8 7 6 5 4 3 2 1

To our children
Eiler, Elena, and Megan
and
Meghan and Allison
Our concern for their welfare piqued our interest in the
welfare of all children.

CONTENTS

ACKNOWLEDGMENTS

First, we wish to thank all the contributors to the four volumes for the exceptional caliber of their research. Their dedication and commitment to understanding the causes of child and family poverty is remarkable. It has been a pleasure to work with such a fine group of scholars. It is noteworthy, too, that more than a few of the contributors endured family emergencies and/or experienced personal crises during the research and writing phase, yet remained committed to the project. For that, we are grateful.

We are honored that Diana Pearce is the author of the Introduction for Volume 1: Families and Children. Professor Pearce has written a thoughtful essay weaving common threads among diverse chapters. She is a tireless researcher who has been a pioneer in examining the causes and effects of poverty in the lives of women and children. Not only has Professor Pearce illuminated the way for other researchers in explaining the complex factors influencing women's poverty, she has been an ardent advocate for ending the feminization of poverty.

Thanks to Rachel Sebastian, graduate student at the University of Cincinnati, who assisted with the project. We appreciate, too, the guidance of Elizabeth Potenza, editor at Praeger, throughout the editorial process, Anne Rehill who assisted early on in the project, Nicole Azze, production manager, Vivek Sood and Saloni Jain who oversaw the copyediting. Finally, thanks to Marie Ellen Larcada, who first approached Barbara about editing the four-volume set.

INTRODUCTION

Barbara A. Arrighi

Give me your tired, your poor, your huddled masses yearning to breathe free the wretched refuse of your teeming shore. send these, the homeless, tempest-tost to me, I lift my lamp beside the golden door!

Emma Lazarus "The New Colossus"

Lazarus's words have been welcoming all who enter New York harbor for decades; however, the same cannot be said of the policies and practices of the United States. Over the course of U.S. history, too often, laws have been less than generous for those who were sick, poor, and/or old. For example, as early as 1720 New Jersey enacted a law that allowed ships to be searched for the elderly, especially older widows who didn't have any means of support.[1]

A century later, Liwwat Boke, a German immigrant who lived between 1807 and 1882, reported her observations of the treatment of the poor, sick, and the elderly in her grueling 75-day voyage from Germany to America. Boke wrote: "when the ship reached land . . . no one is let off the ship except those who had paid their travel cost . . . The others . . . had to stay until they were sold . . . No buyers bought the sick, the blind, or the elderly. Healthy persons were bought at once. The suffering and the crippled often lay on the ship two or three weeks until they died. The chosen one is bound in writing on paper for 5 or 10 years; they can't read English . . . Families are broken up, children are lost!"[2] Boke's words describe an American welcome at variance with Lazarus's, yet both capture a part of America: Come able, prepared to work hard, and be self-sufficient.

The notion of self-sufficiency in the United States has its roots in the views of Herbert Spencer,[3] an Englishman, and his followers who, in the 1800s, advocated Social Darwinism—survival of the fittest. Spencer's ideas were imported to the United

States by the likes of William Graham Sumner[4] who believed the fittest humans survive and thrive because of their ability to adapt to their environment. Conversely, those who cannot adapt will not survive. From the perspective of Social Darwinists, any form of external intervention in the struggle to survive operates against natural selection and weakens society. Amos Griswold Warner, perhaps the first to publish a social welfare tome, argued that welfare was an "... expense to the community, and the degradation and increased pauperization to the poor."[5] Warner, like the others, maintained that providing help for those in poverty would be detrimental to society.

Over time, aspects of Social Darwinism have remained part of the national discourse about the poor. Vestiges of it can be found in Congressional and presidential debates concerning welfare, Medicaid, food stamps, and other social programs. Thus, there exists tension between Social Darwinism and the notion of the *deserving* poor that gets played out in policy debates. Should it be government's responsibility to provide for its citizens or just some of its citizens? Who? How much assistance? For example, in the last century many programs were established for those considered to be the *deserving poor*. One program, Aid for Dependent Children, was passed by Congress in 1935 to provide assistance to widows with children. Other programs like Social Security and Medicare were implemented, although not without resistance, to help lift the elderly (a *deserving* group) out of poverty.

The resistance of the United States to become a "welfare state" sets it apart from other industrialized countries, especially concerning families and children. Embedded in the political and economic structures of other countries are pro-family policies that reflect a philosophy that children are societal resources who represent an investment in the future. The policies illustrate a collective belief that whatever the circumstances of birth (whether poor, within or out of wedlock), if the youngest and most vulnerable citizens have a healthy start in life, they will become healthier, productive adult citizens. In turn, healthy citizens foster stronger societies.

The United States, on the other hand, is beholden to the ideology of individualism and vestiges of the survival of the fittest. Encapsulated within both is the belief that if a person has the "the right stuff," success will come. From this perspective, success is primarily dependent upon an individual's gene pool and the will to succeed. Adherence to individualism means societal factors matter only somewhat in one's life—one's present or past socioeconomic status has little or no bearing on future outcomes. Individualism, as such, is compatible with a *blame the victim* stance—the individual is poor because s/he lacks ambition and motivation. Then, too, individualism perpetuates a rags-to-riches mythology that the middle- and upper-class structures are more permeable than they, in fact, are.

If anything the evidence suggests, instead, an increasing gap between the wealthy and poor. The Brookings Institute found that in the 100 largest metropolitan areas the percentage of middle-income neighborhoods declined by 41 percent and central cities, which had a 45 percent share of middle class in the 1970, now had only 23 percent.[6] If, as expected in the next 10 years, over half of the fastest job growth will be in low-wage occupations, moving out of poverty will be less likely for families.[7]

Although the job and city evidence reflect systemic economic conditions beyond individual solutions, during the last two decades, U.S. policymakers have frequently blamed families for their economic downslide. Indeed, policymakers have frequently questioned the values of U.S. families. The rhetoric often reaches fever pitch at the height of political seasons. The closer the race, the more intense the finger pointing. In one presidential election of the 1980s, a vice-presidential candidate even cited the out-of-wedlock TV birth on a sitcom as somehow contributing to the rise of unmarried parenthood. Earlier in the same decade, a presidential hopeful referred to "welfare queens" who were, in his mind, milking the system by staying at home with their children, rather than working in a paid job.

In the 1990s, a Democratic presidential candidate stole the thunder of the Republican Party by appropriating its Welfare Reform platform. The campaign sound bytes implied that families living in poverty were shirking their responsibility and must be made accountable. The title of the legislation eventually resulting from that election: The Personal Responsibility and Work Opportunity Reconciliation Act, arguably reflects the attitude of policy makers. Bill Clinton, who was elected President, in large part, due to his Welfare Reform stance, decreed that people with children who worked 40 hours a week would rise out of poverty.[8] He said: ". . . this legislation provides a historic opportunity . . . by promoting the fundamental values of work, responsibility, and family."[9]

It is true, that millions of people have been removed from welfare within the last decade. It is also a fact that millions of people who were poor on welfare have now joined the working poor ". . . and a portion of them are significantly worse off than before," says Evelyn Ganzglass, of the Center for Law and Social Policy.[10] If, as reported, the median wage of a mom who transitions from welfare to work is about $8.00 an hour, her gross wage (if she worked 40 hours a week) would be $15,406 a year. Although her annual income would then be more than the income ($11,800) of a family receiving welfare, she would still be poor.[11] The difference: Now she has to pay for childcare, if it is available (and not necessarily high quality care), her food stamp allotment will be cut, she will have to rely on food pantries to make up the food insufficiency, she will spend less time with her children and she will now work a *second shift* (paid work on the job and unpaid work at home). For those who earn less than $8.00 an hour, the situation is even more critical. The bottom line is: "using a variety of measures, relatively more U.S. children are born into disadvantaged environments compared to 40 years ago"[12] The safety net essentially has been removed for poor families and it would appear that policymakers on both sides of the aisle no longer view moms and their children as the *deserving poor*.

Every 4 years politicians spend an inordinate amount of time drawing voters' attention to just 3 to 4 percent of the federal budget—the part that addresses the 13 million children who live in poverty (20 percent of whom are under age 6, 20 percent who live in extreme poverty, and the 17 percent of households with children who experience food insecurity)—and vow to hold down the spending on such "entitlements." During the 2004 presidential campaign, a year in which billions of dollars were unaccounted and/or misspent by independent contractors in Iraq, the focus of the 2004 election once again was family values not government waste.

Political candidates will use "value baiting" as long as it wins elections, but the more important question is: Does the United States value *all* of its families or just some families? What are the values of a nation that allows 13 million children to live in poverty, of which 2 million live in extreme poverty? Currently, U.S. welfare policies focus on the so-called pathology of "needy" families, a term that implies inherent, negative familial characteristics. A more fruitful way to pose the question is: Why are so many families in "need" in the midst of so much plenty? Useful analyses of poverty require examining the systemic constraints that hold families down while at the same time policy measures are passed that allow some families to thrive. A useful analysis includes an examination of the political, educational, and economic institutions within which family life is played out day-by-day.

For example, since 1979 the after-tax income of the wealthiest Americans jumped 370 times that of the lowest income. The change for the wealthy cannot be explained simply by individual characteristics. It represents, in part, systemic tax law changes implemented by Congress. On the other hand, a proposal to raise the minimum wage from \$5.15 to \$7.25 an hour over the next 3 years—which would have represented a systemic change—was defeated in the Senate in 2006. It is instructive that even if the bill passes it would provide families just over *half* the costs of raising two children. One could ask what kind of values are at work in Congress—a body that has voted 6 pay raises in the last 10 years for its members, while the minimum wage has not been raised once in the same time period.

One way to answer that question is to offer a comparative analysis of the families and children policies enacted by other industrialized societies. Table I.1 illustrates just a few basic forms of assistance that nation states provide for children and families. Although not an exhaustive list, it is revealing. All information was obtained from the Clearinghouse on International Development in Child, Youth, and Family Policies at Columbia University.[13]

Because fertility rates in Western industrialized countries are below replacement level, many of the policies are meant to encourage pro-natalist behavior and therefore, increase the fertility rate. Countries like France, Italy, and Sweden have made deliberate pro-family decisions. Sweden has the most generous benefits for children and families and as a result has the lowest child poverty of all the countries listed. Sweden's 14-week maternity leave and 18-month parental leave with 80 percent of one's pay for 13 months are unparalleled. Sweden also allows parents to have up to 60 days off a year to care for a sick child or if the child's caretaker is ill.

In France prenatal and birthing expenses are paid by the state. Parents have available a 16 week, 100 percent paid leave and time off from work increases with the number of children. Then, too, France has universal, free preschool for 2- to 6-year-olds. In addition to a 5-month leave with 80 percent of one's wages, Italy also provides working mothers a 2-hour rest period per day for the first year of a child's life. Although Germany lags behind the other countries, especially in child care policies and early childhood education (Germany has part-time kindergarten), one policy

Table I.1

Cross National Comparison of Selected Family Policies for Seven Advanced Industrialized Countries*

Country	Maternity	Sick Leave	ECFC[a]	Health	Child Care	Direct Benefits
Canada	Maternity 50 weeks 55% of average weekly (80% for low wage) (Prenatal & postnatal covered)	6 weeks for gravely ill child/spouse/parent	Kindergarten 1/2 day	Universal (Provinces vary in coverage)	"Fragmented Data" Mostly unregulated family day care private pay	(Means-tested) Nat'l Child Benefit and Child Tax Benefit (80% of Fams.)
Germany	14-week benefit (Mom's earn pension 3 yrs. Credit equal to 3 years of work) Parental leave—2 years (income tested)	10 days per year, sick child <12 years old	3–5 years old 1/2 day	Mandated 90% population Preventive health care for children	Subsidized pre-school 1/2 day	Universal until 18 years of age Low-wage more (Child Tax Allow.) (Educ. Tax Allow.)
Italy	5 months paid Job protected	6 months job protected 30% of pay for sick/ disabled child	3–6 years old federal Paid 95%	Universal: children to age 12	Publicly funded/ Operated 3 months to 3 years old	Cash allow. (means-tested)
France	16 weeks (6 Pre-/10 Post-) Increases with no. of children (Universal maternity/ childbirth allow)	5 days for kids < 16 years old	2–6 years old Free	National: children < 19 years old	Public 3 months through 2 years old 1/4 paid by family	Cash (Not means-tested)

	Maternity leave	Family/sick leave	Early childhood education*	Health	Child care	Cash benefits
UK	26 weeks paid/job protected 26 weeks unpaid/job protected	13 weeks ill child Parental leave	Creating universal schools 3–4 year olds Part-time	National health	Few children in out-of-home care	Child benefit Work tax credit
US	No national maternity	12 weeks family leave unpaid Job protected (Companies with 50 or more employees)	No national Head Start (Means tested)	No national Medicaid <19 year old (Means tested) SCHIPS children	Subsidized (Means Tested)	Means-tested: Food stamps Public housing Earned income credit Child care credit
Sweden	14 weeks parental 2 weeks paternity Parental leave 18 months (80% of wages for 13 months)	60 days for ill child or ill caregiver	Publicly funded (municipalities must provide)	National for children	Universal	Housing allowance Child allowance

*Early Childhood Education and Care.
Source: The Clearing House on International Development in Child, Youth and Family Policies US, (2004 Germany) (2005 Sweden, Canada, France, Italy, UK).

worth noting is a 3-year state contribution to mothers' pension funds when mothers choose to stay home with their children for up to 3 years.

The table shows that the United States' closest ally, the United Kingdom, has a limited family-friendly system. Even at that, it is the United States that stands out as having the fewest family-friendly policies. The United States has no maternity leave per se. The Family Medical Leave provides for 12 weeks unpaid leave; however, the policy applies only to companies that have 50 or more employees. The United States has no national health care system, no national day care, and no national early education program except Head Start (a means-tested program unless a child is disabled). The United States does have Medicaid (a means-tested health care program) and a federal/state children's health insurance plan (SCHIP) for low-income children not covered by other health plans. Not only does the United States stand alone in the paucity of programs, but what programs do exist are not universal, as many are in other countries. One program that has been touted as a success by U.S. policy makers is the Earned Income Tax Credit (EITC) that allows low-income families to receive a portion of their taxes back. Though welcomed by those who can take advantage of it, families living on the edge have severe cash flow problems and should not be made to wait for a tax return to be able to pay for rent, heat, or groceries. One study found evidence that, in fact, 83 percent of families use the EITC to pay for their family's basic needs.[14]

Although the U.S. federal government has been reluctant to institutionalize universal family-friendly programs, some states are taking the lead. For example, California has enacted a paid 6-week leave at 55 percent of wages for births or illness. Unlike the U.S. Senate, California passed a measure to raise the minimum wage by $1.25 over the next few years. Other states have put minimum wage initiatives on their ballots. Massachusetts recently passed legislation to create statewide universal health insurance. A few states are considering paid leave for parents to attend children's school meetings and proposing tax credits to employers who offer family time off.[15]

The contributions of the authors in this text represent disparate analyses of systemic fault lines beneath families living on the edge—issues addressing the creation of better housing for families, research about how children in foster care have fared since the implementation of Welfare Reform, teens and inadequate shelter life, the unmet needs of children who are refugees, as well as the structured educational disparities in the public schools in the United States, especially for poor minority students. Although seemingly disconnected, taken together, the collective analyses shed light on a pattern of systemic failure to support children and families, especially those living in poverty. Each author offers recommendations for future directions.

Although ethnographic methods provide qualitative evidence, Armaline's analysis of an emergency shelter addresses the intersection of structured inequalities—race, class, and gender—for teens without homes. Families, especially single moms and kids, make up 40 percent of those without homes. Armaline reports that two systemic factors have precipitated increased homelessness: rising unemployment and the continued elimination of low-income housing stock in cities.

However, at the shelter level, Armaline finds that staff members treat the *social* problem of homelessness as the *individual's* trouble, clearly demonstrating a lack of what Mills refers to as sociological imagination. Thus, the focus of shelter treatment for teens is a program designed to facilitate the child fitting in and getting on track. Rather than addressing the causes and conditions of poverty—the extra familial, the staff's focus is on the teens' *unproductive responses*—the intra—to poverty. In this way the system remains intact, unchallenged and the individual is to be changed.

Wells analyzes the effect of welfare reform for families living in poverty in Cuyahoga County, specifically, those coping with issues of foster care. Wells notes that the child welfare system isn't in business to enhance the lives of families and children, but rather exists simply for the purpose of child protection. Wells' research finds a pattern: foster care children tend to be from impoverished homes with more than 75 percent falling below the poverty level. The mothers lacked transportation, a high school diploma, and have insecure housing arrangements. Before welfare reform, over 124,000 families received cash assistance; 4 years later, a little over 34,000 did. While politicians, policy wonks, and pundits extolled the declining welfare numbers, families suffered.

It is well established that child welfare policies aren't enacted to revolutionize the economic and political systems. If the system is ok, then it must be the individual who needs changing. If policy makers and social workers begin with the premise that the poor need to be changed, then mining for familial pathology yields individual problems (private troubles) and individual solutions. Welfare Reform of 1996, touted as the panacea to end poverty by making families responsible, limited assistance to families and shifted much of the fiscal responsibility for the poor to states. If Cuyahoga County is any indication, it hasn't made the lives of poorly educated women and their children any better. In fact, from Wells' analyses, it appears that under welfare reform in Cuyahoga County, foster care has been significantly extended for low-income children because fewer resources are available to help stabilize the families.

Henrici, Angel, and Lein's chapter uses an ethnographic study (part of a three-wave survey of 2400 families) and the interview of one participant to illustrate the multiple variables—education, health, housing, employment, child care, transportation issues—that often are the reason families stay impoverished. It could be viewed as an elaboration of issues families in Wells' study might have faced before becoming completely destabilized. The low-wage jobs that exist for poorly educated single mothers end up being more costly to them than beneficial because of the lack of child care and transportation. There are costs, too, from the physical and emotional demands of low-wage service jobs. Then, too, low-end jobs often require irregular hours, increasing the difficulty of obtaining child care. The authors maintain that in the face of the obstacles that Teresa (the interviewee) and others who share her experience, it is difficult to achieve familial stability. With the federal and state budget cuts to means-tested programs, the authors are warranted in their concern about the risk of intergenerational poverty.

Using a random sample of families in six California counties who reached their maximum time on Temporary Assistance for Needy Families (TANF), Gilbert-Mauldon, London, and Sommer ended up with 1,058 respondents. The researchers uncover the complexity of poverty and multiple variables that impact families' ability to escape it—physical and mental health factors, family members with health issues, no public transportation. The researchers found that 60 percent of those without any barriers to employment—physical and/or mental health factors, transportation, housing issues, child-care problems—were employed. They found, too, that the more barriers, the less likely respondents were employed. Only 9 percent of those with four barriers were employed at the time of Wave 3 of the study. The authors conclude that CalWorks—California's welfare program provided a "cushion" for families who reached the 5-year limit of TANF, but have barriers to employment that California recognizes including: having a disability, caring for an ill or incapacitated person in one's home, being a victim of domestic violence, residing in a high-unemployment reservation or rancheria, or participating in a teen–parent welfare program. Gilbert-Mauldon, London, and Sommer's research is rich in the data they present to the reader, but a key factor in their study is that state and federal legislatures enact policies that impact families in need and decide a course of action based on the ideology of individualism or civitas. California has opted for less individualistic policies and implemented more humanistic policies for their families than those that exist at the federal level.

Curley's chapter analyzes the issue of concentrated neighborhood poverty. Federal programs in the 1970s provided the means for families living in poverty to move to white higher-income neighborhoods and had a positive effect on educational achievement for children and employment patterns for the mothers. The premise is that neighborhood matters. Curley's study presents more recent efforts, specifically, a five-city program implemented by HUD called: Moving to Opportunity (MTO) that relocates families to better neighborhoods and HOPE VI, a program initiated in 1993 to redevelop "failed" housing projects. Curley's findings illustrate how complex poverty is. While there is evidence that a "better neighborhood" improved mental health, there has been little positive impact on other basic needs areas and, to some extent, may have even had a negative effect on social networks and health of boys. However, Curley notes that the children may be the ultimate beneficiary of HOPE VI and MTO.

Three chapters provide analyses of public education in the United States, but from different vantage points. Tajalli's chapter offers an historical analysis of education as a source of inequality; Flores provides some historical background for her discussion of the No Child Left Behind Act of 2001. Finally, Duncan and Wolfe's chapter is a treatise on public education, but especially for black children living in poverty.

Tajalli examines the systemic inequities of public education and provides a discussion of the ideological roots of public education—from ideas of liberty and social justice to what he sees as failed neoconservativism. He points to the narrow, market-oriented approach today in public education in which blacks and Hispanic students are not segregated by law but by wealth. Blacks and Hispanic students are concentrated in high-poverty schools that have escalated de facto segregation and the inequities of public education.

A comprehensive analysis of the No Child Left Behind Act of 2001 is provided by Flores. A careful historical overview of public education in the United

States reveals that the major purpose was to ameliorate poverty and crime. Initially, it was offered to young children and then to adolescents as means for assimilating recent immigrants. Some children were excluded, some marginalized. By 1954, the Supreme Court ruled that segregation was illegal and Flores chronicles the subsequent legislative initiatives over the years to right the historical wrongs. For example, 12 years after Brown versus the Board of Education, President Lyndon Johnson signed a law authorizing federal funds to aid students deprived of an education. One program instituted was Head Start. Then in the 1980s, "A Nation at Risk" reported the deficiencies of public education, but little was done to effect change.

In 1994, President Clinton signed the Improving America's Schools Act to improve education for disadvantaged children. And in 2001, President Bush's No Child Left Behind was enacted to close the achievement between children's whose parents are poor and children whose parents are middle class. However, down Flores points out that the effect has been for teachers to teach to the test, watering down academic content. She reports that there is some evidence that students are not becoming better readers, but are learning a limited vocabulary and basic level reading skills. Flores also critiques the voucher system for those wishing to transfer from a low-performing school as not sufficient for full tuition of higher quality school.

Duncan and Wolfe' have written a cogent analyses addressing the state of public education in the United States especially as it continues to disadvantage black children living in poverty. The authors cite numerous variables including: funding inqualities, the lack of black educators, white flight to private schools, under-qualified teachers, dated curriculum, lack of modern technology even when it's available, resegregation within schools and within courses, adultrification of young black boys, and underfunding of No Child Left Build. Finally, the authors pay homage to the remarkable feat of countless unsung heroes whom they refer to as "gap closers"—those who are able to elicit academic excellence from students who have been summarily "written off" by the educational system.

Finally, in an insightful and thorough discussion of the difficulties that refugee parents and children face while attempting to adjust to life in the United States, Xu and Pearson examine Somali and Somali Bantu families in Denver, Colorado, in 2004. The difficulties stem not only from the differences between Somali and United States culture (though many), many of the problems stem from the inadequacy of U.S. policies for aiding in the settlement of refugee families. Refugee families are expected to become employed and self-sufficient within the first 8 months of their arrival as refugee cash assistance and refugee medical assistance are provided up to that point. Although families struggle with English, after 8 months, they must obtain Temporary Assistance for Needy Families. Xu and Pearson note that children's needs and needs assessment are not spelled out in the refugee resettlement program. The authors note that the number one priority for refugee resettlement is employment. The emphasis on employment harkens back to the notion of individualism and the need to be self-sufficient; however, is it a realistic expectation for those who have been traumatized to the point that they have sought refuge in a foreign country? Is it a realistic expectation for those who have language barriers and dramatic cultural differences?

NOTES

1. David Fisher, *Growing Old in America* (New York: Oxford University Press, 1977)

2. Luke B. Knapke, editor, *Liwwat Boke 1807–1882 Pioneer* (Minster, Ohio: The Minster Historical Society, 1987), 51.

3. Richard Hofstadter, *Social Darwinism in American Thought* (New York: Braziller, 1959).

4. Bruce Curtis, *William Graham Sumner* (Boston, MA: Twayne).

5. David Wessel, "In Poverty Tactics: An Old Debate: Who Is At Fault," *The Wall Street Journal* (June 15, 2006), 1, A10.

6. Janny Scott, "Cities Shed Middle Class, And Are Richer and Poorer for It," *The New York Times* (July 23, 2006), 1, 4 wk.

7. Ibid.

8. Wessel, "In Poverty Tactics, An Old Debate: Who Is at Fault?"

9. "Welfare Reform: Ten Years Later," *The Wall Street Journal*, August 26–27, 2006, A9.

10. Ibid.

11. Ibid.

12. James J. Heckman, "Catch 'em Young," *The Wall Street Journal* (January 10, 2006), A14.

13. The Clearinghouse on International Developments in Child, Youth and Family Policies, Columbia University, available at www.childpolicyintl.org/countries/.

14. "Family Income & Jobs: Raising Children Out of Poverty," *State of America's Children 2005* (Washington, DC: Children's Defense Fund), chapter 1, 22.

15. "Some States Consider Paid Family Leave," *The Cincinnati Enquirer* (June 16, 2006), A10.

CHAPTER 1

(RE)CONCEPTUALIZING ADOLESCENT HOMELESSNESS: MISDIRECTION OF THE STATE AND CHILD WELFARE

William T. Armaline

Conventional definitions of homelessness (roughly, those without consistent shelter of their own) are at best incomplete in defining the conditions of adolescents[1] who populate city streets and shelters. Studies of homelessness typically focus on adult and family populations, without giving much attention to the unique experience of unaccompanied minors whose homeless experience may also be defined by periods of exposure to child welfare agencies. The inadequacies of conventional approaches to homelessness became quite clear to me while conducting qualitative research at an emergency youth shelter for adolescents (Faulk House). Drawing from relevant literature and ethnographic field work conducted at Faulk House emergency shelter, I address the following questions here concerning adolescent homelessness and the connection between marginalized adolescents and the state: *What would a useful, accurate conceptualization of "adolescent homelessness" include? How might this inform child welfare policy and the role of child welfare agencies in the treatment of marginalized youth?*

I (re)conceptualize adolescent homelessness as a (re)produced social problem that may be primarily understood as an expression of intersecting structured inequalities (along lines of class, "race,"[2] and gender). The defining characteristics of adolescent homelessness are tied to and shaped by child welfare policies, an interaction with or aversion to child welfare agencies, and patterns in child removal. Data collected at Faulk House shelter supports the (re)conceptualization offered here, as it is consistent with the narratives and observations of shelter residents and staff. Further, data from Faulk House and recent studies of the foster care system suggest that child welfare systems (the state) take an approach of child "protection," implicating adolescent homelessness as the result of individual pathologies (of guardians or youth involved). Finally, I argue that this approach is problematic in that it fails to 'treat,' and potentially exacerbates adolescent homelessness as a *social* problem linked to (re)produced inequalities.

Existing demographic information and academic research on youth and adult homelessness tend to employ a conventional, or "literal" definition of homelessness as, "those who sleep in shelters provided for homeless persons or in places, private or public, not intended as dwellings."[3] While many of these studies[4] point to the importance of researching and alleviating literal homelessness, (1) conventional definitions of homelessness are conceptually insufficient to explain the full range of experiences unique to ambiguously labeled "homeless" adolescent populations; (2) the experience of adolescents and adults differ in their connection to structured inequalities and their options out of poverty and marginalization, which exclude (for the most part) entrance into the formal labor market.

LITERAL HOMELESSNESS IN THE UNITED STATES

Families (particularly single women of color with children) and children are still the fastest growing homeless populations in the United States and are generally the largest poverty-stricken groups.[5] Under the current federal administration homeless populations have expanded largely due to rising un/underemployment rates and elevated housing costs.[6] In an atmosphere of state fiscal crises and the funneling of federal spending away from social services toward "national security" and the military industrial complex, the G.W. Bush administration has done little to combat the rising number of dislocated adults, families, and children. For example, the department of Housing and Urban Development (HUD) received an increase of $35 million while Congress simultaneously cut public housing operating funds by 30 percent in mid-January of 2003. "To give a sense of how much that means in Washington budgetary terms, $35 million is equal to the money set aside to help keep insects from crossing the border."[7] In sum, conditions for those who are homeless or "at-risk" are becoming more and more difficult in the context of rising poverty and shrinking welfare benefits.[8]

Meanwhile, many efforts have been made on the part of local and state politicians to sweep homelessness under the rug in many large U.S. cities such as New York, Chicago, and Seattle.[9] Problems faced by homeless populations have "not provoked the outcry that the rise in homelessness did in the 1980s . . . You don't see homeless people as much as you did in the '80s because the one great policy initiative of the past 20 years has been to move them from grates into the newest form of the poorhouse, the shelter."[10] As a result of antivagrancy laws, many U.S. cities have also detained and/or incarcerated homeless populations, keeping them (temporarily) out of the public eye at public cost.

Children make up 40 percent of the nation's "literally" homeless population, and for the time they remain without homes or families, and for indeterminate periods of time after, homelessness may be the defining feature of their lives.[11] Studies of homeless families by the Department of Education and by those in the field of social work suggest that homeless children face a number of challenges both academically and socially.[12] These challenges include "exhaustion, lack of time and a place to do homework, coordinating school schedules with work schedules, instability, out of school periods, frequent changes of school, and stigmatization,"[13] not to mention any number of potential problems associated with extreme poverty (such as not having resources for nutrition or medical care). Further, homeless youth are disenfranchised by the competitive/corporate structure of schooling, which systematically discriminates against poor and transient groups of youth.[14] For example, contemporary educational policies such as those outlined in the No Child Left Behind Act[15] emphasize "high-stakes" and proficiency testing as primary measures for educational credentialing. Where success on these tests is dependent on a consistent exposure to test-related curriculum, cultural capital, and household resource, they have been shown to disenfranchise poor youth—especially in non-"white" communities.[16] Youth without consistent shelter often spend periods of time out of school, transfer schools more often than other youth, and experience the multitude of problems related to severe poverty, educational credentialing, and establishing self-sufficiency.

Literal homelessness can then be viewed as a barrier to youths' educational and economic success, and a contributing factor to the reproduction of socioeconomic inequality. As such, "literal" youth homelessness is an important issue for sociological inquiry geared to inform and influence social policy.[17] It is somewhat simple to recognize poverty and homelessness among young populations as "bad" for the well-being of affected communities. Still, efforts to define and theoretically conceptualize youth or adolescent "homelessness" as a unique social phenomenon that goes beyond "literal" homelessness have proven difficult and largely unsuccessful in various fields of research. Logically, this contributes to our collective inability to address it.

A CHALLENGE TO CONVENTIONAL EXPLANATIONS OF "LITERAL" HOMELESSNESS AND POVERTY: MATTERS OF AGE AND STATE INTERVENTION

Sociological work on the topic of youth homelessness, specifically those unaccompanied by or separated from parents, is virtually nonexistent. "There is relatively little written [on homeless children], and the studies that do exist refer primarily to children living with their parents in shelters."[18] Media coverage and mainstream studies of homelessness largely fuse adult, youth, and family populations into a single category that typically describes "street" populations. In what is still considered a fundamental work on adult homelessness, Snow and Anderson[19] investigate how different groups of adults become homeless, and how each group deals with the realities of homeless life and rationalize their own existence on the street. Their work highlights the issue of inadequate resources and ineffective social programs for those affected to obtain and sustain shelter. For instance, Snow and Anderson point to a lack of reasonable employment and the various barriers that homeless adults encounter in getting and keeping jobs. While their research and others like it provide insight for understanding adult homelessness, the experience of homeless youth must be seen quite differently.

To a degree, the socioeconomic situation of impoverished youth can be related to the problems of un/underemployment and poverty among adult guardians. In other words, it points to the connection between poverty and homelessness for all of those unable to afford sustainable housing. But this approach cannot explain the experience of youth who, once disenfranchised from home and school, cannot look to the formal labor market for options out of poverty. Instead, legal minors turn to, or are taken by state agencies through the child welfare and juvenile justice systems, or must survive through methods of street life.

The study of inequality as it affects homeless children and adolescents fundamentally challenges some previously conventional approaches to stratification and poverty. Mere age prohibits most youth from gaining legal, economically sustainable employment. Consequently, the socioeconomic situation of most youth is not a function of their individual participation in the labor market. This should be seen in contrast to: (1) conventional approaches to inequality that reduce socioeconomic or class mobility to "a matter of individual responsibility,"[20] and (2) "culture of poverty" explanations of inequality suggesting that populations such as the "urban poor" develop culture in opposition to conventional employment,[21] and thus remain impoverished. The erroneous suggestion that poor populations have a culture that values poverty, denigrates hard work and education, and values welfare benefits over jobs is insufficient in explaining socioeconomic inequality among youth *or* adults. These previously conventional arguments place little importance on the effects of institutional constraints, such as the class/"race"/gender-oppressive structure of public schooling,[22] public assistance programs,[23] the criminal justice system,[24] and child welfare policy[25] on marginalized populations. The experience of "homeless" youth cannot be explained through a perspective of inequality centered on participation in the labor market, and one's willingness or cultural susceptibility to work. Instead, an appropriate conceptualization of youth or adolescent "homelessness" must begin with an approach that recognizes the structural barriers involved in escaping both "literal" homelessness and poverty.

The experiences of minors with poverty and "homelessness" are unique in that their exposure to social institutions and position within the political economy are significantly different than adults. Poverty and "homelessness" among youth are more likely expressions of the socioeconomic conditions of their families and communities rather than of individual behavior and employment. In addition, *poor or "homeless" minors are more likely than adults to encounter state welfare agencies due to child welfare and child "protection" policies.*

At this juncture, the experience of unaccompanied minors, particularly adolescents, may be separated from that of accompanied youth (families). Youth in homeless and/or impoverished families are still under the legal custody and protection of their parent(s) or guardian(s). In this sense their experience with social welfare agencies and their socioeconomic position are directly mediated by their adult guardian(s). In short, they are much less alone in their dealings with life in and outside of streets and shelters. The failure to differentiate between accompanied and unaccompanied homeless minors is problematic in that many residents populating youth shelters were removed from their previous homes or the street, and placed in shelters by state agencies.

Further, once removed by or placed under the custody of the child welfare system, the experience of *adolescents* may differ greatly from that of younger children and infants. Adolescents can be, and typically are, placed in a variety of disciplinary or "treatment" institutions that cannot or do not house younger children such as group homes, juvenile detention, "independent living" arrangements, and shelters for un-accompanied youth. Adolescents are also much less likely candidates for adoption,[26] ensuring longer periods of exposure to shelters and temporary "placements."

A working definition of "adolescent homelessness" should apply to the unique social situation of adolescents in the context of inequality. The socioeconomic situations of all youth are not simply functions of personal choice. They are more often and more likely to be expressions of the socioeconomic position of their guardians and communities. Unlike adults or entire family units, homeless minors may be taken out of the home or off the street, via law enforcement, social workers, and the child welfare system. Adolescents have unique experiences with the child welfare system, particularly regarding their limited chances for successful, permanent adoptive placements. In sum, unlike its adult, family, or much younger counterparts, *adolescent* homelessness should be defined by a lack of housing and the exposure or aversion to child welfare agencies and state custody. As the site of my research, Faulk House shelter is one such agency.

DATA COLLECTION METHODS: THE STUDY OF STATE WARDS

Faulk House shelter is located in an economically depressed neighborhood of color (primarily African American and Puerto Rican) in a mid-sized New England city. The shelter, run collaboratively by a charitable organization and the state's Department of Child Welfare (DCW), is designed to house up to 14 children at a time from ages 12–17 who have been displaced by the state (removal) or by circumstance ("off the street"). Because of its state regulated partnership with DCW, all Faulk House residents must be (re)entered into state custody.

I gathered data as a volunteer at Faulk House shelter. Work as a volunteer included participating in youth programs and spending time with staff and adolescents in activities, field trips, mealtimes, and most all other daily routines. This provided a wealth of data on "the physical and institutional setting in which [homeless adolescents] live, the daily routine of their activities, the beliefs that guide their actions, and the linguistic and other semiotic systems that mediate all these contexts and activities."[27] I used participant observation to develop intimate knowledge of state and shelter policy, how it is or isn't actually applied, and the environment it creates for adolescent residents. Further, intimate qualitative data was most appropriate for understanding the history and experiences of residents from direct observation/interaction, rather than from secondhand surveys and records.

These qualitative data were collected over the course of approximately 9 months (about 250 hours) at Faulk House shelter. To avoid the ethical problems involved with more covert research,[28] I conducted research "in the open" as a graduate student interested in shelter life and in volunteering for the youth program. Time sampling (conducting fieldwork on a variety of times and days) was used to collect a more exhaustive set of observational data.

In the interest of ethics and sound methodology, any field study of minors deserves particular consideration. Studies on youth in various settings have employed the use of relatively nonauthoritative adult roles such as volunteers or classroom participants.[29] This helps to reduce the power disparity that affects interaction between the youth informant and adult researcher, and increases access to observing and partial inclusion into adolescent "peer culture."[30] In playing my role as a volunteer at Faulk House, I avoided taking on the disciplinary responsibility of a staff member (with obvious safety-related exceptions). This undeniably decreased the level of authority that the youth residents attributed to my role in the shelter. Such practices are also consistent with feminist methodologies that recognize the importance of identifying, addressing, and minimizing the collection and reporting biases caused by differential "positionalities" between researchers and informants.[31] As also suggested by feminist methodology, researchers must be constantly "reflective"[32] and conscious of these disparities in the collection and reporting of data. Reflective practice was particularly useful in determining when and how to approach residents with questions (especially concerning histories and traumatic experiences), and in determining how, and whether to report particular data based on personal and professional ethical standards.

In total, I was able to observe and interact with 26 shelter residents over the course of my research. While I was unable to conduct formal interviews with shelter residents (state law), informal interviews were conducted with all residents through conversations over meals, recreational activities, and general "down time" in the shelter lounge or on the shelter playground. Many of these conversations were fruitful and typically instigated by residents. In these scenarios, conversations about the everyday interests of the adolescents would often expand into discussions of their histories and shelter experiences. Further, these scenarios presented environments in which residents were not "put on the spot" as subject to a questioning authority figure, producing what seemed to be more candid and culturally situated interactions. In the interest of ethical methodological practice, a great deal of discretion was used in recording data on some interactions. Though this meant not using some interesting and useful data, it seemed questionable to violate even informal agreements of personal confidentiality (marked by comments like, "no one really knows this," or "you're not going to tell anyone, right?" or "I don't really talk about it") with those potentially marginalized by their need for care and support.

Power differentials and issues of "positionality" were less problematic in the observation of shelter staff. Many of them were young adults (six women/three men)—some even graduate students in the field of social work. In addition to informal interaction with and observation of the staff, I employed eight semistructured interviews, informed by previous observational data to probe for staff member accounts of particular social events that were unavailable or previously unobservable.

The semistructured, in-depth interviews with Faulk House youth staff, the shelter social worker, and program coordinator reinforced and supplemented data collected through participant observation and informal interviews with all informants.

FAULK HOUSE APPROACH TO ADOLESCENT HOMELESSNESS: "PROVIDING STRUCTURE"

For purposes of this study, the experiences of Faulk House residents and the knowledge of shelter staff may be used to inform a sociological (re)conceptualization of adolescent homelessness. In contrast, an analysis of Faulk House shelter curriculum illuminates the state definition and approach to adolescent homelessness employed by child welfare agencies. Specifically, I maintain that Faulk House Shelter propagates a curriculum of "treatment" emphasizing "structure" and "consistency" in terms of discipline in daily life.

This emphasis became clear in several conversations and all interviews with staff about their jobs, and the attempt to "give something positive" to their adolescent clients. The program coordinator explained:

> I think what most of us try to do is show the kids how much better it is to live in a structured environment. Structure is good, 'cause these kids don't have any structure, because if we can form a routine with them and make it comfortable, I think they open up a lot more . . .'Cause I think they don't have that where they're coming from.

The basis for addressing the problems of homeless adolescents according to Faulk House is not only to supply physical necessities (food, shelter, etc.), but also to provide the "structure" that adolescents may not have experienced in their previous environments. As the shelter social worker explained, "a lot of the kids really have not had that (structure) through a lot of the placements they've lived, either there hasn't been good family life or good supervision in the home." Faulk House shelter provides "structure" through operating as a "quasi-total institution"[33]: providing routinization, strict boundaries, and evaluation of individual behavior within the institution without providing complete, or "total" social control.[34]

Shelter staff and policy manuals presented this approach as a strategy to provide predictable and safe environments for youth to learn responsibility and self-discipline. According to one Faulk House staff member,

> It's not like we lock 'em down, but we lock 'em down. You know, they don't get a chance to go out and do, you know, like a regular 15 year old—get to hang with their friends with your friends and at like this time come back. Because we're so structured and our job here is like to keep 'em safe. That's my first main goal is to keep them safe. And I think that's like every staff. We're so concerned with them being out there, that, you know, I think it's on us that we come down so hard. Because we don't want them to be out there, you know, because we don't think it's safe out there or whatever.

As temporary guardians for residents, the shelter must ensure safety for the adolescents it houses as an organizational necessity. Most staff members seemed to internalize the policy goal of "protection" as a response to the great deal of abuse some residents experienced before entering the shelter. Part of the shelter's effort to protect its residents is to condition them to avoid interactions that may "get them into trouble." Theoretically, residents learn to avoid potentially abusive relationships or interactions with those who may be a "bad influence." Further, "providing structure" serves the purpose of social control in providing predictability for shelter staff and safeguards for the shelter and the Department of Child Welfare (DCW), who are both liable for the well-being of youth residents.

Most importantly, the shelter's approach to treatment and operation reflects an image of adolescent homelessness as an *individual* rather than *social* problem.[35] During a conversation about the shelter's client population at the intake desk, two staff members discussed their perspectives on treatment and the child-care "system":

> Staff 1: "These kids [residents] think that none of us had problems. The system makes them think that they've had the worst life. That's what be messin' them up, yo . . . My foster daughter tries that shit at school—saying some things about her mother and stuff to the school and to me. I tell the school, 'she may not have had control of what happened to her then, but she'—you have control over what you do right now—that stuff [life before state custody] is over. So you follow the rules and take responsibility for what you do!"

> Staff 2: "It's like some of these parents just be droppin' their kids off."

> Staff 1: "YES. It's the parents, they drop off their kids and go on with their lives like they don't have any . . . I was eighteen when I had my daughter. You have nine months—you know that shit is coming. I worked three jobs to make sure that my daughter didn't grow up on welfare. The system doesn't teach them anything, they just go around in circles, it's a cycle. The skills they learn, they need . . . they don't learn that stuff really. They don't have the life skills."

Though the staff members identified that residents may find themselves in a "cycle," they clearly emphasized the individual behaviors of adolescents and their parents in explaining their path into and out of marginalized positions. This perspective mirrors the dominant ideology on child care where "in contemporary U.S. society, both being employed and caring for children are seen as individual responsibilities."[36]

In addition, "taking responsibility," hard work, and picking up "life skills" were seen as the lessons residents "need." According to program manuals and staff accounts the discipline and "life skills" learned at the shelter are to "get the kids on track" for finishing school, working a job, or living in their new placement. Part of providing "structure" is to teach shelter residents to restrict, redirect, and routinize their individual behavior in ways that conform to the demands of school, work, and life. From an institutional policy standpoint, this reflects an approach to treatment or "care as instruction,"[37] where residents are meant to develop particular skills in addition to receiving provisions of biological necessity and physical protection. Through efforts to "keep kids safe" and to provide "structure" to the lives of residents, shelter curriculum emphasizes the individual behaviors of residents and previous guardians as the defining factors behind residents' marginalized positions.

In the following section I problematize this approach as inappropriate and ultimately ineffective, and as connected to the larger movement toward child "protection" as the primary strategy of child welfare systems in caring for (typically) impoverished youth. Drawing from data collected at Faulk House and from contemporary research on public assistance and foster care, a more accurate and appropriate conceptualization of adolescent homelessness comes into focus.

(RE)CONCEPTUALIZING ADOLESCENT HOMELESSNESS

Connections: Structured Inequalities, Literal Homelessness, and Child Removal

As noted above, "literal homelessness" provides us a starting point, but is insufficient in capturing the unique nature of the adolescent experience as described in the sections above. In contrast to adults, minors may enter "shelters provided for homeless persons" through a forceful and lawful removal from their home and guardian(s).

In the United States, the social problems of youth and adolescent (literal) homelessness, child abuse, and general child "protection" are simultaneously addressed and constructed mainly through the state (DCW) and child welfare agencies (Faulk House). Adolescents removed from the home (voluntarily, by court order, after being arrested, or found without housing by public authorities) generally enter a series of state, or state-sponsored institutions designed to temporarily or permanently house them. During their displacement, adolescents within the system remain under state custody, supervised in a variety of institutional or foster care settings, until they are either returned to their previous guardians, age out of the system, or until parental rights are terminated (resulting in permanent state care or adoption). This is the case for all adolescents within the child welfare system, whether removed by the state based on substandard living conditions (as one form of "neglect" or parental negligence), removed as the result of physical or sexual abuse, abandoned by guardians (also "neglect"), left unattended after the imprisonment of parents, or willfully turned over to state custody on their own or guardian's behalf.

Patterns in child (including adolescent) removal are strongly connected to patterns of inequality and literal homelessness. Child welfare policy has formed in concert with economic welfare reform to shrink antipoverty and family preservation programs while increasing the rate of parental rights termination and the removal of minors from poor, especially African American families.[38] This exacerbates the oppressive effects of economic and racial inequality for the affected families and minors. Perhaps "the fundamental flaw" of the child welfare system is its formation as a child protection agency.[39] In the name of protecting children from neglect, unfit housing, and/or abuse, minors are removed from the home and placed within the child welfare system.

Many of the conditions from which minors are "protected" may actually be symptoms of poverty, rather than poor parenting, degenerate culture, or parental immorality. Dorothy Roberts explains how "most cases of child maltreatment stem from parental neglect,"[40] and those cases of "neglect" typically result from conditions of poverty. Poor parents who are economically unable to provide enough food, clean and safe housing, medical care, child care while away at work, transportation to school or other appointments, or proper clothing for their children (forms of "neglect") may have their children removed and/or parental rights terminated by child welfare authorities. Poor parents also lack the economic cushion to handle personal crises that more affluent parents would have. These crises may include, "becoming sick or injured or losing a job; splitting up with a spouse or partner; developing a drug or alcohol or gambling problem—[all of which] can result in a child being suddenly without a home."[41]

Several Faulk House residents had experienced literal homelessness and/or child removal as the result of such "neglect." Katrina, a 16-year-old African American, entered Faulk House when she was found to be caring for her younger sibling in the absence of parents who had both recently gone to prison for drug-related offenses. Talking one day in the lounge, she told me how she was "picked up":

> It wasn't even that late or nothin'. My older brother had come around [to their house] and we had some of our people over—a party or whatever. I guess it was too loud, cause our neighbor—nosey, for real!—whatever—called the cops. The cops came and everyone took off. When the cops were like, 'where are your parents?'—Well, it was only me and my little brother staying at the house so they took us. My mom wanted me to watch him and the house and everything so we didn't get all split up.

Katrina had no relatives capable of caring for her (her aunt, battling a drug addiction, was not seen fit by Katrina or DCW to take custody) and chose to take care of her siblings so not to be "split up" or placed in foster care. Upon entering state custody, Katrina bounced in and out of Faulk House shelter while her younger siblings were placed in separate foster homes.

The connection between poverty and the increased likelihood of imprisonment in the United States is widely documented.[42] Several studies also point to the operation of institutional racism in the U.S. criminal justice system, and the intersection of "race" and class in the increased likelihood for (especially poor) people of color to experience imprisonment.[43] Thus, the likelihood for Katrina and others like her to experience literal homelessness as the result of imprisonment may be connected to the intersection of racial and class inequalities. Katrina entered state custody because of her family's lack of human and material resources to care for her and her siblings following the imprisonment of their parents. Her entrance into state custody was as much a matter of poverty, and potentially institutional racism, as "neglect."

Also consider the case of Maria, a small, quiet, 13-year-old Puerto Rican girl from an area neighborhood, who stayed with her grandparents out of economic necessity and in an attempt to continue attending her middle school while living with her own family. Upon inspection by state social workers, the home of Maria's grandparents did not meet the size requirement necessary for the amount of people in the home (they were already caring for at least one other grandchild). As a result, Maria was removed from the home and placed under state custody. As explained by a staff member,

It's a shame because, [the grandparents] are good people. They come to visit her like, every other week—you know, when they're allowed. They're already taking care of some of her cousins—that's the thing, they didn't have enough room in the house. DCW says you have to have so many rooms for so many kids. They've been trying to find a bigger place, but it's hard 'cause, you know, they're older and don't make much money.

Over the course of a year, efforts by Maria's grandparents to meet the standards of DCW continually failed—she remained in Faulk House for the entire duration of my research. The ability for Maria's parents and grandparents to care for her (to state standards) was limited by *poverty*. She entered and stayed in a shelter for homeless adolescents because her grandparents could not afford a large enough home. In any case, Maria was removed from what all accounts described as a "caring home" as a result of poverty, masked and labeled as parental "neglect." Again, Maria's case illustrates the connection between structured inequalities and both the experience of literal homelessness and life under state custody in shelters and state agencies.

In addition, both "race" and socioeconomic status affect the likelihood of child removal in a more direct sense. Poor, especially African American, parents are more likely to be reported to child welfare authorities for parental neglect or mistreatment.[44] This is primarily due to increased, and, in many ways, oppressive exposure to the state through welfare authorities, social workers, and the police. Further, poor parents are less likely to exercise their legal rights through the assistance of private attorneys.[45] In contrast, problems concerning child care among more affluent and/or "white" families are more often treated as "private matters."[46] In the child welfare system's definition and detection of inappropriate living conditions for minors, "poverty—not the type or severity of maltreatment—is the single most important predictor of placement in foster care and the amount of time spent there."[47] This applies not only to foster care, but also to placement in other child welfare institutions more often experienced by adolescents such as group homes and emergency shelters.

Even forms of maltreatment such as physical, mental, or sexual abuse may be primarily connected to poverty and access to resources—the same factors that contribute to literal homelessness. For instance, "poor parents can't afford to seek counseling, hire a nanny, or take a vacation"[48] in order to alleviate stress (only made worse by poverty), or to treat psychological conditions that may contribute to such abuse. One's socioeconomic condition (affected by class inequality and through structured racial and gender inequality) affects the likelihood of abuse to take place, and state reaction to that abuse.[49] Further, Hill[50] points out that though African American youth are disproportionately taken into state custody via the child welfare system, "black families do not maltreat their children more often than white families . . . and, when

class and other risk factors are controlled for, blacks have *lower* rates of abuse and neglect than whites." Again, we see how structured inequalities—including institutional
racism—contribute to the state removal of adolescents who are disproportionately
poor and/or youth "of color."

We may also consider the role of gender inequality here: take for example, the case
of a mother whose male partner abuses her and her children. The mother's ability
to remove herself and her child from the potentially dangerous environment is based
on her own resources, web of support, and the degree to which she depends on the
support of her abusive partner. This was the case for the Smith sisters (one 13 and one
16), who I grew to know through the duration of my research. Over the course of 2
years they were beaten and sexually abused by their stepfather and his acquaintances,
who paid the stepfather for access to the sisters. Their mother was both economically
and chemically dependent (he supplied drugs for her addiction) on the stepfather,
who also physically abused her. The younger sister on one occasion showed me the
scars from falling off the motorcycle of her "boyfriend" (an acquaintance of the
stepfather). Here we see first, the great adversity faced by homeless adolescents, which
understandably fuels policy initiatives toward child "protection." Second, and more
importantly, we see how gendered inequality (manifested in the poverty and gendered
oppression of women and single mothers) influences the ability of parents to care for
their *own* children, increasing the potential for child removal, and/or entrance into
literal homelessness.

We must also consider how the reduction of social services and public assistance
may also decrease many parents' ability to care for their children or deal with environments and effects of abuse. The connection between systemic/institutional racism,[51]
socioeconomic inequality and patterns of child (including adolescent) removal goes
beyond the policies of the child welfare system to include recent cuts and revisions of
welfare benefits by the state:

> The federal welfare law contains funding provisions that are more likely to disrupt than
> strengthen poor families. It leaves federal funds for foster care and adoption assistance
> as an uncapped entitlement while reducing and capping federal funds for cash assistance
> to families and for child welfare services that support families . . . A child welfare agency
> faced with a family whose TANF benefits have expired may choose to place the children
> in out-of-home care rather than find the funds needed to preserve the family.[52]

Because of reduced welfare benefits, already poor families lose more resources
needed to provide adequate childcare. Rather than providing parents and families the
support needed for family preservation, the state expends *eleven times* more funding
toward removing minors from the household on the basis of parental "neglect."[53]
Instead of treating the causes and conditions of *poverty* through providing benefits,
educational training, or health services, the state often responds to the situation of
poor families by simply removing minors from the home, often resulting in the
termination of parental rights.

The "Runaway" Question

Do cases of "runaway" or previously *un*impoverished youth challenge the model for adolescent homelessness under construction here? One body of literature, commonly mistaken for the study of homeless youth, is the sociological, social-psychological, and criminological study of "runaways," or "runaway adolescents." This literature is of limited use here for several reasons: (1) only about 2–11 percent of literally homeless adolescents (on the street or in shelters) are runaways;[54] (2) many studies of runaways actually concentrate on runaway behavior, or the phenomenon of leaving the home;[55] (3) it would be a grave mistake to approach adolescent homelessness as a behavioral issue—for most literally homeless adolescents, a moment of *choice* may not have led to their compromised position. As Schaffner explains, "the experience of poverty, disadvantage, and need will influence the New York City (homeless) street survivor differently from a Palm Beach teen crashing at a friend's pad."[56] Both of these adolescents would exhibit "runaway behavior," though only the one living on the street would be conceptualized here as "homeless" because their impoverished position did not allow for other options for survival outside of street life or entrance into state custody.

It should also be noted that not all literally homeless adolescents come from impoverished homes, particularly in the case of some long-term runaways. Yet the general patterns of literal homelessness, and the likelihood for adolescents to become and remain literally homeless and to depend on welfare support structures (the outcomes of runaway behaviors) are strongly linked to socioeconomic factors. Once detached from other support systems (if they previously existed), all literally homeless youth may face similar barriers to succeeding in the worlds of school and work while literally homeless, or while in state custody. Further, for those who manage to stay on the street, the street experience for adolescents is mediated by an aversion to child welfare agencies. That is, rich or poor, they are only on the street for as long as they can slip (consciously or unconsciously) under the radar of police and social workers.

Literal Homelessness and State Custody as Overlapping Experiences

Where "neglect" is increasingly used as the grounds for child removal/entrance into state custody, it is also the grounds for taking in (literally) homeless adolescents or potentially removing them from (literally) homeless families. As explained in previous sections, literal homelessness typically includes those who stay in emergency shelters designed for homeless populations. At Faulk House (as with any other shelter in its resident state), any unattended minor *must* be reported to DCW. In fact, most Faulk House residents were actually placed at the shelter by DCW rather than entering from "the street." In short, for many shelters and agencies like Faulk House, entrance into a shelter means entrance into the child welfare system.

The overlap between literal homelessness and state custody is also reflected in the correlations found between histories of foster care and literal homelessness. A report by the National Alliance to End Homelessness found from an analysis of previous studies, records of foster care histories, and surveys of homeless populations in several urban areas (Chicago, NYC, etc.) that:

> There is indeed an overrepresentation of people with a foster care history in the homeless population. The research also demonstrated that childhood placement in foster care can correlate with a substantial increase in the length of a person's homeless experience and that people who are homeless frequently have had multiple placements as children, both in foster care and in the homes of families and friends (unofficial placements). The Alliance also discovered that homeless people with a foster care history are more likely than other people to have their own children in foster care.[57]

Put simply, entrance into state custody does not ensure an exit from literal homelessness.

It is also a common mistake to assume that the current methods employed to house state wards (typically foster care) ensure the safety and well-being of young clients. Recent events suggest that foster care populations may suffer different rather than fewer problems than those who are literally homeless. For example, reports in 2003 showed that Florida's agencies could not even find entire populations of their state wards after reports of abuse and poor records.[58] Thus we cannot simply assume that entrance into state custody ensures long-term escape from poverty, abuse, or a return to literal homelessness. If one were to follow a conventional definition of homelessness as it applies to adolescents, entrance into state custody, foster care for example, would indicate the temporary or permanent end of one's homeless experience. I suggest instead that an adolescent's involvement with child welfare agencies is a *defining characteristic* of their homeless experience and of "adolescent homelessness" as a social phenomenon. From this perspective, it is also possible to view adolescents who are *removed* from the home as part of the adolescent homeless population.

Child Welfare Policy and Adolescent Homelessness

Adolescents, especially those from poor and/or African American families, may be removed from the home and placed in shelters (like Faulk House) or other institutional arrangements created to house adolescents during their displacement. As already suggested, it is possible to include adolescents who are removed from their home as part of the homeless adolescent population in their (often) sharing of the overlapping experiences of state custody and literal homelessness. *Therefore, in an effort to "protect" adolescents from inappropriate living conditions the state, by removing adolescents from the home, while cutting antipoverty/economic welfare programs,[59] may actually CREATE adolescent homelessness.*

The reasons behind adolescent poverty and homelessness are thus mystified through public policy in "protecting" children—treating the problem as the pathology, immorality, or cultural deficiency of parents rather than as a social problem of extreme and oppressive economic inequality. This is *not* to suggest that all adolescents are removed from the home unjustly, or that none benefit from home removal or shelter under state custody. Instead, it suggests that the public response to adolescent homelessness and "child welfare" as a *social problem* is at least misdirected in not recognizing poverty and structured inequalities as the key contributing factors to the marginalized position of many families and youth.

This misdirection is clearly manifested in the curriculum of Faulk House emergency shelter that emphasizes providing "structure" to residents through routinizing and evaluating their behaviors while also "keeping them safe" from outside influences (such as previous guardians, friends, etc.). Again, this is not to suggest that the shelter "does no good," or that shelter staff are not dedicated, or are lazy, or naïve. Like the rest of us, they are forced to work within the restraints set by structure and policy. In fact, many Faulk House shelter staff expressed the desire to "do more for the kids" but were restrained by rules (some of which were broken by giving residents personal money, buying them clothes/supplies with personal money, etc.), time, and resources. Nevertheless, the problematic features of child "protection" are heavily manifested in the policies and curriculum of Faulk House. Faulk House curriculum attempted to address adolescent homelessness as a function of the individual behaviors of residents and previous guardians rather than as related to poverty, social exclusion, and inequality.

A NEW MODEL

The preceding discussion underscores the need for the concept of adolescent homelessness to go beyond the previous, conventional interpretations of "homelessness" to include the role of the state and child welfare system. The public response to adolescent poverty in the United States may effectively create adolescent homelessness, as conceptualized here, among many of those already marginalized in an attempt to protect adolescents from environments characterized as unfit. Further, adolescent homelessness is more an expression of structured inequalities, child welfare policy, and the problems faced by impoverished populations than simply a problem of pathological parenting, degenerate culture, or parental immorality.

As I have argued here, adolescent homelessness as a (re)produced social problem may primarily be understood as an expression of structured inequalities (socioeconomic, raced, and gendered). A visual illustration may be useful in understanding the complexity of this argument (see Figure 1.1), with numbers corresponding to the ones below):

(1) Structured inequalities (primarily raced, classed, and gendered) expressed in part
through socioeconomic status and as a result of the related conditions of shrinking
welfare benefits, rising unemployment, and rising housing/living costs serve as primary
determinants of literal homelessness for adolescents and families. Remember that the
socioeconomic position of adolescents, and their ability to maintain consistent and satisfactory living conditions, are mainly expressions of the socioeconomic conditions of
their families and communities.

Structured Inequalities
(Race, Class, and Gender)
Expressed mainly through Socioeconomic
status, partially a condition of shrinking
welfare benefits, rising unemployment, etc.

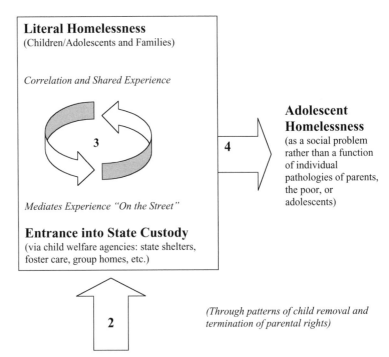

Literal Homelessness
(Children/Adolescents and Families)

Correlation and Shared Experience

3

Mediates Experience "On the Street"

Entrance into State Custody
(via child welfare agencies: state shelters,
foster care, group homes, etc.)

4

Adolescent Homelessness
(as a social problem
rather than a function
of individual
pathologies of parents,
the poor, or
adolescents)

2

*(Through patterns of child removal and
termination of parental rights)*

Structured Inequalities
(Race, Class, and Gender)
With respect to an increased exposure
to state intervention and policing.

(2) Structured inequalities also determine the likelihood of adolescents' removal from the home, placement under state custody, and the length of time spent in state custody.

(3) We have already explored the strong correlation between literal homelessness and entrance into state custody. An understanding of literal homelessness and child welfare/child removal policies illuminates the overlapping experience of adolescents on the street and in state placements. Many of those youth who spend time in state custody have or will experience extreme poverty and/or literal homelessness. Also, the literally homeless experience of adolescents is mediated by their (or their guardians') ability to

avoid state actors, thus avoiding state custody. In sum, it is questionable whether or not these make up two discernable populations.

(4) Finally, I argue that adolescent homelessness may be defined as a fluid condition, caused primarily by structured inequalities, and manifested primarily in the correlating experiences of literal homelessness and entrance into state custody.

Child welfare policies, and the structural arrangement and curriculum of agencies such as Faulk House, do not reflect the *causes* of adolescent homelessness and the reality of the adolescent homeless experience as a fluid condition and social problem. As a result, these policies ultimately fail to address adolescent homelessness, reflected in its perpetuation and the growing caseloads of social workers nationwide. Further, contemporary policy approaches contribute to the ideological "victim blaming" also attributed to welfare reform.[60] The positions of homeless adolescents and their families are defined and addressed largely in terms of their personal behaviors and deficiencies rather than in terms of their marginalized positions within systems of inequality—both mystifying social reality and legitimating their suffering under the rubric of individual responsibility and rational choice. Again, current state/child welfare policies may actually *increase* populations on the street and in state systems as a result of cutting antipoverty programs and focusing on the reactionary measures of child removal and imprisonment rather than on preventative measures such as family and community preservation and reinvestment.

Employing the conceptualization of adolescent homelessness offered here would first contribute to a theoretical lens for critical analysis of relevant public policies. This (re)conceptualization of "adolescent homelessness" may be more theoretically useful in studying marginalized youth/adolescents that simultaneously populate the street, shelters, and child welfare system. Finally, this conceptual framework could inform child welfare policy in avoiding behavioral pathology models that target parents, kids, and marginalized populations rather than structured inequality and its many symptoms.

NOTES

1. I (subjectively) define "adolescents" as between the ages of 12 and 17. For those 18 and above, the homeless experience changes with regard to state agencies as a result of reaching legal adulthood.

2. References to "race" or racial categories will appear in single quotes to indicate their complete and total social construction as oppressive, hierarchical concepts that I do not seek to reify.

3. David Snow and Leon Anderson, *Down on Their Luck: A Study of Homeless Street People* (Berkeley, CA: University of California Press, 1993).

4. Irene Glasser, *Homelessness in Global Perspective* (New York: G.K. Hall, 1994); James Farrow, M. D. Deisher, M. D. Brown, M. D. Kulig, and M. D. Kipke, "Health and Health Needs of Homeless and Runaway Youth," *Journal of Adolescent Health* 13(1992): 717–726; Majorie J. Robertson, Paul Koegel, Linda Ferguson "Alcohol Use and Abuse among Homeless Adolescents in Hollywood," *Contemporary Drug Problems* 16(3) (1989): 415–452; Elisa J. Sobo,

Gregory D. Zimet, Teena Zimmerman, and Heather Cecil, "Doubting the Experts: AIDS Misconceptions among Runaway Adolescents," *Human Organization* 56(3) (1997): 311–320; Y. Rafferty, "Developmental and Educational Consequences of Homeless on Children and Youth," in *Homeless Children and Youth: A New American Dilemma*, ed. Julee H. Kryder-Coe, Lester M. Salamon, and Janice M. Molnar, (New Brunswick, NJ: Transaction Publishers, 1991); Snow and Anderson, *Down on Their Luck*.

5. Julee Kryder-Coe, Lester M. Salamon, and Janice M. Molnar, *Homeless Children and Youth: A New American Dilemma* (New Brunswick, NJ: Transaction Publishers, 1991); Ralph Nunez, *Hopes, Dreams, and Promise: The Future of Homeless Children in America* (New York: Homes for the Homeless Inc., 1994); Dorothy Roberts, *Shattered Bonds* (New York: Basic Civitas Books, 2002); US Census Bureau, available at www.census.gov/hhes/poverty (2006).

6. Joel Stein, "The Real Face of Homelessness," *Time Magazine*, January 20, 2003, 52–57.

7. Stein, "The Real Face of Homelessness," 54.

8. Ken Neubeck and Noel Cazenave, *Welfare Racism: Playing the Race Card Against America's Poor* (New York: Routledge, 2001); Roberts, *Shattered Bonds*; Stein, "The Real Face of Homelessness."

9. Jennifer Egan, "To be Young and Homeless," *The New York Times Magazine*, March 24, 2002, 32–37/58–59; Peter Marcuse, "Neutralizing Homelessness," *Socialist Review* 18(1) (1988): 69–96.

10. Stein, "The Real Face of Homelessness," 54.

11. Egan, "To be Young and Homeless."

12. Mark Nord and A. E. Luloff, "Homeless Children and Their Families in New Hampshire: A Rural Perspective," *Social Science Review* Spring (1995): 461–477. Kryder-Coe, Salamon, and Molnar, *Homeless Children and Youth*; Nunez, *Hopes, Dreams, and Promise*.

13. Nord and Luloff, "Homeless Children and Their Families in New Hampshire," 461

14. Jean Anyon, "Social Class and the Hidden Curriculum of Work," *Journal of Education* 162(1) (1980): 67–92; Jean Anyon, *Ghetto Schooling: A Political Economy of Urban Educational Reform* (New York: Teachers College Press, 1997); Kathleen DeMarrais and Margaret LeCompte, *The Way Schools Work: A Sociological Analysis of Education* (New York: Longman Publishers, 1995); Jay McLeod, *Ain't No Makin' It: Aspirations and Attainment in a Low-Income Neighborhood* (Boulder, CO: Westview Press 1995); M. Robertson, "Homeless Youth: An Overview of Recent Literature," in *Homeless Children and Youth: A New American Dilemma*, ed. Julee Kryder-Coe, Salamon, and Molnar. (New Brunswick, NJ: Transaction Publishers, 1991).

15. No Child Left Behind, available at US Dept. of Ed., www.nochildleftbehind.gov, 2006.

16. William T. Armaline and Donald Levy, "No Child Left Behind: Flowers Don't Grow in the Desert," *Race and Society* 7(1) (2004): 31–62.

17. Irene Glasser and Rae Bridgeman, *Braving the Street: The Anthropology of Homelessness*, (New York: Berghahn Books, 1999).

18. Glasser and Bridgeman, *Braving the Street*, 23

19. Snow and Anderson, Down on Their Luck.

20. Anthony Giddens, *Central Problems in Social Theory: Action, Structure, and Contradiction in Social Analysis* (Berkeley, CA: University of California Press, 1979); Ruth Horowitz, "Barriers and Bridges to Class Mobility and Formation," *Sociological Methods and Research: Ethnographies of Stratification* 25(4) (1997): 502.

21. Winter Alan, *The Poor: A Culture of Poverty, or a Poverty of Culture?* (Grand Rapids, MI: Eerdmans, 1971); Eleanor Leacock (ed.), *The Culture of Poverty: A Critique* (New York: Simon and Schuster, 1971); Lewis Oscar, *La Vida: A Puerto Rican Family on the Culture of*

Poverty—San Juan and New York (New York: Random House, 1966); Horowitz "Barriers and Bridges to Class Mobility and Formation."

22. Stanley Aronowitz and Henry Giroux, *Education Under Siege* (South Hadley, MA: Bergin and Garvey, 1985); DeMarrais and LeCompte, *The Way Schools Work*; McLeod, *Ain't No Makin' It.*

23. Neubeck and Cazenave, *Welfare Racism.*

24. Tera Herivel and Paul Wright (eds), *Prison Nation: The Warehousing of America's Poor* (New York: Routledge, 2003).

25. Robert Hill, "Institutional Racism in Child Welfare," *Race and Society* 7(2004): 17–33; Roberts, *Shattered Bonds.*

26. Kryder-Coe, Salamon, and Molnar, *Homeless Children and Youth*; Roberts, *Shattered Bonds.*

27. Donna Eder and William Corsaro, "Ethnographic Studies of Children and Youth: Theoretical and Ethical Issues," *Journal of Contemporary Ethnography* 28(5) (1999): 521–531.

28. Robert Emerson, *Contemporary Field Research: Perspecitves and Formulations* (Prospect Heights, IL: Waveland Press, 2001); John Lofland and Lyn Lofland, *Analyzing Social Settings: A Guide to Qualitative Observation and Analysis* (U.C. Davis: Wadsworth Publishing, 1995).

29. Emerson, *Contemporary Field Research*; Eder and Corsaro, "Ethnographic Studies of Children and Youth."

30. Barrie Thorne, Gender Play: Girls and Boys in School (Rutgers University Press, 1993); Eder and Corsaro, "Ethnographic Studies of Children and Youth."

31. Nancy Naples, *Feminism and Method: Ethnography, Discourse Analysis, and Activist Research* (New York: Routledge, 2003).

32. Ibid.

33. Douglas Kivett and Carol Warren, "Social Control in a Group Home for Delinquent Boys," *Journal of Contemporary Ethnography* 31(1) (2002): 3–32.

34. William T. Armaline, "'Sheltered Struggle': Negotiating Rules, Power, and Social Control in an Emergency Youth Shelter," *American Behavioral Scientist* 48(8) (2005): 1124–1148.

35. Ibid.

36. Anita Garey, "Social Domains and Concepts of Care: Protection, Instruction, and Containment in After-school Programs," *Journal of Family Issues* 23(2002): 772–773.

37. Ibid.

38. Roberts, *Shattered Bonds*; Neubeck and Cazenave, *Welfare Racism*; Hill, "Institutional Racism in Child Welfare."

39. Roberts, *Shattered Bonds*, 74

40. Ibid., 34

41. Egan, "To be Young and Homeless," 56

42. Jeffrey Reiman, *The Rich Get Richer and the Poor Get Prison: Ideology, Class, and Criminal Justice* (Boston, MA: Allyn and Bacon, 1998); Herivel and Wright, *Prison Nation.*

43. Joe Feagin, *Racist America* (New York: Routledge, 2001); Hank Kalet, "Unequal Justice," *Progressive Populist*, June 1, 2000; Christopher Stone, *Race, Crime, and the Administration of Justice* (Washington, DC: NIJ, April 1999: 26–32). Herivel and Wright, *Prison Nation.*

44. Roberts, *Shattered Bonds*; Hill, "Institutional Racism in Child Welfare."

45. PBS, Frontline, "Failure to Protect: The Taking of Logan Marr" and "The Caseworker Files," 1/30/03, 2/6/03. Barry Feld, *Bad Kids: Race and the Transformation of the Juvenile Court* (New York: Oxford University Press 1999); Hill, "Institutional Racism in Child Welfare."

46. Roberts, *Shattered Bonds*; Feld, *Bad Kids*; Hill, "Institutional Racism in Child Welfare."

47. Roberts, *Shattered Bonds*, 27

48. Ibid., 32

49. R. L. Hampton, "Child Abuse in the African American Community" in Child Welfare: *An Africentric Perspective*, ed. J. E. Everett, S. S. Chipungu & B. R. Leashore (New Brunswick, NJ: Rutgers University Press, 1991, pp. 247–265); J.K. Holton, *Black Families and Child Abuse Prevention* (Washington, DC: CWLA, 1990).

50. Hill, "Institutional Racism in Child Welfare," 18; See also: A. Sedlak and D. Broadhurst, Executive Summary of the Third National Incidence Study of Child Abuse and Neglect (Washington, DC: US Dept. Health and Human Services, 1996); A. Sedlak and D. Schultz, "Race Differences in Risk of Maltreatment in the general Child Population," in *Race Matters in Child Welfare*, ed. D. Derezotes (Washington, DC: CWLA, 2004).

51. Feagin, *Racist America*; Neubeck and Cazenave, *Welfare Racism*; Roberts, *Shattered Bonds*; Hill, "Institutional Racism in Child Welfare."

52. Roberts, *Shattered Bonds*, 190–191.

53. Ibid., 191

54. Laurie Schaffner, *Teenage Runaways: Broken Hearts and "Bad Attitudes"* (New York: Haworth Press, 1999).

55. Loring Jones, "A Typology of Adolescent Runaways." *Child and Adolescent Social Work Journal* 5(1) (1998): 16–29; Joseph Palinski, *Kids Who Run Away* (Saratoga, CA: R & E Publishers, 1984); Jane Powers and Barbara Jaklitsch, *Understanding Survivors of Abuse: Stories of Homeless and Runaway Adolescents* (Lexington, MA: Lexington Books, 1989); Schaffner, *Teenage Runaways*.

56. Schaffner, *Teenage Runaways*, 14.

57. Nan Roman and Phyllis Wolfe, "The Relationship Between Foster Care and Homelessness," *Public Welfare* 6(3) (1997): 7.

58. Dana Canedy, "Two Years After Girl Disappeared, Little Has Changed in Florida Agency," *New York Times*, January 19, 2003.

59. Dorothy Roberts, *Killing the Black Body*, (New York: Pantheon Books, 1997). Roberts, *Shattered Bonds*; Neubeck and Cazenave, *Welfare Racism*.

60. Neubeck and Cazenave, *Welfare Racism*.

CHAPTER 2

CHILD WELFARE AND WELFARE REFORM: A STUDY OF ONE COMMUNITY

Kathleen Wells*

This chapter focuses on one group of economically impoverished children, children involved in the child welfare system, and examines how such children in one community fared under conditions of welfare reform. To do so, it presents a general overview of a program of research on this issue and speculates as to its significance for child welfare policy.

POVERTY AND CHILD MALTREATMENT

A large number of factors are associated with the likelihood that a child will be maltreated, that is, neglected, physically abused, sexually abused, and or psychologically maltreated. These factors pertain to characteristics of the parent, the child, and the interactions between the two; the social and institutional networks in which they are embedded; and the social structure of which parents and children are a part.[1] One of the central conditions that characterize maltreating families, however, is poverty.[2] Although most poor parents neither abuse nor neglect their children, poor children are more likely than are nonpoor children to be reported to authorities as possible victims.[3] For example, the risk for poor children of being reported is 6.8 that of nonpoor children.[4]

Children who have been found to be maltreated, moreover, come from those who are "among the poorest of the poor."[5] For example, when maltreating parents who received public assistance were compared with their nonmaltreating counterparts, it was found that they were more likely to be living in crowded households, to inhabit substandard housing, and to have gone hungry.[6] More than half of all maltreated children are considered to be neglected, that is, their basic needs for food, shelter, protection and supervision, health care, and education have not been met.[7]

Not surprisingly, therefore, the majority of maltreated children who have been separated from their parents and placed in foster care come from families headed by poor, unmarried mothers eligible for receipt of public assistance.[8] Indeed, unstable parental income has been associated with placement of children in foster care.[9]

While it is clear that poverty does not cause child abuse and neglect, most scholars agree with the conclusion drawn by Pelton[10] that poverty provides the ground in which abuse and neglect may flourish, and that the factors that mediate the relationship between poverty and maltreatment "have more to do with the ability or inability to cope with poverty and its stresses than with anything else (p. 42)."

CHILD MALTREATMENT AND THE CHILD WELFARE SYSTEM

United States policy mandates a broad range of goals for child welfare agencies that provide services for families who maltreat their children.[11] Agencies are expected to promote children's well-being, to keep them safe from harm, to provide them with stable families, and to enhance the well-being of their families.[12] Families who have maltreated their children typically receive either in-home services such as parenting classes or mental health outpatient treatment, or out-of-home services such as placement of their children in foster care.

However, the child welfare system in the United States is not designed currently to promote child and family well-being broadly defined or, for that matter, to address poverty. Over the past several decades it has evolved from a system intended to help parents to care for their children through the provision of supportive services to one that is dominated by its child protection function.[13] As a result, most of the work of state or county child welfare agencies is devoted to screening reports of child abuse and neglect, investigating the veracity of such reports, and providing services to children identified as abused or neglected, as defined by state law.[†]

CHILD WELFARE AND PUBLIC WELFARE POLICY

Over the past decade, child welfare policy has become more punitive toward biological mothers of children in foster care than in the past.[14] For example, the Adoption and Safe Families Act of 1997 built upon prior child welfare legislation but emphasized that a child's health and safety is of critical concern in determining whether reasonable efforts to preserve the child's family or to reunify the child with his or her families have to be made. It also identified circumstances in which such efforts are not required. The act specifically mandates that the rights of parents of children under age 10 who have been in foster care for 15 of the most recent 22 months be

---

[†] This is a daunting task. The number of reports is substantial. In 2002, for example, approximately 2.6 million reports of abuse and neglect were filed (representing 4.5 million children); 67 percent of those reports were investigated; 27 percent of the reports were substantiated (found to be true) and 4 percent were indicated (found to be possibly true); and 59 percent of those received some kind of child welfare service.[15] In that same year, approximately, 303,000 U. S. children entered foster care. A total of 532,000 children were in care on September 30, 2002.[16]

terminated. Consequently, reunification of children with their parents hinges upon the speed with which parents can safely resume the care of their children.

Public welfare policy evolved also during this same period of time. It has changed from a system intended to improve the material conditions of impoverished parents, typically single mothers, through the provision of cash grants and other forms of concrete assistance to one that promotes work. For example, the Personal Responsibility and Work Opportunity Reconciliation Act of 1996 (Public Law 104-193), commonly known as welfare reform, was designed to promote paid employment among those who had historically relied on cash assistance; to make work pay by promoting welfare recipients use of all of the government benefits for which they were eligible; and to promote the formation of two-parent families. Two primary features of this legislation were the elimination of the entitlement to cash assistance that had been available under the prior welfare policy[17] and the restriction of the access to cash assistance to 60 months.

THE PROBLEM

At the time welfare reform legislation was being debated, some child welfare advocates raised the concern that its effect on families at high risk of involvement in the child welfare system or on families already involved in the child welfare system would be negative.[18, 19] The concern grew out of the recognition that a majority of families involved in the child welfare system were also recipients of cash assistance[20] and, as a result, child welfare families would be affected by welfare reform. Moreover, these families were known to have severe, complex, and chronic problems, such as drug addiction[21] and domestic violence,[22] in addition to poor parenting skills. Some expected these problems would make it difficult for parents to obtain and retain paid employment with the level of support that was anticipated and within the proscribed period of time.[23] Given the strong link between poverty and child maltreatment, the over-arching worry was that if poverty increased, so too would child maltreatment and, in particular, placement of children in foster care.[24]

Several hypotheses were advanced regarding the mechanisms through which loss of income[25] or poverty would increase abuse and neglect.[26] However, the specific ways in which welfare reform would affect the child welfare system were unclear. Federal welfare reform legislation made few specific changes to child welfare policy, and the States were allowed considerable latitude as to how to implement the federal legislation. As a result, the effects of reform could be expected to depend on how legislative mandates to promote work, to protect children, and to preserve families were implemented in a specific economic, social, and policy context.[27]

THE PROGRAM OF RESEARCH[†]

In 1998, we launched a program of research to address the concern that welfare reform would negatively affect children at risk of involvement in the child welfare

---

[†] This chapter's description of the research program relies on the prior work of the author and her colleagues.[28]

system. The research program was an in-depth case study, a study that relied on multiple methods, of the child welfare system in one large urban county—Cuyahoga County, Ohio. As such, findings from this program cannot be used to show definitively that welfare reform caused the findings obtained.

This community exemplified the social and economic trends observed in other northern industrial cities over the past 30 years: loss of heavy industry and associated jobs; loss of population, particularly two-parent families, to the suburbs; and continued racial segregation of housing.[29] Cuyahoga County is the largest of Ohio's 88 counties. It has a population of close to 1.4 million.[30] It is dominated by its largest city, the City of Cleveland, where approximately one third (34.3%) of county residents live.[31] Despite the economic growth and the decrease in poverty that occurred in the county during the 1990s, the social and economic conditions in Cleveland had become depleted. For example, in 1999, 48 percent of city children were living in single-parent households; 38 percent of city children were living in poverty; and 65 percent of all births were to women who were unmarried prior to the birth of their child.[32] In 2000, 51 percent of city residents were African American.[33]

The program was comprised of four interrelated but separate components: a Policy Study, a Caseload Study, a Cohort Study, and an Interview Study conducted in collaboration with the Cuyahoga County, Ohio Department of Children and Family Services, the community's child welfare agency. These studies allowed, in turn, an examination of the implementation of welfare reform in the county; of whether child welfare caseloads increased; of whether rates of reunification of foster children declined; and of the nature of the needs and resources of biological mothers with children in foster care under conditions of welfare reform in the community under study.

At the time the study began, it was affected by State of Ohio welfare reform implementation legislation.[34] This legislation indicated the State's concurrence with the federal welfare reform legislation and, in some places, contained more restrictive requirements.[35] For example, under the State's program, cash assistance was limited to 36 months rather than the 60 months allowed under federal law, though after 2 years parents could apply for an additional 2 years of aid. Each county in the State was to devise a plan to implement the State's welfare reform plan so that all county plans could be responsive to local conditions. This county-by-county flexibility was a major feature of reform in Ohio.[36]

In light of the socio-economic conditions and the legislative mandates affecting the county, we reasoned that if welfare reform were going to have negative effects on families involved in the child welfare system, we should be able to detect these effects in Cuyahoga County, Ohio.

CASELOAD STUDY

Aim

This study was intended to describe how the child welfare caseload changed under conditions of welfare reform in order to provide a context for the other studies in the program. At the time the study began, it was unclear as to how welfare reform might affect specifically the child welfare system. Reform might affect the population of families at risk of abuse and neglect and promote an increase in the number of child abuse and neglect reports. Alternatively, reform might affect the way in which the system responded to those reports and promote an increase in the number of children with substantiated reports referred to county foster care. To examine whether any such changes occurred, we examined Cuyahoga County child welfare caseloads from January 1995 through August 2001, an 80-month period of time of which 33 months were prior to welfare reform and 45 were after.

Methodological Approach

Study questions were examined with a time-series design (see Wells, Guo, Shafran, and Pearlmutter 2004 for study questions and other methodological details of this study.)[37] This is a quasi-experimental design in which an individual or group is measured at regular intervals and in which an intervention such as welfare reform is introduced during the measurement period.[38] In this analysis, the number of cases for each child welfare variable under study was counted for each of 80 months and plotted on a graph.

Study data came from three administrative data bases: the Cuyahoga County Department of Children and Family Services data set that contains basic demographic and service-use data for children and their families; the State of Ohio Income Maintenance System administrative data set that contains information on monthly cash assistance payments; and the State's Unemployment Insurance administrative data set that contains wage data, with the exception of data from employers outside Ohio, from those who are self-employed, and from those who are engaged in informal work.

Study data were analyzed with two statistical techniques—"curve smoothing,"[39] a procedure to remove random fluctuations so that actual decreases or increases in monthly counts plotted over time are easier to identify, and an autoregressive regression model using maximum likelihood estimation.[†] In these analyses, there were three independent variables: the number of recipients of cash assistance, 5 months prior to the current month; a dichotomous variable indicating whether the current month is a pre- or a post-welfare reform month; and the current month's unemployment rate. The dependent variable was the count of the child welfare variable of interest in the current month.

Key Findings

During the months under study, the Cuyahoga County cash assistance caseloads declined, the unemployment rate remained relatively low and steady,[‡] and the child

---

[†] This technique allows an assessment as to whether a dependent time-series variable for a given month is related to an independent variable for that same month, after controlling for a third variable.

[‡] There was a steady decline from January 1995 through August 2001 in the number of recipients of cash assistance in Cuyahoga County. For example, in January 1995 there were 124,527 recipients; in September 1997 there were 95,796 recipients; and by August 2001, there were 34,061 recipients. By way of contrast, the unemployment rate in the county remained relatively steady throughout the study period.

welfare caseloads showed evidence of increasing child maltreatment in the community.[40] Between January 1995 and August 2001, there were increases in the number of children with substantiated reports referred to protective supervision, and in the number of children with such reports referred to foster care on a monthly basis. For example, between May 1995 and January 1996, there was a decline in the number of children with substantiated reports; after that month, the number of children each month varied between 336 and 370 until September 1997. After 1997, the number of children with substantiated reports varied, but the trend was upward so that by June 2001, the number of children with substantiated reports was 593. The statistical analysis of these data showed that this increase was related to the decrease in cash assistance counts in Cuyahoga County to a statistically significant degree ($p < .001$).

COHORT STUDY

Aim

Although it is useful to document the changes in Cuyahoga County child welfare caseloads under conditions of welfare reform, such data do not reveal whether length of stay in foster care is increasing or whether it is related to children's mothers' access to cash assistance or to wages. The Cohort Study focused on this issue.

The Cohort study examined three cohorts of children and their biological mothers: one cohort of children entered foster care prior to welfare reform, one entered foster care after the onset of welfare reform, and the third entered foster care after welfare recipients could begin to lose cash assistance in the county under investigation. This study tested whether a mother's economic circumstances delays the speed with which her children in foster care return home and, if negative economic circumstances are related to such a delay, whether the relationship is greater after welfare reform than before (see Wells and Gao 2006 for a list of specific study questions and other methodological details of this study.)[41]

Methodological Approach

We sought to achieve this aim with a staggered multiple-cohort design, a nonexperimental design which compares cohorts gathered at different times.[42] The study population of 2,128 children is comprised of all children entering foster care in Cuyahoga County between October 1 and March 31 for the following years: 1995–1996; 1998–1999; and 2000–2001. Each child also had to be age 16.5 years or less, from a single-mother home, and in foster care for the first time. Of these, 1,560 are in the study sample or 73 percent of the study population.

Children in the study samples were placed in foster care at different points in time during the three 6-month enrollment periods. They also remained in care for differing lengths of time. To manage this variability, we selected the 12 months after each child's entry into foster care as the period in which to examine reunification speed. This period of time is compatible with the permanency-planning deadline established under the Adoption and Safe Families Act of 1997.

After securing appropriate contracts and confidentiality agreements, we linked data from the three administrative data sets that we used in the Caseload Study. Study data are examined using event history analysis in general and the Cox proportional hazards model in particular.[43] In this study, the event of interest is reunification. Study data met the statistical requirements for use of the Cox model and the analysis was not threatened by multicollinearity among the independent variables.

Key Findings

When the three cohorts of foster children were compared, children who entered foster care after welfare reform are reunified with their biological mothers more slowly within 12 months of their placement than are children who entered care before reform. For example, children in the first post-welfare reform sample ($n = 522$) were reunified at a speed that is 42 percent slower than were children from the prewelfare reform sample ($n = 378$) ($p < .05$), after controlling for other variables with which speed of reunification has been associated in prior research.[44] Children from the second post-welfare reform sample ($n = 657$) were reunified at a speed that is 48 percent slower than were children from the prewelfare reform sample ($p < .01$), after controlling for other variables in the analysis described above.

In addition, after welfare reform, compared to before, a higher percentage of children are first placed in foster care, a higher percentage remain in care for more than 12 months, and a lower-percentage exit care within 12 months in the care of guardians. For example, before welfare reform, 37.3 percent of children were in care for more than 1 year compared to 45.7 percent and 53.4 percent (for post-reform samples 1 and 2, respectively), after reform.

Both before and after welfare reform, however, family income has a strong relationship to the speed with which children are returned home. For example, children whose mothers lose a significant amount of cash assistance, defined as a mother's first loss of $75 (or more) in cash assistance after her child's placement and before reunification or until her child has spent 12 months in foster care, whichever comes first, are reunified more slowly than are children whose mothers received cash assistance and did not lose such cash assistance ($p < .001$), after controlling for other variables in the analysis. The rate is 86 percent slower for the former than for the later group. Alternatively stated, 87 percent of children whose mothers received but lost a significant amount of cash assistance were in care 12 months after placement; this percentage differs dramatically from the percentage of children whose mothers received cash assistance but did not lose a significant amount of cash assistance—41 percent—at that same point in time.

INTERVIEW STUDY

Aim

While it is useful to know whether children's mothers economic circumstances are related to the speed with which they return home within the first year of placement, these findings do not reveal the full nature of mothers' economic circumstances, the obstacles they face to employment in the low-wage labor market, or suggest the full effects of mothers' economic circumstances on their children, as depth and duration of poverty has been linked strongly to poor child outcomes.[45]

The Interview Study focused on this issue by addressing the following questions: (1) What is the prevalence of mothers' material hardship and obstacles to employment? (2) Is maternal substance abuse either alone or in combination with other obstacles to employment related to a lowered likelihood that mothers are employed? (3) Is a mother's substance abuse related to the speed with which her child is reunified primarily through the effect such abuse has on a mother's loss of cash assistance? (4) What do mothers report that they need in order for their children to be returned to them, and what do they recommend regarding improvement of welfare and child welfare services? (see Wells, Gao, Shafran, and Pearlmutter 2004 for a more detailed articulation of this study than is presented here.)[46]

Methodological Approach

These questions were addressed with a subset of children and their biological mothers drawn from the Cohort Study's second post-welfare reform sample—those mothers who were 18 years of age at the time of data collection and who spoke English. Of the 436 mothers in the population, 178 provided informed consent to participate. The remaining 258 mothers were not interviewed for the following reasons: interviewers could not contact them, despite information as to their location ($n = 126$); interviewers (and the child welfare agency) lacked information regarding their locations ($n = 72$); interviewers did not contact mothers because the data collection period had ended ($n = 37$); or the mothers refused to be interviewed ($n = 23$). Thus, the study sample was 54 percent (178/327) of those eligible to be interviewed.

Study data were obtained from two sources: an in-person interview and administrative data pertaining to mothers' wages, use of cash assistance, and use of and treatment for substance dependence. The interview contained multiple measures drawn from those used in the Michigan Women's Employment Study,[47] the Illinois Family Study,[48] and in other components of our research program because these studies relied on concepts under examination in this investigation (see Wells and Shafran 2002 for a full description of the measures used in this study.)[49]

Interviews took place, on average, within 3 months after the mothers' children's placement in foster care. Each mother was interviewed once by one middle-aged female interviewer whose race matched her own. Interviewers were trained by principal investigators. Each interview lasted approximately 2 hours. Each mother received a cash payment of $40 for participation in the study.

Research question 1 was examined with descriptive statistics; question 2 with logistic regression analysis to determine whether employment outcomes differ for mothers with substance use alone or in combination with other obstacles to employment;

research question 3 was examined using event history analysis; and research question 4 was examined with content analysis.

Key Findings

Mothers with children in foster care are economically impoverished. Over three quarters (81.1%) had incomes that fall below the poverty level and over half (58.6%) had incomes that fall below the extreme poverty level. Thirty percent had no wages from work in the year after their children's placements and 47 percent had average total monthly wages of less than $500. About half (49.1%) had at least one significant material hardship beyond insufficient income from wages such as food insecurity, substandard housing, housing insecurity, and economic insecurity, variously defined.

Mothers also had multiple obstacles to employment and to a greater degree, on some obstacles, than do mothers in the general welfare population. Of the eleven obstacles studied, the most common obstacles to employment, in order of magnitude, were transportation (74.1%); lack of a high school education or a General Educational Degree (48.1%), and a substance use problem (48.1%).

Mothers with co-occurring obstacles to employment, especially obstacles posed by substance dependence, are less likely to be employed (at least 10 hours per week) than are mothers without such problems. For example, mothers with co-occurring substance use and human capital barriers (i.e., women with two of the following three barriers to employment—education, work, or job experience) were about 93 percent less likely to be employed than were mothers who did not have those barriers ($B = -2.65$, $Exp(B) = .07$, sig. $< .05$). Mothers with co-occurring substance use and mental health barriers were about 84 percent less likely to be employed than were mothers who did not have those barriers ($B = -1.81$, $Exp(B) = .016$, sig. $< .01$).

Moreover, children whose mothers abuse substances are reunified more slowly within 12 months of their placements than are children whose mothers do not; however, the effect of substance abuse on reunification speed is mediated through its effect on loss of cash assistance. Statistical analyses support the hypothesis that although a mother's substance use influences the rate at which her child returns home, the effect operates mainly through the effect a mother's substance use has on her loss of cash assistance postplacement. (See Wells, Gao, Shafran, and Pearlmutter 2004 for a more detailed discussion of this analysis.)[50]

Three quarters of mothers expected their children to return home, but stated that they needed concrete material assistance pertaining to, for example, housing and transportation in order for reunification to occur. Difficulties meeting the child welfare agency's expectations centered on lack of financial resources, conflicts between work and caring for others, and substance dependence.

Conclusion

Taken together, the findings from these studies suggest that child welfare families deteriorated under conditions of welfare reform in the county under study. I draw on several strands of evidence to support this conclusion—increases in child welfare caseloads; decreases in the speed with which children, once placed in foster care, are returning home; mothers living in extreme poverty; and mothers' loss of cash assistance slowing the speed with which their children in foster care return home. In addition, substance use emerges as a critical problem for this population. Indeed, the child welfare system has become the de facto substance abuse treatment system for very poor mothers.[†]

Alternative interpretations of these findings are, of course, possible, because the studies are not experiments. One such explanation is suggested by the policy study. In that study we found that although foundational aspects of the State's welfare reform strategy had been implemented, some elements had not.[51] For example, by mid-2000 only five of the eleven neighborhood-based centers through which services were to be available to county mothers were in place.[52] Moreover, at this same point in time, the mechanisms through which public agencies were to coordinate their efforts on behalf of impoverished parents were cumbersome, at best. As a result, subgroups that required services from more than one service system such as poor addicted mothers with children in foster care were unlikely to receive the help that they needed to ameliorate the problems that brought them to the attention of the child welfare system and to find or to keep paid employment. Thus, child welfare families may have deteriorated under conditions of welfare reform because services were unavailable or insufficient.

Nonetheless, mothers state that they need concrete help and study data to support their claim. However, the kinds of help needed—transportation, housing, or a living wage—are beyond the purview of a public child welfare agency. As a result, it is not surprising that recent calls for reform of the child welfare system emphasize the importance of integrating services to protect children with those designed to support their families.[53] What may be at issue is not only mothers' abilities to regain custody of their children but also their status in society. Without minimizing mothers' strengths[54] or the risks some mothers may pose to the safety of their children, it is important to recognize the extent of their victimization. "Perhaps the Declaration of Human Rights, designed to fight discrimination and oppression throughout the world, is the appropriate framework in which to develop a response to this highly disadvantaged population."[55]

NOTES

*This research program was funded, in part, by The Annie E. Casey Foundation, The Cleveland Foundation, The George Gund Foundation, the Ohio Department of Mental Health, as well as by its sponsoring institutions, the Mandel School of Applied Social Sciences

---

[†] Recent research suggests why prototypical treatment programs do not work well for this population. Substance dependence among women develops in response to preexisting anxieties, phobias, or psychiatric disorders and in relationship to significant incompletely or, more relationship difficulties. As a result, their neuropsychological functioning is impaired and the likelihood that they will recover quickly from addiction is low.[56]

at Case Western Reserve University, and the Cuyahoga County Department of Children and Family Services. I am also grateful for the assistance provided by the Cuyahoga County Department of Job and Family Services with data required for the conduct of this program and to Mandel School's Center on Poverty and Social Change for preparation of these data.

1. Neil B. Guterman and Catherine A. Taylor, "Prevention of Child Abuse and Neglect," in *Child Welfare for the Twenty-First Century: A Handbook of Practices, Policies, and Programs*, ed. Gerald Mallon and Peg McCartt Hess (New York: Columbia University Press, 2005), 270–289.

2. Leroy Pelton, *For Reasons of Poverty* (New York: Praeger, 1989).

3. Greg J. Duncan and Jeanne Brooks-Gunn, "Making Welfare Reform Work for Our Youngest Child," *Child Poverty News and Issues* 8(1) (1998). Available at http://www.nccp.org/media/spr980text.pdf (accessed on March 9, 2006).

4. Ibid.

5. Pelton, *For Reasons of Poverty*.

6. Isabel Wolock and Bernard Horowitz, Child Maltreatment and Material Deprivation among AFDC Recipient Families, *Social Service Review* 53 (1979), 175–194.

7. Diane Depanfilis, Child Protective Services, in *Child Welfare for the Twenty-First Century: A Handbook of Practices, Policies, and Programs* (New York: Columbia University Press, 2005), 290–301.

8. U.S. Department of Health and Human Services, Office of the Assistant Secretary for Planning and Evaluation, *Dynamics of Children's Movement Among AFDC, Medicaid, and Foster Care Programs Prior to Welfare Reform: 1995–1996* (Washington, DC: U.S. Government Printing Office, 2000).

9. Pelton, *For Reasons of Poverty*.

10. Ibid., p. 42.

11. *Adoption Assistance and Child Welfare Act of 1980*, Public Law 96-272.

12. *Adoption and Safe Families Act of 1997*, Public Law 105-189.

13. Duncan Lindsey, *The Welfare of Children* (2nd ed.) (Oxford: University Press, 2004).

14. Leslie Doty Hollingsworth, "Birth Mothers Whose Parental Rights are Terminated: Implications for Services," in *Child Welfare for the Twenty-First Century: A Handbook of Practices, Policies, and Programs*, ed. Gerald Mallon and Peg McCartt Hess (New York: Columbia University Press, 2005), 469–481

15. Depanfilis, "Child Protective Services."

16. U. S. Department of Health and Human Services, *The AFCARS Report*, Available at http://www.acf.hhs.gov/programs/cb/stats_research/afcars/tar/report9.htm (accessed on March 9, 2006).

17. Social Security Act of 1935, Title IV: ADC, and Title V: Child Welfare Services Program.

18. Mark Courtney, "Welfare Reform and Child Welfare Services," in *Child Welfare in the Context of Welfare Reform*, ed. Sheila Kamerman and Alfred Kahn, Report V 1-35 (New York: Columbia University School of Social Work, Cross National Studies Research Program, 1997).

19. Mark Hardin, "Sizing Up the Welfare Act's Impact on Child Protection," *Clearinghouse Review* (Jan.–Feb., 1997), 1061–1068.

20. Rob Geen and Karen C. Tumlin, *State Efforts to Remake Child Welfare: Responses to New Challenges and Increased Scrutiny*, Washington, DC: The Urban Institute Occasional Paper no. 29 (1999), available at http://www.urban.org/Content/Research/NewFederalism/Publications/PublicationbyTopic/Income/Childwelfare/child.htm (accessed on August 15, 2003).

21. U.S. Department of Health and Human Services, *Blending Perspectives and Building Common Ground: A Report to Congress on Substance Abuse and Child Protection* (Washington, DC: U.S. Government Printing Office, 1999).

22. National Council of Juvenile and Family Court Judges, *Effective Intervention in Domestic Violence and Child Maltreatment Cases: Guidelines for Policy and Practice* (Reno, NV: Author, 1999).

23. SAMSHASA, *Exploring Opportunities for Addressing Children's Mental Health and Child Welfare Issues* (Washington, DC: U.S. Department of Health and Human Services, Administration for Children and Families, 2000).

24. Courtney, "Welfare Reform and Child Welfare Services."

25. Kristin Shook, "Does the Loss of Welfare Income Increase the Risk of Involvement with the Child Welfare System?" *Children and Youth Services Review* 21(9/10) (1999), 781–814.

26. Rutledge Q. Hutson, *Red Flags: Research Raises Concerns about the Impact of Welfare Reform on Child Maltreatment* (Washington, DC: Center for Law and Social Policy, 2001).

27. Courtney, "Welfare Reform and Child Welfare Services."

28. Kathleen Wells, Shenyang Guo, Robert Shafran, and Sue Pearlmutter, *The Impact of Welfare Reform on Child Welfare in Cuyahoga County, Ohio, Project Final Report*, Final Report Submitted to the Annie E. Casey Foundation, the Cleveland Foundation, and the George Gund Foundation (Cleveland, OH: Case Western Reserve University, Mandel School of Applied Social Sciences, 2004); Kathleen Wells, *The Impact of Welfare Reform on the Child Welfare System in Cuyahoga County*, Ohio, 2995-2001, Policy Brief 06-1 (Cleveland, OH: Case Western Reserve University, College of Arts and Sciences, The Schubert Center for Child Development, 2006).

29. Claudia J. Coulton, Jill E. Korbin, Marilyn Su, and Julian Chow, "Community Level Factors and Child Maltreatment Rates," *Child Development* 66 (1995), 1262–1276.

30. U.S. Census Bureau (2003).

31. Thomas Brock, Claudia Coulton, Andrew London, Denise Polit, Lashawn Richburg-Hayes, Ellen Scott, and Nandita Verma, *Welfare Reform in Cleveland: Implementation, Effects, and Experiences of Poor Families and Neighborhoods, Report on the Project on Devolution and Change, 2002*. Available at http://www.mdrc.org/Reports2002us_cleveland/uc_ cleveland_fullreport.pd (accessed on August 15, 2003).

32. Annie E. Casey Foundation, "CLIKS: County-City-Community-Level Information on Kids 2003." Available at http://www.aecf.org/cgi-bin/cloks.cgi (accessed on March 18, 2003).

33. U. S. Census, *Fact Sheet: Cleveland City Ohio 2000*. Available at http//quickfacts. census.gov/qfd/states/39/3916000.html (accessed on March 21, 2006).

34. Ohio H. R. 408, 1997–1998 General Assembly, 122nd session, 1997.

35. Brock et al., *Welfare Reform in Cleveland*.

36. Charles Adams and Miriam Wilson, "Welfare Reform Meets the Devolution Revolution in Ohio," in *Learning from Leaders: Welfare Reform Politics and Policies in Five Mid-western States*, ed. Carol Weissert, 25–49 (Albany, NY: State University of New York, 2000).

37. Wells et al., "The Impact of Welfare Reform."

38. Donald Campbell and Julian Stanley, *Experimental and Quasi-Experimental Designs for Research* (Chicago, IL: Rand McNally, 1967).

39. Robert S. Pindyk and Daniel L. Rubinfeld, *Econometric models and economic forecasts* (4th ed.) (New York: McGraw Hill, 1998).

40. Wells et al., "The Impact of Welfare Reform."

41. Ibid; Kathleen Wells and Shenyang Guo, "Welfare Reform and Child Welfare Outcomes: A Multi-cohort Study," *Children and Youth Services Review* 28 (2006), 941–960.

42. Stephen Feinberg and William M. Mason, "Specification and Implementation of Age, Period, and Cohort Models," in *Cohort Analysis in Social Research: Beyond the Identification Problem*, eds. Stephen Feinberg and William M. Mason, 44-88 (New York: Springer, 1985).

43. Paul Allison, *Survival Analysis Using the SAS System: A Practical Guide* (Cary: SAS Institute, Inc., 1995).

44. Kathleen Wells and Shenyang Guo, "Reunification and Entry of Foster Children," *Children and Youth Services Review* 21(4) (1999), 273–294; Kathleen Wells and Shenyang Guo, "Reunification of Foster Children Before and After Welfare Reform," *Social Service Review* 78(1) (2004), 1–22.

45. Jeanne Brooks-Gunn and Greg J. Duncan, "The Effects of Poverty on Children," *The Future of Children* 7(2) (1997): 55–71.

46. Wells et al., "The Impact of Welfare Reform."

47. Women's Employment Study—Wave 1 Instrument (University of Michigan, School of Social Work, Michigan Program on Poverty and Social Welfare, Survey Instrument, Wave 1, 1997). Available at http://www.fordschool.umich.edu/poverty/wes/instrument/coverqn.pdf (accessed on October 14, 2002); Sandra Danziger, Mary Corcoran, Sheldon Danziger, Colleen Hefler, Ariel Kalil, Dan Rosen, and Diane DePanfilis, "Barriers to the Employment of Welfare Recipients," in *The Impact of Tight Labor Markets on Black Employment*, ed. Robert Cherry and William M. Rodgers, 239–269 (Ann Arbor, MI: University of Michigan Program on Poverty and Social Welfare Policy, 2000).

48. Dan A. Lewis, Kristen Shook, Amy Stevens, Paul Kleppner, James Lewis and Stephanie Riger, *Work, Welfare, and Well-Being: An Independent Look at Welfare Reform in Illinois* (Evanston, IL: Northwestern University, Institute for Policy Research, 2000).

49. Kathleen Wells and Robert Shafran, "Mental Health Needs of Biological Mothers of Children in Foster Care," Final Report Submitted to the Office of Program Evaluation and Research, Ohio Department of Mental Health (Cleveland, OH: Case Western Reserve University, Mandel School of Applied Social Sciences, 2002).

50. Wells et al., "The Impact of Welfare Reform."

51. Ibid.

52. Cuyahoga Work and Training, *2000 Annual Report* (Cleveland, OH: Author, 2000).

53. U.S. Department of Health and Human Services, *National Study of Child Protective Services Systems and Reform Efforts Review of State CPS Policy* (Washington, DC: U.S. Department of Health and Human Services, 2003). Available at aspe.hhs.gov/hsp/cps-status03/state-policy03/.; James Whittaker and Anthony Maluccio, "Rethinking 'Child Placement': A Reflective Essay," *Social Service Review* (March 2002), 108–134.

54. Gretchen Kirby, Thomas Fraker, LaDonna Pavetti and Martha Kovac, *Families on TANF in Illinois: Employment Assets and Liabilities* (Washington, DC: Mathematica Policy Research, 2003).

55. United Nations General Assembly, *Universal Declaration of Human Rights,* Adopted and Proclaimed by General Assembly Resolution 217 (III) of 10 December 1948. Available at http://www.un.org/overview/rights.html (accessed on December 16, 2003); Kathleen Wells and Robert Shafran, Obstacles to Employment among Mothers of Children in Foster Care, *Child Welfare* LXXXIV(1) (2005), 67–96.

56. Paige Quimette and Pamela J. Brown, *Trauma and Substance Abuse: Causes, Consequences, and Treatment for Co-morbid Disorders* (Washington, DC: American Psychological Association).

CHAPTER 3

NAVIGATING THE WELFARE TIME LIMIT IN CALIFORNIA: HOW DO FAMILIES FARE?*

Jane Gilbert-Mauldon, Rebecca A. London, and Heidi Sommer

The welfare reform law of 1996, PRWORA (the Personal Responsibility and Work Opportunity Act), which authorized the new TANF (Temporary Assistance to Needy Families) program, was heralded as a route to self-sufficiency for millions of low-income families who had been languishing on the welfare rolls. Government was no longer to be complicit with a culture of despair and victimhood, within which—it was said—entire generations grew into adulthood dependent on government aid, with no prospects of decent employment and its attendant benefits. Rather, state welfare agencies would, by prodding, encouragement, training, practical assistance, and ultimately through sanctions and grant terminations, help welfare recipients step from dependency onto the escalator of gainful employment. They would gradually be carried upward toward economic self-sufficiency, self-respect and full participation in the American economy, and in the process transform the prospects for their children—a transformation which was, in the minds of many, the most cherished hope but also the greatest and riskiest challenge of welfare reform.

In the 10 years since PRWORA passed, all 50 states have renovated their welfare programs to conform to the TANF mandates, and in the process greatly reduced their caseloads. State policies differ widely, most especially in how they include (or do not) families who seem reluctant or unable to step onto the employment escalator, or who fall off it, or abandon it. When states provide additional supports beyond the minimum mandated by PRWORA, these are often justified as aid to the neediest children, rather than to adults.

In this chapter we use data from one such relatively generous state, California, to explore how parents and children fare as they pass through the federal 5-year welfare time limit. We look at parents' abilities to provide for their children: What barriers do they face in navigating the world of work, and what supports does government provide for them? Are they employed, and how much are they earning? A child's well-being is intimately tied to his or her family's resources: How much money do families have, before and after reaching the time limit—is it enough to escape poverty? What does this income translate into, in terms of quality of life: Does the family have adequate housing, enough food, and basic utilities; can they get medical care when needed? And finally, how are children themselves faring: Are they healthy? Do they have regular medical care? As teenagers, how are they coping with the transition to adulthood?

Yet showing, as we do, that these post-time limit children typically live in deep poverty, often experience material hardship, and encounter a rocky adolescence is perhaps not of great value to policymakers. After all, this has always been true of children in families that receive welfare—by definition, welfare serves those at the bottom of the income distribution. The critical question for policy-makers is how to promote self-sufficiency through TANF policies and still protect children whose parents cannot step on, or stay on, the escalator. That is our focus here: We classify families as those who are relatively self-sufficient, those who are struggling, and those with so many barriers that they are not likely to succeed, and follow their well-being into the next year as they cross the time-limit threshold. By situating the study in a state—California—that has chosen to continue some support to needy families who have exhausted their TANF entitlement, we explore the protective possibilities offered by such policies.

WELFARE POLICY NATIONALLY AND IN CALIFORNIA: AN OVERVIEW

The work-first, time-limited approach mandated by TANF is intended as only a bridge, or a boost, for families needing short-term help to navigate some kind of temporary health or employment setback or family disruption. It was thought that the 5 years of assistance provided by the law would be enough to address deeper-seated barriers to employment among needier families. Children, in this framework, would benefit directly as their parents' earnings increased and indirectly by seeing their parents (and, by extension, themselves) as part of the economic mainstream. The assumption built into TANF that within 5 years almost all families can earn enough to not need welfare was the most controversial aspect of the law.

The dire predictions of PRWORA's harshest critics have not been borne out, but neither have predictions that facing a time limit would generate greater prosperity among welfare leavers. The number of families receiving TANF declined 57 percent between August 1996 and June 2005,[1] but this change in caseload has not universally been associated with greater well-being among families. For example, the Urban Institute's National Survey of America's Families found that while work and median earnings among welfare recipients increased after 1997, poverty remained high—69 percent were still in poverty in 2002 (though families in "deep poverty" declined from 60 percent to 42 percent).[2] Only 57 percent of welfare leavers were working in 2002, at median hourly earnings of $8, and 26 percent returned to welfare within

2 years of exiting (up from 20% in 1997). Receipt of federally funded food stamps and health insurance did increase among welfare exiters between 1999 and 2002—28 to 35 percent for food stamps and 40 to 48 percent for health insurance—indicating that as TANF implementation progressed, state human service agencies became more adept at helping exiting recipients access the programs for which they continued to be eligible even after leaving welfare.

CalWORKs, California's welfare program, serves a broad swath of needy families. The program has a vigorous employment focus: recipients are expected to address and overcome, not be deterred by, their own difficulties in finding and keeping work. Funding is available, although perhaps not always sufficient, to address mental health, substance abuse, and domestic violence problems as well as to cover practical needs for childcare and transportation. Parents can receive up to the full 5 years of lifetime aid permitted under TANF.

Within its strong employment focus, the state permits up to ten reasons for a Cal-WORKs exemption—which stops the time-limit "clock"—and six more reasons for an extension to the time limit.[3] California policy-makers have also adopted policies and programs to aid needy families that become ineligible for the full TANF grant. After timing out, parents can enroll their children in a state-funded child-only program (called the Safety Net), which provides roughly the equivalent of a child-only Cal-WORKs grant. Families sanctioned for noncompliance can also receive a child-only CalWORKs grant.

The diverse program elements in CalWORKs, along with the state's complex demography, combine to create a very heterogeneous (and large) caseload.[4] CalWORKs recipients are almost as likely, as not, to speak English, and there is a wide variety of languages spoken by the non-English speakers. Economically, the caseload is diverse as well. For instance, in the agricultural Central Valley many parents receive large CalWORKs grants during the winter when there is no agricultural work available, and minimal grants (or none) during the peak harvest months when they are fully employed.

THE RESEARCH BEHIND THE FINDINGS

Given the complexity of the CalWORKs program and its interplay with the state's demographic and economic diversity, the legislature mandated an evaluation of the consequences of the time limit for recipient families (and for state and county agencies and budgets), which provided the survey data used in this chapter. A random sample of timing-out families was selected from the welfare rolls in six California counties, with two-parent and non-English-speaking families over-represented. The six counties were: Alameda (covering most the eastern edge of the San Francisco Bay, including the city of Oakland); Los Angeles (with one-third of the population of the state); Orange (a geographically small, prosperous county south of Los Angeles); Riverside (a desert county that is rapidly becoming home to many who work in Los Angeles); Sacramento (home to the state Capitol, with a substantial rural/agricultural population) and Tulare (in the Central Valley, and heavily dependent on agriculture).

These counties, which together account for more than half of California's welfare caseload, reflect the geographic, economic and demographic diversity of California.

Ultimately 1,797 individuals agreed to join the study and were interviewed by telephone between June 2004 and August 2005, the months just prior to the month we expected them to have accumulated 60 months of aid.[5] The majority of respondents to this initial survey were then reinterviewed some 6–9 months later, with a reinterview response rate of 79 percent.[6] Confining the two-interview analyses to respondents interviewed in English, Spanish, or Vietnamese[7] and living with their own children in the same family type in both interviews leaves us with 1,043 respondents for all the analyses reported here (unless indicated otherwise). The data are weighted to be representative of participants in any one of the six focus counties.[8]

In addition to recording basic household demographic information, we asked these parents to explain their welfare status at each interview (whether they were still getting CalWORKs, had gone to the Safety Net, or were off cash aid entirely); and we asked about their current and recent employment, including their hours worked, wages and total household cash income (excluding food stamps). All measures in this chapter, including employment, earnings and CalWORKs receipt, are self-reported by survey respondents.

The survey results indicate that our respondents included some relatively self-sufficient families who in other states would have been excluded from assistance (and welfare studies) because of their more-than-minimal earnings. Parents were working "full-time"—31 or more hours a week currently or during in the previous year—in 32 percent of our respondent families.[9] At the other end of the spectrum, 48 percent were not working at all and had not worked in the preceding year. In many other states these families would have long since disappeared from welfare rolls because of stricter sanctions and time limit policies.

These two completely disparate groups—one not working at all, the other employed essentially full-time—together comprised 80 percent of the sample and, presumably, of the timing-out caseload. Most of the remainder (14%) had "low work hours"—less than 20 hours a week, or 30 hours between two parents.[10] The final 6 percent were a heterogenous left-over group with "intermediate" work hours—single parents currently working between 20 and 30 hours per week and two-parent families in which both parents currently worked part-time totaling more than 30 hours per week.

BARRIERS AND EMPLOYMENT

Previous research from across the country provides ample evidence that many welfare recipients face substantial barriers to work. A Chapin Hall study found that four out of five welfare applicants in Wisconsin reported one or more employment barriers and more than half reported having two or more.[11] Hauan and Douglas reported that among welfare workers in six states, the most common barriers to employment were the presence of health (21%) or mental health (30%) problems; having a child with special needs (29%); having no high school diploma or GED

(40%); having limited work experience (22%); issues with unstable housing (22%) or transportation (27%) and childcare problems (34%).[12] Similarly, Zedlewski found that among welfare recipients nationally, 42 percent did not have a diploma or GED, 35 percent were in poor health and 30 percent had not worked in recent years.[13] This evaluation, based on National Survey of American Families data, indicated that 44 percent of welfare recipients reported two or more barriers to employment.

These studies indicate that employment barriers typically not only persist over time but are in fact correlated with reduced work participation.[11,13] Courtney and Dworsky[11] find that those with more barriers were statistically less likely to be currently employed 3 years after applying for aid. Sixty percent of those reporting no barriers were currently employed at Wave 3 versus 35 percent among those with two barriers, and 9 percent among those with four barriers. After controlling for other personal liabilities, Hauan and Douglas[12] find that only limited education or work experience, poor physical health, childcare issues, or being pregnant had a negative effect on actual employment. Nationally, although those facing barriers increased their employment after the implementation of welfare reform (from 5% in 1997 to 20% in 1999) their work participation decreased to 14 percent in 2002 when the economy weakened.[13]

Unlike many other states, California permits exemptions to the welfare time limit for five possible employment barriers: having a disability that limits work; caring for an ill or incapacitated person residing in the home; being a victim of domestic abuse; residing in an high-unemployment Indian reservation or rancheria; or participating in a teen-parent welfare program (i.e., being a teen parent). We inquired about the first three conditions, confining the questions about domestic violence to the last year, defining "disabled" as a health problem that limited the respondent's ability to work, and asking about caregiving responsibilities for ill or impaired household members that affected the respondents' ability to work We also tried to identify the presence of a likely learning disability, and asked whether any of five mental health problems had, in the past year, interfered with the respondent's ability to work, go to school, or care for children, namely: depression, anxiety, a stressful event (which does not include divorce or childbirth), alcohol use or drug use.[14]

Our survey data confirm that many of California's long-term welfare recipients face health, mental health, caregiving, or other challenges.[15] Twenty-three percent of respondents suffered from a disabling physical or mental health problem that limited their ability to work.[16] Caregiving often imposed barriers: 11 percent had one or more children with a health problem sufficiently severe to limit their parents' ability to work, and 4 percent were limited by caring for a disabled or impaired family member. Eleven percent of respondents had experienced domestic violence in the preceding year. Thirty-four percent reported at least one mental health barrier—depression, anxiety, thoughts of a stressful event, alcohol use, or drug use—that interfered with work, home or school (and that did not trigger a positive response to the preceding question about disabling health conditions that limit ability to work). Finally, we found 15 percent with a likely learning disability.

As Table 3.1 shows, respondents working at least 31 hours a week (called "full-time" in the table) had fewer barriers than those working fewer hours. Conversely,

Table 3.1
Incidence of Barriers to Employment, by Hours of Work at Wave 1

Percent in each category reporting the following:	Full-time workers (30+ hrs/wk)	Low or zero work hours (≤20 hrs/wk)	Intermediate work hours (21–29 hrs/wk)	Total
		Hours of Work		
Has 0 or 1 reported barrier (of 9)	82.2 (Group A)	56.4 (Group B)	67.0 (Group D)	65.4
Has 2 barriers (of 9)	9.6 (Group D)	17.0 (Group B)	18.4 (Group D)	14.7
Has 3 or 4 barriers (of 9)	6.9 (Group D)	18.2 (Group C)	12.8 (Group D)	14.2
Has 5 or more barriers (of 9)	1.3 (Group D)	8.4 (Group C)	1.8 (Group D)	5.7
Sample Size (unweighted)	309	672	62	1043

employment was less among those confronted by more barriers. However, a substantial number of people had relatively few (fewer than three) reported barriers and were nevertheless working only a few hours a week or not at all. Their employment may have been inhibited by external barriers, such as lack of jobs, or lack of appropriate child care, or, perhaps, by personal or family-related barriers that our interview questions did not capture.

The distribution of barriers among the 48 percent of respondents not working at all currently or in the preceding year was very similar to the barriers facing people that worked limited (under 20) hours. These distributions are not shown separately in the table because, being similar, the two categories were combined into "little or no work." Within this combined category, 78 percent were nonworking and 22 percent worked limited hours.

Although each welfare participant's life is unique, we combine the information about barriers and employment to create four family "types," that chart different paths through the critical juncture of the 60-month time limit:

- Those who are relatively self-sufficient, with few barriers and substantial work effort—identified as Group A;
- Those who report few barriers, but with zero or low work hours (defined above)—identified as Group B;
- Those who face multiple barriers and zero or low work hours—identified as Group C; and
- A residual category (mixed) who work intermediate hours (defined above) and face any level of barriers—identified as Group D.

Each of these types of recipients appears in the political rhetoric and debates surrounding welfare and describes a substantial number of welfare participants. Group A, comprising 26 percent of the sample, met our work criteria for full-time and has no, or only one, employment barrier. Group B, the second and largest group with 45 percent of the sample, had zero or "low" work hours (defined above) and two or

Table 3.2
Incidence of Barriers to Employment, by Hours of Work at Wave 1

	Barrier Group				
Percent in each category reporting the following:	Few or no barriers, high work hours (Group A)	Few or some barriers, low work hours (Group B)	Many barriers, low work hours (Group C)	Mixed barrier profile, moderate work hours (Group D)	Total
A health-related barrier that interferes with work					
Own limiting health condition	8.4	21.3	52.1	22.1	23.1
Caregiving for a child with a limitation	2.6	7.2	29.1	16.7	10.8
Caregiving for another family member	2.4	3.8	5.8	5.9	4.0
Domestic violence by spouse/partner in past year	3.1	7.8	30.0	15.7	11.2
At least one mental health barrier— depression, anxiety, recall of a stressful event, alcohol use, or drug use—that interferes with work, home, or school.	8.2	20.7	94.8	53.1	33.7
Likely learning disability	2.2	10.7	35.0	31.7	15.1
Sample Size (unweighted)	309	156	516	62	1043

fewer barriers. Some of this group might have been unable to find work; some may have had significant personal barriers not captured in the available data, and some may have chosen to care for their children, pursue education, or simply stay at home rather than work.

Group C includes recipients who *both* faced multiple (three to nine) barriers to work *and* had zero or low work hours; this group is 16 percent of the sample. All the evidence—descriptions of their health, mental health, and caregiving obligations, as well as their limited or nonexistent participation in the world of work—points to these parents as unusually challenged, even among long-term welfare recipients. Three-fourths of Groups B and C (78 and 77 % respectively) were not working when interviewed and had not worked during the previous year. Finally, the fourth, residual group (Group D) comprises the 6 percent with "intermediate" work hours and a further 7 percent who worked full-time despite having more than three barriers.

As Table 3.2 shows, health and mental health problems are the most common barriers reported by parents in all of these groups. Among Group C respondents, who by definition have three or more barriers, 52 percent were limited in their own health, 29 percent were limited by their children's health problem, 6 percent were caring for an adult household member, 30 percent reported domestic violence in the past year, 95 percent had one or more mental health problems that interfered with work and were not already listed as a limiting health impairment, and 35 percent had a likely learning disability. Among Group B respondents, with fewer problems on average (48% have zero barriers, 29% had one, and 23% had two), 21 percent were also limited in their own health, and 21 percent reported, in addition, a limiting specific mental health problem.

These groups differ in important ways apart from work and barriers—in marriage/cohabitation, ethnicity and language, and education (Table 3.3). Group A respondents, those with few barriers and substantial work, were nearly one-third married or cohabiting, which is double the proportion in the sample overall. Marital status correlates closely with ethnicity: Group A included many Vietnamese speaking Vietnamese (22%, compared to 8% of the entire sample), and Spanish-speaking Latinos (15% compared to 10% overall). These non-English-speaking respondents had somewhat less education than other groups; 39 percent of Group A lacked a high-school diploma and 25 percent had attended any college. Group C, in contrast, was almost all English-speaking (92%) and relatively well-educated, with 42 percent having attended college (and one-quarter of these obtaining a degree). Group C parents were almost all single (95%).

Put differently, the demographic characteristics of these long-term welfare users—their marital status, their ethnicity and their education—are powerfully tied to their employment and the barriers they face. Just over half of the married/cohabiting respondents were in Group A and very few were in Group C. Single-parent respondents were about as likely to be in Group A as in Group C (one-fifth of each). Vietnamese and Spanish speakers were far less likely to be in Group C compared to white and

Table 3.3
Demographic Characteristics for each Study Group at Wave 1

		Barrier Group			
Percent in each category reporting the following:	Group A Few or no barriers, high work hours	Group B Few or some barriers, low work hours	Group C Many barriers, low work hours	Group D Mixed barrier profile, moderate work hours	Total
Marital Status					
Single	67.7	90.0	95.0	85.7	84.5
Married or cohabiting	32.3	10.0	5.0	14.3	15.5
Race/Ethnicity and Language					
White, English speaking	14.3	18.7	22.3	22.2	18.6
African American, English speaking	24.2	36.0	34.3	32.8	32.3
Latina, English speaking	19.8	21.5	19.6	26.3	21.3
Latina, Spanish speaking	14.7	10.7	4.5	6.7	10.2
Vietnamese, Vietnamese speaking	22.1	3.1	3.0	5.0	8.3
Asian or other race/ethnicity, English speaking	3.7	9.6	15.9	6.5	8.7
Education Level					
High school dropout	38.6	39.7	36.4	32.6	38.0
High school diploma or GED	36.3	34.5	21.9	31.1	32.5
Some college or college degree	25.0	25.8	41.7	36.3	29.5
Sample Size (unweighted)	309	156	516	62	1043

African American English speakers, which may reflect different cultural or interpretational responses to the survey questions. Among these long-term users of welfare, more than one-quarter have some college education, but college-educated parents faced more employment barriers than average.

HARDSHIPS AND INCOME AT FIRST INTERVIEW

A central focus of the interview was whether respondents were able to secure a materially stable life for themselves and their children. We asked whether, during the past year (or since the last interview) the family experienced any of 12 "material hardships." We asked whether they: lacked the money needed for (a) their rent or mortgage, (b) paying utility bills, (c) buying food, (d) paying for basic things; (e) shared housing to cut cost, (f) had to move when they did not want to, (g) had their utilities shut off, (h) had their car repossessed, (i) used a food bank or (j) soup kitchen, or (k) borrowed from family; and finally, (l) did they or someone in their immediate family not get medical care when they needed it? We found these indicators of economic stress or hardship to be very widespread (data not shown): virtually all (97%) of our respondents reported at least one within the previous year. About one-third (32%) had two or fewer, 30 percent had three or four, and nearly 40 percent reported five or more hardships. The most common were borrowing money from family (59%), lacking money for utilities (54%) or basic things in general (52%), and using a food bank (45%).[17]

As Table 3.4 shows, Group C, with many barriers and low or no work, stands out as having had many more problems than other groups. The high-barrier low-work families reported 5.5 hardships each, on average, compared to 3.1 problems per family in Group A, 3.7 in Group B and 4.1 in the residual Group D. Because the other three groups largely resembled each other, they are combined in Table 3.4. The biggest proportionate differences were in the rates of not getting medical care when needed (reported by 24% of Group C and 9 percent of others, usually about an adult family member); having had a car repossessed (32% compared to 15%); not having had enough money for food and/or using a food bank (56% versus 35%, and 69% versus 37%), utility shut-offs (35% compared to 21%) and having been compelled to move (29% compared to 19%).

Many of these hardships are likely to have been detrimental to children. Children notice when their family lacks (or, perhaps even worse, loses) basic amenities—utilities are shut off, a car is repossessed, there is not enough food in the house. The dislocations that come with moving—particularly moves that are compelled rather than voluntary—can be very stressful and has been shown to be detrimental to children's future well-being.[18] Knowing that a family member has an untreated medical problem can also be upsetting for children.

The problems just discussed are tangible indicators of a difficult and stressful life. A more widely accepted, although less direct, metric of life's quality is family income, which we report next. We calculated the ratio of the respondent's reported monthly household cash income from all sources (although not in-kind assistance such as food

Table 3.4
Incidence of Material Hardship and Average Numbers of Hardships at Wave 1, Many Barrier/Low Work Group compared to All Others

Material Hardships	Group C: Working little or not at all, and three or more barriers	All other respondents
Housing		
Could not afford rent in last year	49.6	40.7
Currently share housing	22.1	20.6
Had to move in past year	28.9	18.5
Utilities		
Could not afford utilities in past year	64.9	48.8
Utilities shut off in past year	35.3	21.0
Transportation		
Car repossessed in past year	32.2	14.6
Food sufficiency		
Could not afford food in past year	56.3	34.9
Use food bank in past year	69.4	36.6
Use soup kitchen in past year	19.7	9.8
Health Care		
Someone in family did not get needed medical care in past year	24.4	8.8
Other Hardships		
Not enough money for basic things in past year	72.6	47.1
Borrowed money from family in past year	73.3	55.9
Average number of hardships in past year	5.5	3.6
Sample Size (unweighted)	168	875

stamps, housing, or child care) to the federal poverty threshold for each household size.[19] Respondents' household incomes were categorized as less than 50 percent, 50–99 percent, 100–149 percent, 150–200 percent, or more than 200 percent of the poverty threshold. (In 2005, the federal poverty threshold for a single-parent family with two children was $15,735 annually.)

Just as with the material hardship measures, we found large differences between groups. As Figure 3.1 illustrates, virtually all respondent families lived in poverty, and many were below 50 percent of the poverty threshold. Indeed, the majority of families in Groups B and C reported incomes lower than half of the federal poverty threshold.

As would be expected, poverty was most closely tied to employment, but less tied to the number of barriers respondents faced. Whereas the measure of hardships showed the low-barrier groups (Groups A and B) better off than others, the poverty measures showed the most-employed groups (Groups A and D) substantially better off.

In addition to household-level income and hardships, the survey provides some specific information about children's well-being. Figure 3.2 shows that one-quarter (26%) of the families had at least one child who had a "health condition, disability,

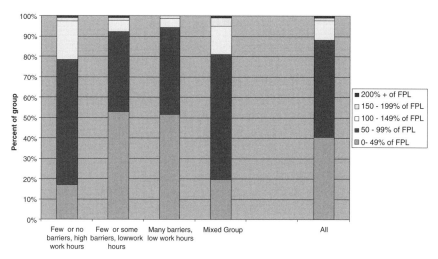

Figure 3.1
Family Income as a % of Federal Poverty Level (FPL) at Wave 1 by Work/Barrier Group

or behavioral condition that limit[ed] the kinds of things or amount of things that they [could] do, such as playing, going to school or participating in family activities;" a quarter of these families (6% of all families) had more than one such child. Among the conditions asked about, the most commonly reported (though not shown here) were asthma or allergies (16 percent of the sample), Attention Deficit Disorder (9%), behavioral or emotional problems (8%) and developmental delays (6%). In sum, child health problems were common and often serious among long-term welfare users.

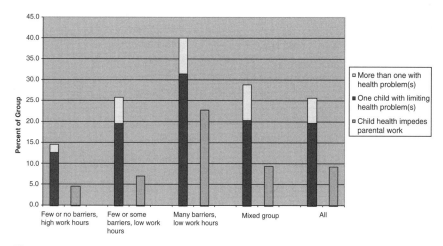

Figure 3.2
Child Health Problems, by Work/Barrier Group

Over a third of these parents—9 percent of all respondents—reported that their child's health problem interfered with their or their spouse's ability to work, so that they could not work at all (3% of the sample), could not work the hours needed (3% of sample), or encountered some other impediment (the final 3%). Child health problems that interfere with work were included in the list of employment barriers, so it is natural they were the most prevalent in the many barriers/low work Group C. Among these families, 32 percent had one child with a limiting condition and 8 percent had two or more, for a total of 40 percent in this group—more than double the rate of 15 percent in Group A. These health problems interfered with work for 23 percent of Group C compared to 5 percent of Group A. Eleven percent of Group C parents had a developmentally delayed child, 8 percent a child with loss of sight or hearing, 19 percent a child with emotional or behavioral problems sufficient to limit their activities, 17 percent a child with ADD and 26 percent a child with asthma or allergies (results not shown here).

HOW DID FAMILIES FARE AFTER REACHING THE TIME LIMIT?

A central part of the analysis was to investigate whether, after the time limit, families became worse off. Reaching the time limit means, in most states, that the entire family becomes ineligible for welfare unless they qualify for an exemption (which, as noted earlier, most states do not offer apart from the exemptions mandated by TANF). In California, families may qualify for the Safety Net if their incomes are low enough. Safety Net grants are lower than regular CalWORKs grants by the amount associated with the (now excluded) adults in the family. The program, therefore, was intended to protect children from extreme poverty but, on the other hand, to ensure that there was some consequence of reaching the time-limit.

We compared numbers of hardships and the prevalence of specific hardships from the first survey to the second, for each group and for the sample as a whole. The results (Figure 3.3) were strikingly similar at the two interviews. Families with full employment and few barriers reported an average of 3.1 hardships at Wave 1 and 3.0 at Wave 2; the low-employment/few barriers group had on average 3.7 hardships, the low-employment/many barriers group 5.5, and the "Mixed" group had 4.1, followed by 4.0, hardships. In short, while individual families fared better or worse in the second year, overall rates did not change.

The income-to-poverty ratios were also remarkably constant across the two interviews. As Figure 3.1 shows, at the first interview 41 percent of the entire sample were below half the poverty level, with 17 percent, 53 percent, 52 percent and 20 percent (respectively) of Groups A, B, C, and D at that level. At the second interview the rates were virtually identical: 40 percent of the sample and 17 percent, 52 percent, 50 percent and 23 percent (respectively) of Groups A, B, C, and D were below half of the poverty threshold.

The only area in which we see any cross-wave differences are in reports of behavior problems among teenagers, which are very prevalent in these families. At the first interview, 29 percent of parents had a teen that had been suspended or expelled from

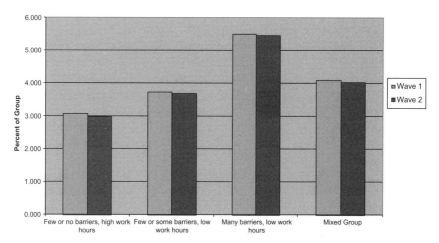

Figure 3.3
Average number of hardships in 12 months at Wave 1 and Wave 2, by Work/Barrier Group

school, 13 percent had a teen in trouble with the police, 2 percent had a teen (age 17 and under) drop out of school, and 4 percent had a teen that got pregnant or got someone pregnant (results not shown here). Figure 3.4 and Figure 3.5 show group differentials between Waves 1 and 2 in school suspension/expulsion and run-ins with the law, behaviors which appear (based on their higher frequency) to be the more sensitive

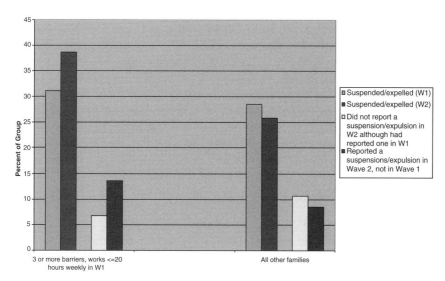

Figure 3.4
Teens Ever Suspended or Expelled, by Work/Barrier Group

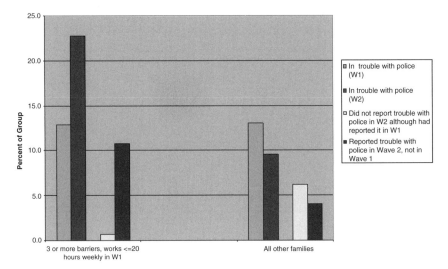

Figure 3.5
Teens Ever in Trouble with Police, by Work/Barrier Group

indicators of well-being among these school-age teens. The other two, rarely reported, problems do not differ significantly across time or across the key study groups.

While in the aggregate these two measures of teen behavior did not change significantly between the two interviews, Group C (those with many barriers and low employment) once again looked different from the rest: Rates did rise significantly from one interview to the next. In the first interview, 31 percent of Group C teens had ever been suspended or expelled and 13 percent had been in trouble with the police. At the second interview these rates had increased to, 39 percent and 23 percent respectively, with many parents newly reporting one of these problems in Wave 2.[20]

These results suggest that the passage of time leads to more negative outcomes for teens in the most-disadvantaged group. It is not clear from these data whether the deterioration was associated with timing out, or simply that the teenagers were growing older and engaging in more risky behavior. In either event, parents and teens in this group clearly face unusual challenges.

CHANGES IN EMPLOYMENT AND EARNINGS

An important result of this study of California families is that in most respects they were not economically worse off after reaching the 60-month time limit. Neither their incomes nor the hardships they reported changed in the aggregate between the months just before the time limit, and a few months after. Individual families became better off or worse off, but overall the measures of hardship and the income-to-poverty ratios hardly changed.

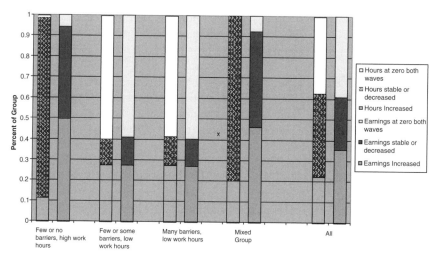

Figure 3.6
Changes in Hours and Earnings, by Work/Barrier Groups

This is a remarkable finding, given that in most states, reaching the time limit leads to a substantial reduction in income for at least some groups of recipients. To understand what happened in California we look first at hours of work and earnings. As noted earlier, many CalWORKs recipients are not employed[21] and most remain so after timing out. Figure 3.6 shows the extent of changes in earnings and hours between the two interviews. Nearly two-fifths of all respondents reported no hours worked (39%) or no earnings (37%) at both Wave 1 and at Wave 2. About one-fifth (22%) reported increased hours, and a larger number (35%) reported increased earnings, suggesting that some respondents enjoyed pay raises between the two interviews.[22] Some worked fewer hours at Wave 2 (21%) and a similar proportion (21%) reported lower earnings. Stability was more common than change: 57 percent had the same hours as before (typically zero), and 44 percent had the same earnings. On average, there was only minimal change in respondents' hours worked by about 30 minutes weekly (those working more balanced out those working less). Earnings, however, increased by an average of $102 per month in the whole sample, or $174 a month for respondents working at either interview. The earnings increase juxtaposed against almost unchanged work hours implies that average wages were higher at the second interview. Wages might have risen for those working at both periods or the people working more at Wave 2 might have been somewhat different from those who reduced their work hours after Wave 1.

Most respondents in the high-employment groups (Groups A and D) saw changes in their hours or earnings. Among Group A respondents, earnings rose for 50 percent and declined for 31 percent, and the average Group A family had $58 more in earnings per month. Group A hours rose for 12 percent and dropped for 38 percent, and dropped overall by 8 hours per week, even while their average earnings rose.

The large majority of Groups B and C were not working at either of the interviews (60% of Group B and 59 % of Group C). However, some previous nonworkers did find jobs and others increased their hours, with the result that 27 percent of each Group worked more hours at Wave 2, and only 9 percent of Group B (6% of Group C) worked fewer hours. Earnings changed at the same rate as hours—27 percent of both Groups were earning more and 12 percent of Group B (13% of Group C) was earning less. The workers in these Groups (respondents with hours or earnings at one of the interviews) worked considerably more at Wave 2 than Wave 1—an average of 15 hours more per week. Among workers, earnings rose substantially, by $351 monthly in Group B and an even larger $430 monthly in Group C. (Averaged across the workers and non-workers, Group B enjoyed an earnings gain of $132 and Group C an earnings gain of $173.) It is noteworthy that despite facing at least three work barriers, Group C had a larger gain in earnings than Group B, facing two or fewer barriers—perhaps because Group C was the best-educated group, with 41 percent having attended college.

Group D respondents, who are a mixture of those working an intermediate amount at Wave 1 and those with many barriers working full-time, are the only group with a (very small) loss in average earnings, of $14 per month, and similar numbers increased as lost earnings (46 and 43%, respectively). This group worked, on average, 9 hours less per week, so the fact that their earnings did not fall noticeably suggests that, like Group A, the average wage for this group may have been higher in Wave 2 than Wave 1.

Given that many in Groups B and C remained at zero hours of work, and that earnings dropped markedly for the full-time workers in Group A, a strict time-limit policy such as awarding few exemptions and terminating aid entirely to all others might have led to substantial reductions in family income. This, however, did not happen. Rather, California's welfare policies seem to have cushioned these families as they reached the 5-year TANF time limit.[23]

WELFARE RECEIPT AT SECOND INTERVIEW

Welfare for many families is a fluctuating source of income, higher when earnings are low, and minimal or zero as earnings increase. Families working full-time, with relatively high earnings, are especially likely to become ineligible for aid if their earnings increase even slightly. This fluidity was evident at the very start of the study: between the time when families were selected for the study and the first interview conducted some weeks or months later, ten percent of the sample left aid. Among the few barriers/high work group, 22 percent had exited by the time of the first interview. Almost everyone (85%) off aid in Wave 1 was still off in Wave 2.

All the respondents who were still on welfare at Wave 1 (90% of the entire sample) had already, according to the welfare records when they were selected for the study, accumulated nearly 60 months of cash aid. Following state policy, as they approached the time limit their files would be reviewed to assess whether an exemption was warranted (either prospectively or retrospectively) to stop the CalWORKs clock.

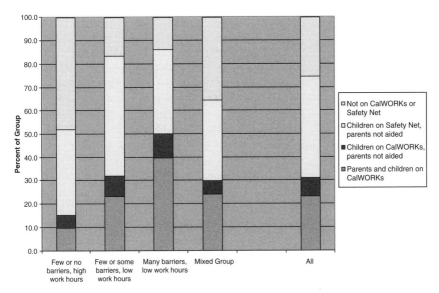

Figure 3.7
Welfare at Wave 2 by Work/Barrier Group among the Aided at Wave 1

Recipients not given an exemption or extension could also be aided through the Safety Net program, which has the same grant levels and eligibility thresholds as CalWORKs but excludes timed-out adults from the assistance unit. Additionally, some respondents' CalWORKs clocks had been stopped because the parents were excluded from the assistance unit and the family received a child-only grant (the same dollar amount as under the Safety Net).[24]

Thanks to these three routes to continued aid, 69 percent of the sample (and 77% of those on aid at Wave 1) were on aid at the second interview. As Figure 3.7 shows, the largest portion, 40 percent of the entire sample, were on the Safety Net, while 21 percent were on full-family CalWORKs because of an exemption or extension and 8 percent were on child-only CalWORKs. Given the large number that switched into the Safety Net from CalWORKs, it is not surprising that 45 percent were receiving a smaller grant than at Wave 1.[25]

Assistance was common across the entire sample, although there were also large differences between groups, as Figure 3.7 shows. Even among the highly employed Group A, only about half of families who had received CalWORKs at Wave 1 (48%) were off aid entirely in Wave 2. The aid received by Group A came mainly from the Safety Net (36%), although 10 percent still qualified for full-family Cal-WORKs. In contrast, families in Group C, with the most barriers, were the most likely to be on full-family CalWORKs (40%). Only 14 percent were off aid entirely. Group B, with fewer barriers but also little or no work at Wave 1, had relatively fewer on full-family CalWORKs (23%) and more on Safety Net or child-only Cal-WORKs (60%).

DISCUSSION

Five themes stand out in this study of families reaching the 5-year welfare time limit in California. First, even before reaching the time limit, virtually all these families faced serious difficulties in their lives, difficulties that are both causes and consequences of poverty. Some of these difficulties appear in this study as "barriers to work," others are counted as "hardships." Both barriers and hardships were widespread among this sample of families approaching 5 years of aid. More than half (57%) faced at least one personal or family-related barrier to employment, such as their own work-limiting health problem, caregiving responsibilities for a child or adult family member with a limiting health problem, a recent experience with domestic violence, a likely learning disability, or a mental health problem that interferes with work or school. Not considered here are barriers that are associated with the economic or service environment, such as a poor local job market, inadequate public transportation, or insufficient child-care options.

The hardships we asked about—including not enough food, utility shut-offs, unstable and crowded housing, difficulty or delay in getting necessary medical care—were experienced by almost all of these families; the average rate was four such problems per family. Furthemore, many children in these families suffer from serious health problems. Teenagers, too, appear to be a high risk for behavior problems, particularly in the many barrier/low-work families. Teens' behavior problems in this group of families were the only indicators that showed significant deterioration from Wave 1 to Wave 2. This does not necessarily suggest any negative consequences of the time limit, but rather, probably highlights how behavior risks increase with age among this group.

The second theme is the striking diversity among these families in the nature and extent of difficulties they faced, and in their work participation. Barriers, while common, were far from universal: 43 percent reported no employment barriers, but at the same time, nearly 20 percent reported three or more. One-third (32%) of the sample worked full-time or close to it, but half (48%) were not working at all and had not worked in the preceding year. The extent of barriers to employment is not nearly as correlated with employment itself as one might expect, particularly given that many of the barriers were defined as interfering with work. Even among people with similar levels of barriers to work, some did not work at all, while others worked full-time.

Our third point is that the time limit does appear to have had the desired effect on work participation among recipients. Most of the gain in work hours is due to the entry into employment of parents who before were working minimally or not at all. However—our fourth point—upon reaching the 5-year time limit, only one-quarter of all families (25%) actually left cash aid. This is the result of an anomaly in the California program, whereby the children of parents who time out can continue to receive aid through the state-funded Safety Net program. Indeed, nearly half (43%) of families that reached the time limit transferred to the Safety Net program, a further 8 percent received child-only CalWORKs (for children whose parents were sanctioned off CalWORKs or others whose parents do not qualify for reasons other than timing out), and nearly one-quarter received full-family CalWORKs. Many of these families continued to combine cash aid with earnings; overall there was a modest gain in average monthly earnings and a minimal gain in weekly hours worked. For those who worked very little or not at all at Wave 1, timing out appeared to have a larger impact on work, with an increase of about 6 hours per week. One-quarter of those who were not working at Wave 1 were working at Wave 2.

Our fifth and final point is that the Safety Net has had the desired effect, to protect children (and, by extension, their parents) from economic destitution. Families had the same average incomes (when scaled to the poverty threshold) at Wave 2 as at Wave 1. The average number of hardships within each group and across the entire sample was also no different at Wave 2 than at Wave 1. This is a critically important result: the welfare time limit as implemented under CalWORKs moderately increased work effort and earnings and did not increase average levels of hardship or drive families deeper into poverty.

As we mentioned at the beginning of this chapter, it is not news that many TANF families nearing the time limit have employment barriers and face substantial material hardship. Our analysis demonstrates that reaching the CalWORKs time limit may not be tremendously detrimental to families, even those that are not stepping onto the employment escalator, due to the safeguards put in place in the CalWORKs program—exemptions/extensions for families who face certain barriers, and for the rest, the state-funded Safety Net program that allows children to remain on aid even after their parents time out.

For those in the most dire situations, with many employment barriers and low work effort at the onset of the time limit, there is no question that use of both these safeguards protected family well-being. However, even among the group with few barriers and high employment, Safety Net use was substantial and points to the fragility of the labor market in moving even the most able to the point of self-sufficiency. One can only speculate about what would have happened to all exiting CalWORKs families in the absence of the Safety Net. The very presence of this program could have led families to different employment and welfare choices than they might otherwise have made. However, given the reliance on Safety Net benefits by nearly half of those who timed out, and the extent of employment barriers among the CalWORKs adults who reach the time limit, it seems likely that this support was critical for protecting California's children against severe poverty and hardship.

NOTES

*The surveys used in this chapter were collected by the Survey Research Center at the University of California, Berkeley. We gratefully acknowledge the excellent work of the SRC staff in fielding the surveys and the work of Yuteh Cheng in providing data support.

This research was supported by funds provided by The Regents of the University of California (Welfare Policy Research Project (WPRP), California Policy Research Center) and the William and Flora Hewlett Foundation. The views and opinions expressed do not necessarily represent those of the William and Flora Hewlett Foundation, The Regents of the University of California, WPRP, its advisory board, or any State or County executive agency represented thereon.

1. US Department of Health and Human Services (2006), "Welfare Rolls Continue to Fall: 2nd Quarter Data Ending June 2005 Show Another Decline in Caseloads." USDHHS News Release, February 9, 2006.

2. Urban Institute (2006). "A Decade of Welfare Reform: Facts and Figures." June 2006.

3. Sarah E. Crow and Jacquelyn Anderson. 2006. *Working Against the Clock: The Implementation of Welfare Time Limits in California.* Oakland, CA: California Policy Research Center, Welfare Policy Research Project (available at the WPRP website: http://wprp.ucop.edu). This report, the first from WPRP's time limit study, has on page 19 a table summarizing the four federal and ten state exemptions. The report provides extensive discussion of the exemptions, including California's unique exemption for court-ordered child support payments.

4. With approximately 24 percent of the nation's welfare caseload but only 12 percent of U.S. the population, California has a much higher per-capita welfare participation rate than other states. See National Conference of State Legislatures, available at http://www.ncsl.org/statefed/welfare/caseloadwatch.htm for welfare caseload data.

5. All had accumulated at least 54 months of aid when they were interviewed, and most were in months 57–59. A few we were not able to interview until their actual month of timing out, or even one month later. This is not a serious flaw, however, because most of the questions pertain to the period immediately prior to the interview, when they had not yet timed out. Additionally, although all were on CalWORKs when they were selected to participate, by the time they were reached for interview about eight percent had left the program and were not on aid. They had not yet timed out, but had left voluntarily.

6. A portion of the full sample had not completed their second-wave interviews when this chapter was prepared.

7. The full study included shorter simultaneously-translated interviews in dozens of other languages, which omitted many of the questions analyzed here

8. As noted, the six counties together comprise more than half the state caseload. In order that the results simply not be driven by the Los Angeles sample we do not weight counties proportionate to their populations but instead give each county equal weight in calculating sample percentages. Supplementary analyses show that the results do not vary greatly under other weighting schemes.

9. Two-parent households are considered working full-time if at least one person worked this much.

10. The complete definition of this group is: a single parent was working less than 20 hours and not working full-time in the previous year; two parents were were working less than 30 hours between them and neither had worked full-time in the past year.

11. Mark Courtney and Amy Dworsky. "Those Left Behind: Enduring Challenges Facing Welfare Recipients." Chapin Hall Center for Children, University of Chicago. Issue Brief #107, May 2006.

12. Susan Hauan and Sarah Douglas. 2004. "Potential Employment Liabilities Among TANF Recipients: A Synthesis of Data from Six State TANF Caseload Studies." US Department of Health and Human Services, Office of the Assistant Secretary for Planning and Evaluation, October 2004.

13. Sheila Zedlewski. 2003. "Work and Barriers to Work among Welfare Recipients in 2002." *Snapshots of America's Families III Number 3.* Washington, DC: The Urban Institute.

14. Our sample excludes teen parents, and also residents of Indian Country, so we did not ask in the surveys about those CalWORKs reasons for exemption.

15. These data refer to barriers that survey respondents faced at Wave 1 of the survey.

16. The health limitations measure is coded 1 if the respondent reported "an ongoing physical, mental, or emotional problem that limits [her/him] in the kind of work or amount of work that [s/he] can do."

17. These percentages refer to the two-wave sample of 1,058, but the entire Wave 1 sample had very similar distributions.

18. Nan Astone and Sara McLanahan. "Family structure, residential mobility and educational attainment." *Demography*, 31(4) (1994): 575–584.

19. The poverty thresholds are typically measured for families rather than households. Because we examine household rather than family income, we may be somewhat underestimating "official" poverty rates for this group.

20. Between the two interviews some 12-year-olds became teens and some 17-year-olds became adults, so the target population changed slightly. When parents are reporting about the same children (the majority of cases), there should only be additional problems reported, and none disappearing, between the interviews, because these are lifetime measures. However, in these as in all other survey questions, some respondents misreport, whether because of stigma, forgetfulness, or because an event no longer seems to fit the question (For example, a teen who dropped out before Wave 1 might not be reported as dropping out if she returned to school before Wave 2). As Figure 3.2 shows, responses did change and, populations differ between Wave 1 and Wave 2, the changes do not always add up to the new rate at Wave 2.

21. Recall that 48 percent of the sample was not working at Wave 1 and had not worked in the preceding year.

22. To minimize the impact of small changes, single parents with changes in hours under 4 hours or changes in earnings under $50, and couples with changes in hours under 8 hours or changes in earnings under $100, were considered to have unchanged hours or earnings respectively.

23. A rigorous assessment of post-time-limit cash aid is beyond the scope of this chapter; the fluidity of individuals' welfare participation and their many possible reasons for welfare exit or re-enrollment make the statistical issues quite daunting.

24. Parents and caregivers are excluded from the assistance unit if they themselves are aided through SSI, if they are sanctioned for program noncompliance, and for a few other reasons. Respondents enrolled in child-only CalWORKs at Wave 1 were counted as "on welfare," not off welfare.

25. Grant levels vary greatly with earnings as well as between programs, and many respondents' earnings fluctuate, so 26 percent had higher grants in Wave 2 and only 3 percent had the same grant.

CHAPTER 4

WOMEN AND CHILDREN IN THE HEALTH CARE GAP

Jane Henrici, Ronald J. Angel, and Laura Lein

In this chapter we consider the insecurities of health care access tied to changing gender roles and family patterns. From our examination of the current socioeconomic context and our data, we find current American policy and practice and its decreasing lack of support for health care for women and their children problematic and in need of change. At the same time that a rising percentage of women in the United States now must work for wages to sustain themselves and their children, many nevertheless go without adequate health coverage and care. This situation relates to two existing gender gaps within the larger socioeconomic context.[1] Both of these gaps affect women as well as other family members including children, and are particularly pronounced for women of color and their families.[2]

The central issue is that for the last several decades the cost of health care has increased at a rate far greater than that of food, transportation, housing, and the rest of the package of consumer goods that a family needs to survive. Meanwhile, as health care has become more expensive it has also become more essential to guaranteeing optimal health at all ages. Modern medical care is expensive largely because it is effective. Unfortunately, even though adequate health care coverage is necessary for a healthy and productive life, a growing number of American families face the possibility of short-term or longer-term gaps in coverage. Faced with the growing costs of group plans many employers have stopped offering health insurance altogether or they require their employees to bear a larger portion of the cost. For many working and middle-class Americans these health care insecurities are a new and discomforting phenomenon, but for minority Americans, the poor and single mothers with children these insecurities are not new. If anything, the vulnerability of these traditionally vulnerable groups has only increased as federal and state governments grapple with the growing cost of public health care.

Single-parent households with children face particular vulnerabilities in health care access as the result of a combination of factors, each of which presents a family with barriers to care and, taken together, place the health of many poor adults and children in jeopardy. Single-parent households tend to be headed by an unmarried female and are disproportionately poor and members of ethnic and racial minorities. Escaping from this situation through employment remains an elusive goal for these families. Most minority single mothers can find work only in the low-wage service sector in which they are not offered benefits and in which employment is episodic and insecure. In this chapter we explore these themes using as a focus a case study of one mother who was part of a large-scale, multidisciplinary study of women, children, and poverty in three large American cities.[3] We conclude that given the inadequacy of the public health care financing system of the United States and the lack of possibilities for work-based health care coverage for poor families, the health care needs of both poor and middle-class families can only be addressed through a system of universal health care coverage.

The original study from which our in-depth examination of one family is drawn was motivated by a desire to understand the potential consequences of the changes in welfare that were introduced by Congress in 1996 on the lives of children and their caretakers in impoverished families. The Personal Responsibility and Work Opportunity Reconciliation Act of (PRWORA) made welfare time-limited and placed new pressures on couples and women on welfare to leave the rolls and find employment. At the same time that welfare reform introduced more stringent work requirements for single women and couples, the nature of low-wage jobs continued to place employer-sponsored coverage out of reach for both women and their male partners. As a consequence, poor families remained dependent on Medicaid and the State Children's Health Insurance Program (SCHIP). What we found in the study is that although almost all young children in families below 200 percent of the official government poverty life qualify for public coverage based on their family's income, obtaining and maintaining coverage for all children in large families required constant effort on the part of parents; and, even when they expended that effort, most families experienced periods in which some children, often the older ones, were without coverage. The adults in these families were rarely able to obtain coverage of any sort for themselves and, as a consequence of inadequate and incomplete health care, their health and productive capacities were undermined.

In what follows, we examine the multiple themes of gendered work, single motherhood, and the impact of both on access to health care.[4] As we will see, poverty and its negative health consequences are not evenly distributed throughout the population; certain segments of the population defined in terms of gender, race, and ethnicity are the most vulnerable.

THE FEMINIZED WORKFORCE AND WAGES

The term "feminized workforce" is used to describe the current dominant work and wage system in which low-wage employment rises within industries and in forms that preferentially select for women and hire all workers with an emphasis on flexible hours, unstable contracts, and no benefits. The gender gaps that affect the health of children of poorer women appear both in the lower salaries that women receive so that they are limited in their ability to pay out-of-pocket for care, and in their larger chance of being employed within these sectors and thus lacking either salaries or health coverage to address their health care needs.

Women earn less than men in general, and minority women earn less than majority women. This results from the fact that even more than the rest of the workforce, employment opportunities available to many minority and poor women are marked by low wages, irregular hours and pay, job insecurity, and often institutional stratification by race and ethnicity.[5] The economic vulnerabilities that women, and especially minority women, face are the result of historical processes and current economic patterns that have restricted educational and occupational opportunities to women, African Americans, and Latinos in particular for generations, and which have placed glass ceilings of color at very low levels in the occupational hierarchy. As our study showed, the combined characteristics of low-wage work and the dependence on public assistance of all sorts undermines a woman's ability to enhance her human capital through education or job training.[6]

The disproportionately low wages that all women in the United States continue to receive relative to men reflect cultural beliefs and practices as well as labor market characteristics and public policies of more than a century of history.[7] Ideas about women's wages can be traced at least to nineteenth century British social structure in which the male breadwinner was viewed as the primary source of the welfare of his wife and children. The welfare of children, and the appropriate social order, required that women should not work outside the home and should devote themselves to domestic labor. Families were the basic production and consumption units and at most charitable religious and social services might assist with unexpected needs so that women need not work while they raised their children.[8]

Despite this primarily middle-class ideal of domesticity, women in the United States, particularly those of the poorer and working classes, have always worked outside the home to help support their families. More recently, mothers have been forced to work in the attempt to secure health care for themselves and their children.[9] Unfortunately, given the types of jobs that poorly educated and low-skill women can get the effort is often futile. The family model that includes a male breadwinner and in which women's salaries are secondary and their independent medical coverage superfluous, obscures the real life situations of many women and their families. Public policies that are based on this increasingly irrelevant male breadwinner model of family income and household employment help perpetuate the gender gap in salary and access to health care.[10] Today it would appear that a large fraction of children will spend at least some portion of their childhoods in a single-parent household headed by a woman with little earning capacity who is dependent on public health care coverage for her children.

Further, as noted, low-wage jobs, and increasingly higher-wage jobs as well, are marked by unstable employment and few benefits in the call for increasing "flexibility" in the workforce.[11] Occupations in the service sector, including medical support staff, and retail industries in which women are overrepresented[12] are often structured around variable schedules, changes in number of hours worked, and a lack of benefits.[13]

MULTIPLE RESPONSIBILITIES

Compounding their difficulties with the feminized workforce is the fact that, although many women in the United States historically have been at least partially responsible for their household incomes, they also bore and continue to bear the major responsibility for child and elder care.[14] Women remain the primary child-care givers among married couples and are the more likely parent to retain responsibility for children in the event of divorce or separation. Traditional family arrangements have also placed the primary responsibility for aging and infirm parents on women. When older relatives need assistance because of poor health or for other reasons, women are the first to respond despite their other domestic and work responsibilities.

Poor women juggle these competing demands of work, family, and an increasingly punitive welfare system as best they can. Women of color, Mexican American women in particular,[15] are likely to experience periods with no health insurance coverage at a time when both employer-assisted programs and publicly funded health programs provide less coverage.[16] We now proceed to a case study to illustrate the ways in which the vulnerabilities we have identified work themselves out in the life of one family.

WELFARE REFORM AND CHILDREN: A THREE-CITY STUDY

Our example is from a study entitled "Welfare, Children, and Families: A Three-City Study," a large, multidisciplinary examination of all aspects of the lives of poor families in the period after the introduction of welfare reform in Boston, Chicago, and San Antonio. Approximately 2400 families were surveyed in three waves in 1999, 2000–2001, and 2004 (under analysis and not used for this chapter) in selected low-income neighborhoods in each city. Each household included at least one child younger than 4, or one child between the ages of 10–14.[17] The survey included a detailed study of child development among preschool children in the sample.

In addition to the survey and developmental assessment, the study included an ethnographic component in which approximately 60 low-income families were followed longitudinally in each city. The ethnography provided far deeper insights into the ways in which these families negotiated work, family, and welfare system demands in the neighborhood contexts in which they lived. Part of the ethnographic sample included a group of families in which at least one young child had a diagnosed disability.

Interviewers recruited welfare-eligible African American, Latin American, and European American families in each city. The ethnographic families were recruited between June 1999 and December 2000. About 40 percent of the families were

Latino, 40 percent African American, and 20 percent of European descent. Ethnographers met with the families monthly over an 18-month period and conducted 6-month and 12-month follow-ups. Most meetings occurred in families' homes, although ethnographers also accompanied family members to the grocery store, family celebrations, welfare offices, and on a number of other family errands and activities.

This chapter focuses on the city of San Antonio. San Antonio's economy is heavily reliant on tourism, light industry, and commerce. Unlike Chicago and Boston, which have historically had more developed industrial economies, San Antonio has less developed social service delivery, transportation, and employment opportunities. Since the introduction of welfare reform public aid has diminished in all three cities, at the same time considerable workforce growth has occurred in the service, freight, construction, and medical sectors. Jobs in these sectors are characterized by part-time work, low-wages, low-benefits, and often relatively unstable employment discussed in the introduction. As low-end wages stagnate and as benefit coverage deteriorates across the United States, all three cities face neighborhood and household changes. San Antonio is a useful example of a mid-sized city with an ethnic minority as the majority population and a core concentration of urban poverty.

The women we spoke to in each city made every effort to get and keep a combination of wages and welfare benefits necessary to support their households and to obtain health care for their children. In their struggle to do so, they often neglected their own health problems. Despite their best efforts, these women faced complex problems and irregularities in social service access that made it difficult to provide even their basic needs. Women with older children, or those with more than one child, found that finding and keeping a job, obtaining public supports, and maintaining health care coverage was often beyond their reach. Families in San Antonio faced particularly serious problems finding and keeping consistent health care.

Over the time we documented the "fits and starts" poorer mothers in San Antonio experienced with employment, child care, education, residency, and medical treatment. Throughout the study their difficulties seemed to multiply rather than diminish. Elsewhere we have presented a broader description of our findings and represented a number of the families interviewed.[15] Here, we concentrate on one household that exemplifies how problems for a woman with few resources and young children escalate over time and create barriers that keep her from dealing effectively with them.

"TERESA"

Teresa, as we will call her, was 33 with two daughters 10 and 12 years old and a 4-month-old son when we met her in July 1999. She and her children lived in a subsidized apartment in a housing development that sprawled across a formerly industrial section on the west side of San Antonio. Teresa participated in the study for over 3 years. She is of Mexican and African parentage and described herself as Hispanic, or simply "Mexican." Soon after the second daughter's birth, Teresa and the girls' father divorced, and in 1988 he was deported to Mexico. Teresa received no support from him. She had severed ties to her son's father since he molested one of her daughters.

Through Teresa's example we will explore the ways in which health status and health care availability interact with the low wages, irregularity, and insecurity of gendered work. The study presents some difficulties faced by Teresa, since the family member's health and her work were intertwined with a host of other issues and problems including those related to the children's schooling, the family's housing, and their access to transportation. While this presentation focuses on the intersection of work and health, we also explore the ways in which both interact with these other problem areas. What was clear from the start was that the multiple responsibilities facing Teresa and her older daughter meant they were forced to sacrifice important elements of health care, as well as educational and work opportunities.[18]

Teresa's Health

When we met her, Teresa had been diagnosed with diabetes for 10 years. Her sister was also diabetic. Following her recent pregnancy, Teresa had experienced numbness in her legs, and by July 1999 had difficulty walking. Although she remained eligible for Medicaid coverage for a while after her last pregnancy, she still had difficulties with health care. Teresa was supposed to visit the physician every month and monitor her diabetes on a daily basis. However, she found it difficult to comply and often missed her scheduled visits because of family responsibilities, her children's health problems, her lack of transportation, or the fatigue and physical difficulties caused by her own worsening health. She also suffered from seasonal pollen allergies and during the study her diabetes-related conditions grew worse. Her vision deteriorated as she developed glaucoma. Her fingers, hands, legs, and feet all became symptomatic. She took three different prescriptions as well as insulin, but her diabetes was affecting her organs, and by May 2000 she learned that her kidneys were severely damaged.

Teresa's Work and Education

Teresa had a checkered educational and work history that was greatly affected by her health problems. She had dropped out of high school and was unable to complete her GED because of her poor health. She had worked as a nursing care assistant, and had been able to support her daughters without welfare in the early 1990s. By 1998, she was pregnant and increasingly diabetic, and had stopped working and applied for welfare but preferred to have stayed employed. She told us that she felt she would be "better off working," but also "would like to have insurance and hospital insurance for my kids" that were unavailable through her job. Her full-time position paid slightly above minimum wage and provided no benefits for her family.

In the summer of 1999, her son was a few months old, and Teresa was aware that she would be under renewed pressure to find a job and face sanctions from welfare if she failed to do so. However, she waited to look for work until she could get some treatment for her diabetes. In early December of 1999, Teresa and her children lived in a shelter because she could not pay her rent, and her welfare funds were cut even further because her oldest child missed a week of school.

She continued to look for work even though she ran the risk of losing welfare and Medicaid if she were to find a job. Teresa worried that the physical demands of a nursing job would injure her health still further so she looked for other work. She found a job as a custodian at a sports arena but quit after 3 weeks. The wages were relatively low ($5.50/hour), the work hard, and the night hours difficult for arranging child care. A major precipitating factor was the hospitalization of her son for pneumonia and her need to stay home with him when he left the hospital. While the boy was sick, Teresa was exempted from the welfare-to-work requirements and regained TANF until her son was better. After that, she took another low-paying job.

Teresa returned to her nursing job in December 2000, and as a result lost her Medicaid and TANF. Unfortunately the job did not offer medical insurance. By February of 2002 her health had deteriorated further and she had difficulty standing or walking due to a pinched nerve in her back. She remained seated much of the day and used a cane to walk outside. As a result, she lost her job and had no way in which to pay for treatment or care. With no other option, Teresa again found herself dependent on welfare that she received for her son and older daughter, and on Medicaid, that the three of them received. Her middle child, who suffered from hyperactivity and attention deficit disorder among other problems, began receiving SSI (Supplemental Security Income) once Teresa was successful in obtaining that disability assistance for her.

Other People's Health

Both of Teresa's daughters suffered from health problems. Both girls were in what are called Special Education classes. Medicaid covered the younger girl's medicine, eyeglasses, and counseling, but Teresa struggled to pay for the nonprescription drugs that had been recommended for both her daughters and herself.

Teresa's son meanwhile continued to suffer from unspecified congenital problems. He was delayed in standing and experienced chronic asthma as well other acute ailments, including ear and eye infections and pneumonia. His health required a great deal of attention, but by his second birthday he was not only standing and walking, but beginning to dress himself. A year later he was toilet trained.

Meanwhile, Teresa's mother was hospitalized repeatedly with asthma and a liver problem, and occasionally stayed in Teresa's apartment when unable to care for herself. Teresa struggled to support the household for the period of her mother's illness with no income other than welfare (TANF) and Medicaid. At the hospital, Teresa and her siblings took turns attending their mother. Her mother died in early 2001.

Transportation

Teresa's ability to attend doctor visits, certification appointments for her Medicaid and other welfare services, and work was limited. Without a car, she had to walk several city blocks to the nearest bus stop. Her physical condition often made this difficult. As a result, despite her impaired vision, Teresa bought a car in order to get to and from the jobs for which she had been told she must apply in order to receive any welfare coverage. Eventually, Teresa applied for a handicapped driver permit. When Teresa began receiving SSI because of her own poor health, she planned to have her elder daughter apply for an unrestricted driver's license in order that she become the family driver although the girl was not yet 16 years old.

Children's Schooling

As Teresa's health deteriorated, her elder daughter's assistance grew ever more essential in dealing with tasks ranging from caring for the baby to grocery shopping. On occasions, the daughter missed school in order to accompany Teresa to the welfare office. She supervised the younger children when Teresa had to rest, and cared for one when Teresa had to take the other to medical appointments or see the doctor herself.

The Fight for SSI

Teresa became increasingly disabled over time. She knew that SSI payments would be higher than what the family received from TANF and the income from that source would be more regular. Given her deteriorating health she did not think she could work much longer. After her younger daughter's ADD was diagnosed, Teresa applied for SSI for both herself and her daughter. Her younger daughter became eligible for SSI by February of 2000. Although the SSI allowance was more than TANF provided, her daughter also had new medical expenses but the family's total TANF cash benefits were lowered and their Food Stamps were cut because of the additional SSI income. Meanwhile, Teresa continued to be denied SSI for her own health problems.

By December 2000, Teresa's vision was deteriorating. She continued to drive her car to get to work, although her weak vision made this difficult. Without a workplace sick leave policy, she missed three doctor's appointments rather than lose her job. Finally, Teresa was approved for SSI in August of 2002, and automatically qualified for Medicare benefits. She gained access to new treatments and attended "diabetes classes" to learn about proper diet and exercise for diabetics. By the fall, Teresa was working to make her house wheelchair accessible and hoped that Medicare would pay for the chair.

Chronic Struggles

Teresa's story, although a single case, exemplifies the extensive and interrelated problems that mark the lives of most of the low-income single mothers that we interviewed. They struggled in low-wage and irregular jobs and had to deal with multiple complex responsibilities for children and older adults. Most had only transitory and limited assistance from what, for many, was a deteriorating safety net. Using this narrative as a base, we now return to the general themes with which we introduced the chapter.

Low-Wage Jobs

Unlike many of the women interviewed in San Antonio, Teresa had the benefit of a skill set in which she had been trained and as a result could earn somewhat above minimum wages on those occasions when she could work. In that regard she may have been better off than many other single mothers. However, like many other mothers, for Teresa, the jobs she could get did not improve the family's economic situation. Working cost her a great deal financially since it involved multiple expenses for transportation, child care, and basic needs that welfare would not cover if she was working. This is a dilemma that has been described by other researchers as well.[19]

Further, in addition to their economic costs, the jobs Teresa could get took a physical toll on her. The physical demands required that she take time off from work for medical care or to recuperate and the illnesses generated additional health care costs. Financially, for Teresa, as for other single mothers, work was more of an economic loss than a means to economic self-sufficiency.

Irregular Jobs

Teresa, like many of the other mothers in the study, held jobs with irregular hours and hours outside the "normal" working day. Even these jobs were often hard to find and keep. Indeed, many of the mothers we spoke with worked at jobs in which their hours changed on a weekly or even daily basis. They worked different schedules each week, with changes in income depending on the number of hours assigned. This irregularity in employment had ramifications for a range of family functions from child care and homework supervision to transportation issues.

Multiple Responsibilities

Teresa faced a daunting and sometimes conflicting set of responsibilities. As a result of the new requirements that were part of welfare reform Teresa was required to look for a paid job in order to qualify for housing, for her children's medical care, and for cash assistance. In addition to these requirements, she was expected to find transportation, buy healthy food for the family on a limited budget, make and keep medical appointments for herself and her children, document all of these activities as part of the certification procedures for assistance, and somehow do it all without missing work. The result was that while she clearly provided for her children as best she could, she also depended on her children for essential services. Without her daughter's assistance it was clear that Teresa would simply have been overwhelmed.

The Unraveled Safety Net

The economic foundation upon which a poorer family's economic welfare depends is rarely firm. As for Teresa, their dependence on jobs that offer no benefits and the continuous uncertainty of their welfare benefits means that low-income mothers must engage in an ongoing search for necessary services for their families. Teresa's struggle was one that seemed to have no potential positive outcome. As her health deteriorated her capacity to work or to manage the complexities of her life did as well. She was engaged in a constant struggle to locate medical care and other services, while she also tried to find and keep jobs, none of which offered enough income or stability to improve the family's situation.

Even when Teresa was eligible for services, the application process could be difficult and lengthy. Many families in our study found the application process for social and medical services complicated. Maintaining their eligibility requires continual recertification and interactions with the bureaucracy. As a result, they often faced interrupted or delayed medical coverage. Many families lost coverage because they did not bring all necessary records to meetings with caseworkers. Missing required documentation is easy since so many are required, including original records of income, children's birth and health, and the father's capacity to support the child. If any of these documents are missing or lost in the application process itself, families may lose or face delays in their Medicaid coverage. Although SCHIP has been a great boon to a number of families, others find the application procedure confusing since they must document their ineligibility for Medicaid before they can apply for SCHIP.

Teresa, like many mothers, did not understand her own or her children's eligibility for transitional benefits after the loss of TANF. Although Teresa continued to apply for what she needed, many families were troubled by the stigma associated with public assistance, and in some cases they faced barriers resulting from the inability to speak English.[20] Families struggled to understand the different messages from caseworkers, physicians, educators, and the larger society about welfare eligibility and use.

As a result of the pressures of multiple responsibilities and limited resources mothers often experienced a cascade of negative consequences as difficulties in one domain fed into and exacerbated difficulties in another. Teresa's precarious health, as well as her children's health problems, made it difficult for her to keep a job or to keep her children in school or in child care, and for a time they were homeless. Her work, the overall condition of the family, and the family members' education all were undermined by poor health. Yet, when Teresa lost a job, health care remained unavailable.

Policy Responses

Without more regular jobs and assistance in meeting basic needs for medical and other services, it is hard to see how families like Teresa's and the others in our study could become stable. Even full-time minimum wage jobs can leave families with incomes below the poverty line. Jobs that offer irregular, part-time work almost assure that a family will remain in poverty and that they will be worse off than on welfare. Low-wage jobs leave single mothers unable to support their households without on-going assistance and they make frequent crises almost inevitable. For the families we studied, even if they were willing, fathers were unable to contribute enough to make a real difference in household finances. While the fathers of Teresa's children made no attempt to contribute to their children's support, many mothers reported receiving aid, however, it usually consisted of small and unpredictable donations from fathers whose jobs were as irregular and low-paid as those of the mothers. Without higher wages and more regular work, as well as the critical addition of subsidized health coverage, single mothers will be unlikely to support stable households.

Given the nature of the low-wage labor force, even mothers with regular, but low-paid employment required the assistance of public services. Even working mothers often need assistance with child care, medical care, Food Stamps and other problem areas to make ends meet. At the bottom of the income hierarchy even the most diligent budgeting and money management cannot make a limited income stretch as far as is needed to meet a family's needs. A brief analysis of our medical system as it relates to the needs of low-income families illustrates the problems associated with a means-tested approach to basic service needs. Indeed, there have been some important attempts to make these programs more accessible to working mothers. However, while mothers must meet eligibility requirements and seek recertification for services while juggling the demands of work and family on a poverty budget, they are unlikely to be able to stabilize their families.

Innovations in Medicaid and other programs can certainly help impoverished families but even with reforms such means-tested programs are unlikely to result in stability in health care access over the long term. In recent years the Medicaid application process has been simplified and the state-funded and federally matched SCHIP has been introduced to insure that children in families ineligible to receive Medicaid are covered. These reforms and programs extended coverage to a large number of children in families with incomes well above poverty. In the face of shrinking state revenues, expansion of SCHIP or Medicaid seems unlikely, and in Texas and some other states funding has been cut and many women and their children again find themselves without coverage.[21]

Although federal and state governments provide health care coverage for children in poor families, almost no programs provide similar coverage to their parents, unless they are pregnant or disabled.[22] As a result of economic stagnation, smaller state budgets, and rising health insurance costs both Medicaid and private health insurance coverage for children have diminished following welfare reform[23] in spite of increased federal spending on Medicaid.[24] Nearly 11 percent of all children (8.2 million) lacked health insurance coverage in 2002.[25] Yet nearly half of these children qualify for public care on the basis of family income.[26] This fact illustrates the impact of the barriers to accessing and maintaining coverage. The situation is unlikely to improve in the short term since states have instituted methods to cut their share of the Medicaid costs.[27] These strategies include limits on services, caps on enrollment, and restrictions on prescriptions covered.[28]

As this chapter goes to press, the federal budget cuts rather than maintains public health care coverage. Poorer and working-age families with children will be among the most seriously affected.[29] Established research, in addition to our study, documents the association between a lack of health insurance coverage, inadequate health care, and poor health outcomes.[30] That is, the diminished health care coverage will increase the probability of serious illnesses for children.[31] Lowered vitality and educational deficits resulting from poor health then increase the risk of intergenerational poverty.[32]

Elsewhere, we have presented a full argument in support of universal health coverage in the United States.[33] As part of the public debate over health care reform in the United States we must investigate avenues that move us toward a more egalitarian and universal medical care system that does not penalize specific segments of the population based on gender, marital status, race, ethnicity, and income. We must also address the serious problems associated with the decentralized and fragmented programs that provide other necessary services such as child care, public housing, and adult training and education if we are to truly stabilize impoverished families headed by workers in low-wage jobs. Finally, the problems of poor families cannot be addressed without critically assessing the liberalized low-wage labor market, what is called the feminized workforce, and its growing rather than diminishing gender gaps which provide inadequate income, irregularity, and no benefits to workers that undermine even the most diligent efforts to get ahead.

NOTES

1. Elsewhere we have discussed health coverage and care in the United States and other nations in a more comparative manner, in *Poor Families in America's Health Care Crisis*, ed. Ronald Angel, Laura Lein, and Jane Henrici (New York: Cambridge University Press, 2006).

2. Pamela Braboy Jackson and David R. Williams, "The Intersection of Race, Gender, and SES: Health Paradoxes," in *Gender, Race, Class, and Health: Intersectional Approaches*, ed. Amy J. Schulz and Leith Mullings (San Francisco: Jossey-Bass, 2006); Sara McLanahan, "Family, State, and Child Well-Being," *Annual Review of Sociology* 26 (2000): 703–706; Alice O'Connor, "Poverty Research and Policy for the Post-Welfare Era," *Annual Review of Sociology* 26 (2000): 547–562; Ruth E. Zambrana and Bonnie Thornton Dill, "Disparities in Latina Health: An Intersectional Analysis," in *Gender, Race, Class, and Health: Intersectional Approaches*, ed. Amy J. Schulz and Leith Mullings (San Francisco: Jossey-Bass, 2006).

3. We are grateful for both the funding support we received for this project, the help of multiple study team members, and the families and agency workers who so generously gave us their time and views. For more information about all of these please see www.jhu.edu/~welfare.

4. Elsewhere we have discussed health coverage and care in the United States and other nations in a more detailed and comparative manner, in *Poor Families in America's Health Care Crisis*, ed. Ronald Angel, Laura Lein, and Jane Henrici. (New York: Cambridge University Press, 2006).

5. Jackson and Williams, *Gender, Race, Class, and Health: Intersectional Approaches*; McLanahan, "Family, State, and Child Well-Being"; O'Connor, "Poverty Research and Policy

for the Post-Welfare Era"; Zambrana and Dill, *Gender, Race, Class, and Health: Intersectional Approaches*.

6. Jane Henrici and Carol M. Miller, "Work First, Then What? Families and Job Training after Welfare Reform," in *Doing Without: Women and Work after Welfare Reform*, ed. Jane Henrici (Tucson, Arizona: University of Arizona Press, 2006).

7. Suzanne M. Bianchi and Daphne Spain, "Women, Work, and Family in America," *Population Bulletin* 51(3) (Washington, DC: Population Reference Bureau, Inc., December 1996).

8. Jane Lewis, "Gender and the Development of Welfare Regimes," in *Power Resources Theory and the Welfare State: A Critical Approach*, ed. Julia S. O'Connor and Gregg M. Olsen (Toronto: University of Toronto Press, 1998); apparently, there was one decade in U.S. history in which this elite British model was also the American average and that was, as popular culture leads us to expect, during the late 1940s through mid-1950s; however, according to research on this topic, there has never been a period in which the majority of American men were able to pay all household expenses with only their wages and without help from other sources (if not from women's incomes then, for example, from their parents).

9. That includes women receiving cash benefits, or welfare, as a number of researchers have shown: Kathryn Edin and Laura Lein, *Making Ends Meet: How Single Mothers Survive Welfare and Low-Wage Work* (New York: Russell Sage Foundation, 1997).

10. Bianchi and Spain, "Women, Work, and Family in America"; Lewis, *Power Resources Theory and the Welfare State*.

11. Holly Bell, "Putting Mothers to Work: Caseworkers' Perceptions of Low-Income Women's Roles in the Context of Welfare," in *Doing Without: Women and Work after Welfare Reform*, ed. Jane Henrici (Tucson, Arizona: University of Arizona Press, 2006); Laura Lein, Alan F. Benjamin, Monica McManus, and Kevin Roy, "Without a New, Without a Job: What's a Mother to Do?" in *Doing Without: Women and Work after Welfare Reform*, ed. Jane Henrici (Tucson, Arizona: University of Arizona Press, 2006).

12. Marlene Kim, "Women Paid Low Wages: Who They Are and Where They Work." *Monthly Labor Review* 123(September 2000): 26–30.

13. S. Lambert, E. Waxman, and A. Haley-Lock (2002). *Against the odds: A study of instability in lower-skilled jobs*. Working paper, Project on the Public Economy of Work. Chicago, IL: University of Chicago.

14. Philip N. Cohen and Danielle MacCartney, "Inequality and the Family," in *The Blackwell Companion to the Sociology of Families*, ed. Jacqueline Scott, Judith Treas, and Martin Richards (London: Blackwell Publishing, 2004).

15. Ronald Angel, Laura Lein, and Jane Henrici, *Poor Families in America's Health Care Crisis*. New York: Cambridge University Press, 2006.

16. Ronald J. Angel and Jacqueline L. Angel, "Family, the State, and Health Care: Changing Roles in the New Century," in *The Blackwell Companion to the Sociology of Families*, ed. Jacqueline Scout, Judity Treas, and Martin Richards (London: Blackwell Publishing, 2004); Ronald J. Angel and Laura Lein, "The Myth of Self-Sufficiency in Health," in *Doing Without: Women and Work after Welfare Reform*, ed. Jane Henrici (Tucson, Arizona: University of Arizona Press, 2006); Angel, Lein, and Henrici, *Poor Families in America's Health Care Crisis*; Cohen and MacCartney, *The Blackwell Companion to the Sociology of Families*; Jackson and Williams, *Gender, Race, Class, and Health: Intersectional Approaches*; Zambrana and Dill, *Gender, Race, Class, and Health: Intersectional Approaches*.

17. At the time of the interview, 40 percent of the survey families were receiving cash assistance and few had private health insurance.

18. Angel, Lein, and Henrici, *Poor Families in America's Health Care Crisis.*

19. Edin and Lein, *Making Ends Meet.*

20. Glenn Flores, M. Abreu, M.A. Olivar, and B. Kastner. "Access Barriers to Health Care for Latino Children," *Archives of Pediatric Adolescence Medicine* (1998): 1119–1125; Janet Perloff. "Insuring the Children: Obstacles and Opportunities," *Families in Society: The Journal of Contemporary Human Services* 80(1999): 516–530; Mae Thamer and Christian Richard. "Health Insurance Coverage Among Foreign-Born US Residents: The Impact of Race, Ethnicity, and Length of Residence," *American Journal of Public Health* 87(1997): 96–102.; Robin Weinick and Nancy Krauss. "Racial/Ethnic Differences in Children's Access to Care." *American Journal of Public Health* 90(2000): 1771–1774.

21. Wendy Chavkin, Diana Romero, and Paul Wise, "State Welfare Reform Polices and Declines in Health Insurance," *American Journal of Public Health* 90(2000): 900–908; Carol Kohn, Susan Hasty, and C. Henderson, "State Welfare Reform Polices and Declines in Health Insurance," *Managed Healthcare Information* September(2002): 10–11; Weinick and Krauss, "Racial/Ethnic Differences in Children's Access to Care"; Stephen Zuckerman, Genevieve Kenney, Lisa Dubay, Jennifer Haley, and John Holahan. "Shifting Health Insurance Coverage, 1997–1999: Economic expansion, Welfare Reform, and SCHIP Have Changed Who Has Insurance Coverage, but Not Across the Board." *Health Affairs* 20(2001): 169–77.

22. Anne Dunkelberg and Molly O'Malley, "Children's Medicaid and SCHIP in Texas: The Impact of Budget Cuts," Report No. 7123, The Kaiser Commission on Medicaid and the Uninsured (Washington, DC: The Henry J. Kaiser Family Foundation, 2004).

23. Chavkin, Romero, and Wise, "State Welfare Reform Polices and Declines in Health Insurance."; Committee on Child Health Financing "Implementing Principles and Strategies for the State Children's Health Insurance Program," *Pediatrics* 107(2001): 1214–1220; Leighton Ku, and Shannon Blaney, "Health Coverage for Legal Immigrant Children: New Census Data Highlight Importance of Restoring Medicaid and SCHIP Coverage" (Washington, DC: Center for Budget and Policy Priorities, 2000); Diane Rowland, Alina Salganicoff, and Patricia Seliger Keenan, "The Key to the Door: Medicaid's Role in Improving Health Care for Women and Children," *Annual Review of Public Health* 20 (1999): 403–426.

24. John Holahan and Brian Bruen, "Medicaid Spending: What Factors Contributed to the Growth between 2000 and 2002?" (Washington, DC: The Urban Institute, 2003).

25. Kohn, Hasty, and Henderson "State Welfare Reform Polices and Declines in Health Insurance."

26. Barbara Starfield, "Evaluating the State Children's Health Insurance Program: Critical Considerations," *Annual Review of Public Health* 21(2000): 569–585.

27. Vernon K. Smith, Rekha Armes, Kathleen Gifford, Helen Ellis, Victoria Wachino, and Molly O'Malley, "States Respond to Fiscal Pressure: A 50-State Update of State Medicaid Spending Growth and Cost Containment Actions," Report No. 0000, The Kaiser Commission on Medicaid and the Uninsured (Washington, DC: The Henry J. Kaiser Family Foundation, 2004).

28. Peter J. Cunningham, "Medicaid Cost Containment and Access to Prescription Drugs: States' Efforts to Contain the Rising Costs of Medicaid Prescription Drugs Are Reducing Enrollees' Access to Needed Medications," *Health Affairs* 24(2005): 780–789; Nancy E. Morden and Sean D. Sullivan, "States' control of Prescription Drug Spending: A Heterogeneous Approach," *Health Affairs* 24(2005): 1032–1038.

29. Edwin Park, "New Congressional Budget Office Estimates Indicate Millions of Low-Income Beneficiaries Will Be Harmed by Medicaid Provisions in Budget Bill," *Center for Budget*

Policy Priorities Report (January 29, 2006), available at http://www.cbpp.org/1-29-06health.htm (accessed January 29, 2006).

30. Institute of Medicine, *Care Without Coverage: Too Little, Too Late* (Washington, DC: National Academy Press, 2002).

31. Nancy Adler and Katherine Newman. "Socioeconomic Disparities In Health: Pathways and Policies." *Health Affairs* 21(2002): 60–77; Amy Davidoff, A. Garrett, Diane Makuc, and Mathew Schrimer. "Medicaid-Eligible Children Who Don't Enroll: Health Status, Access to Care, and Implications for Medicaid Enrollment." *Inquiry* 37(2000): 203–218; Institute of Medicine. *Coverage Matters: Insurance and Health Care* (Washington, DC: National Academy Press, 2001); Institute of Medicine, *Care Without Coverage: Too Little, Too Late*; Rowland, Salganicoff and Keenan, "The Key to the Door: Medicaid's Role in Improving Health Care for Women and Children"; C. Schur and L. Albers. "Health Care Use by Hispanic Adults: Financial vs. Non-Financial Determinants." *Health Care Financing Review* 17(1995): 71–89; Starfield, "Evaluating the State Children's Health Insurance Program: Critical Considerations."

32. Sara MacLanahan and Gary Sandefur. *Growing up with a Single Parent: What Hurts, What Helps* (Cambridge, MA: Harvard University Press, 1994).

33. Angel, Lein, and Henrici, *Poor Families in America's Health Care Crisis.*

CHAPTER 5

DISPERSING THE POOR: NEW DIRECTIONS IN PUBLIC HOUSING POLICY

Alexandra M. Curley

The 2000 census revealed that 2.3 million children in the United States live in extremely poor neighborhoods (poverty levels of 40% or more).[1] The growing field of "neighborhood effects" research suggests that neighborhood poverty, as opposed to just family poverty, can play an important role in child and family outcomes, such as employment, welfare participation, child development, and delinquency.[2] As a result, theorists and policymakers have argued that if concentrated poverty contributes to social problems and reduced life chances, then deconcentrating poverty should reverse this effect. This rationale has led to housing dispersal programs and mixed-income housing initiatives that intend to deconcentrate poverty, and consequently reduce the social problems attributed to the extreme poverty concentration in urban public housing developments.

This chapter reviews two large public housing initiatives that seek to deconcentrate poverty: Moving to Opportunity (MTO) and HOPE VI. These programs hope to improve the lives of poor families by changing the neighborhood environments in which they live through relocation to different communities and/or the redevelopment of public housing developments. The chapter reviews research on the effects of these two programs on low-income families and highlights key areas that could be strengthened in order to better help improve the lives of low-income families.

NEW DIRECTIONS IN PUBLIC HOUSING POLICY

In the 1930s and 1940s, public housing policy in the United States focused on constructing housing for working families. By the 1960s, the targeted recipients of public housing had shifted to those most in need of housing assistance. As tenant selection and rent calculation procedures changed, many working families moved out of public housing.[3] These communities turned into blighted pockets of extreme isolation and disadvantage, and the physical and social conditions of the developments deteriorated. As a result, public housing policy has been criticized for contributing to the concentration of poverty, race, and social problems in urban communities across the nation.

Policymakers and scholars have realized that concentrating extremely poor households in large superblock public housing projects in low-income communities leads to further racial and economic segregation, as well as isolation from opportunities. One early policy response to this practice was the Section 8 program (recently renamed the Housing Choice Voucher Program), a housing assistance program created in 1974 that provides portable vouchers for people to rent in the private housing market. Rather than concentrating people in public housing developments, the vouchers allow low-income families to rent apartments throughout different communities. More than 1.4 million households currently receive housing vouchers.[4]

In response to the growing concentrations of low-income families of color in public housing, the Gautreaux program was established by the courts in 1976 to desegregate Chicago's public housing. Gautreaux provided vouchers to low-income black families living in high-poverty public housing communities to relocate to predominantly white higher-income suburbs. Research found that the children of the families who moved to the suburbs were more likely than those who remained in the city to graduate from high school, enroll in college, and obtain jobs with benefits.[5] However, there were no differences in adult wages or the percentage of families living in poverty. Yet, mothers who moved to the suburbs were more likely to be working.[6]

MOVING TO OPPORTUNITY (MTO) PROGRAM

Inspired by some of the positive results of the Gautreaux program, HUD's Moving To Opportunity (MTO) demonstration program was created in 1994 as an experimental initiative to assess the effects of relocating public housing residents from concentrated developments to low-poverty communities. The five-city program (Baltimore, Boston, Chicago, Los Angeles, New York) randomly assigned public housing residents to one of three groups: (1) an experimental group, which received housing counseling along with Section 8 vouchers that could only be used in low-poverty neighborhoods (poverty rates of less than 10 percent); (2) a Section 8 group that received traditional vouchers (not restricted to low-poverty communities); or (3) a control group that remained in public housing. The random assignment was used to improve researchers' ability to attribute measured differences to the intervention (relocation to low-poverty neighborhoods) and not to differences in family characteristics or motivation.[7] Yet, only about half of those who were offered the opportunity to relocate to low-poverty neighborhoods took up the offer, making strong conclusions difficult.[8] Still, much can be learned about the program's impact from research so far.

Early short-term impact studies were conducted by different groups of researchers in different MTO sites about 2 to 3 years following implementation. In addition to these site-specific studies, an interim evaluation was conducted to measure mid-term impacts across all five MTO sites about 6 years following implementation. Research has focused on assessing whether moves to low-poverty neighborhoods resulted in positive neighborhood effects such as improvements in self-sufficiency, health, child development and achievement, and delinquency. Previous research suggests that neighborhoods can shape access to opportunity through factors such as neighborhood resources (schools, institutions, proximity to jobs), neighborhood characteristics (crime, disorder, violence), and social capital (social networks, middle-class role models, job contacts). Overall, MTO findings suggest that relocating low-income families from high-poverty public housing developments to low-poverty communities can lead to substantial improvements in housing quality, neighborhood safety, and mental and physical health.[9] Findings on self-sufficiency, child development, educational achievement, and delinquency are less encouraging.

Neighborhood and Housing Quality

Research indicates that the MTO program was successful in dramatically improving housing and neighborhood conditions for families in the experimental and Section 8 groups who relocated out of poverty concentrated public housing. Families in the experimental group moved to neighborhoods with lower rates of poverty, welfare receipt, female-headed households, higher rates of employment and education, higher percentages of professionals, two-parent families, and homeowners.[10] Families in the Section 8 group who moved also made gains in these neighborhood traits, but only about half as large as the gains experienced by the experimental group families.[11] The findings demonstrate that portable vouchers enable families to move to better neighborhoods, and that those who receive counseling and vouchers restricted to low-poverty areas make greater gains in neighborhood quality.[12] It should be noted, however, that although families in the experimental group moved to low-poverty communities, these new neighborhoods were not affluent communities.[13] In addition, the MTO program had only a small impact on neighborhood segregation. For families in the experimental group, relocation reduced the concentration of minority residents in their new neighborhoods by less than 10 percent.[14] Nearly two-thirds of the experimental group families relocated to neighborhoods where 80 percent or more of the residents are minority.[15]

Families who moved out of public housing through the MTO program also experienced improvements in neighborhood safety, exposure to violence, and reduced victimization. For example, 40 percent of families in Boston reported feeling unsafe in their communities prior to moving. After relocation, 24 percent of families in the experimental group reported feeling unsafe, compared to 39 percent of those in the control group.[16] Families in the experimental group were also more likely to move to neighborhoods with higher levels of social organization and social control.[17] Movers in both the experimental and Section 8 groups reported large reductions in neighborhood problems such as litter, trash, graffiti, abandoned buildings, public drinking, and people hanging around. Movers also felt safer in and around their homes, had less difficulty getting police to respond to calls, and reported more satisfaction with their current housing and neighborhoods than families in the control group. These improvements were consistently about 10 percentage points greater for families in the experimental group compared to those in the Section 8 group.[18] In addition, mothers in the experimental group were also much less likely than those in the Section 8 and control groups to report problems with crime, violence, disrespectful neighbors, and widespread idleness (i.e., lots of people who cannot find work).[19]

Findings also suggest that families in the experimental group were more likely to move to neighborhoods with greater collective efficacy. Collective efficacy refers to the social cohesion and shared expectations among residents and is believed to be important for reinforcing community norms and social order.[20] MTO research has found that mothers who moved to low-poverty neighborhoods reported that their new neighbors were more likely to share information about children's misbehavior than their old neighbors.[21] In addition, significantly more mothers in the experimental group reported that their new neighborhoods were good places for their families to live and that if there were problems in their new communities their neighbors could help solve them.

Self-Sufficiency

It was expected that moving families from high-poverty public housing developments to low-poverty neighborhoods might improve employment prospects and decrease welfare use by increasing families' proximity to jobs, middle-class role models, and community norms that are more supportive of employment than welfare. Yet, moving also means disruptions in the supportive social networks that many low-income people rely on for emotional support, job referrals, child care, and small loans, suggesting that relocation could lead to short-term setbacks.

Findings on outcomes related to self-sufficiency, such as employment, welfare use, and income, have not been consistent across sites.[22] Some earlier studies found small positive effects on the welfare receipt of families that moved.[23] Yet, the more recent interim impact study indicates that MTO participation across all sites had no positive impact on welfare participation, income, or food security.[24] In fact, the cross-site interim evaluation actually found a slight reduction in the employment rate for adults in the experimental group 2 years after the program was implemented.[25]

Social Capital

In addition to economic outcomes, it was also expected that MTO relocation might have an impact on residents' social capital. William Julius Wilson's (1987) social isolation theory suggests that people living in communities of concentrated poverty are isolated from middle-class people and working role models.[26] This isolation limits their access to important job networks and mainstream norms pertaining to work, family, and community. In contrast to this perspective, others argue that residents of poor communities often have well-functioning social networks that provide an important safety net and help residents cope with the hardships of poverty.[27] Through extensive support networks, families access needed social and instrumental support. Thus, one perspective suggests that the relocation of poor residents from their communities may decrease social isolation and enhance social capital, and another perspective suggests that relocation may disrupt support systems and lead to further instability.

Of the few studies that have included social capital measures, findings are mixed. One study found little significant evidence that movers experienced changes in social capital relative to nonmovers.[28] Yet, there is some evidence that moving to low-poverty areas could improve people's job networks in the long run. Moving to a low-poverty neighborhood increased the chances that adults would have friends who graduated college or earned more than $30,000 a year.[29] These better-educated and steadily employed neighbors could turn into useful job contacts in the future. However, only 8 percent of the participants in the same study said they had found a job through someone living in their neighborhood, and there were no differences across the three groups.

Adult Health

Research suggests that relocation to low-poverty neighborhoods can lead to improvements in both physical and emotional well-being. Individuals in the experimental and Section 8 groups in one site were more likely to report "good or better" overall health than the control group.[30] Findings from another site were similar, and the improvements in the overall health of parents in the experimental group were linked to dramatic improvements in emotional well-being.[31] The more recent cross-site study found a large and statistically significant effect of relocation on only one measure of physical health: obesity. There was a large reduction in the incidence of obesity among experimental and Section 8 adults, but no significant effects on hypertension, asthma, or self-reported overall health. The authors suggest that the effect on obesity could be related to reduced psychological distress and increases in exercise and nutrition observed for the Section 8 and experimental groups.[32] In addition, although there was no significant impact of relocation on overall physical health for the entire adult population, there was a significant positive impact on physical health for the younger adults. The authors suggest this could be indicative of younger people being more responsive to changes in habits and behaviors due to a change in neighborhood environment.

Both the short-term and interim studies found positive impacts on the mental health of adults in the experimental group, and sometimes for those in the Section 8 group. Adults in the experimental group experienced a reduction in psychological distress, a reduction in depression, and an increase in feelings of peacefulness and calmness.[33] Researchers believe that the reduction in stress experienced by families who moved away from dangerous public housing communities is likely a key factor contributing to the improvements in mental health.[34]

Educational Achievement

Although it was anticipated that the quality of schools would improve for children who moved to low-poverty neighborhoods, evidence indicates that gains in school quality were modest. The children who relocated with vouchers were attending schools that performed only slightly better on state exams than their old schools.[35] In fact, nearly three-quarters of the children in the experimental group who moved were attending schools in the same school district. Many remained in the same large urban school districts, and some did not change schools at all due to school choice options and/or families not moving very far away. In addition, the MTO program had no significant effect on teacher-to-pupil ratios.

Early research revealed that the MTO program was having a mix of positive and negative effects on children's educational outcomes.[36] On the one hand, elementary and middle school students in the experimental and Section 8 groups were more likely to improve their math and reading scores compared to those in the control group (gains were more pronounced among the experimental group). Yet, evidence from the same study revealed *increases* in grade retention, suspension, and expulsion for teenagers in the experimental group and increases in grade retention for teens in the Section 8 group. Higher rates of disciplinary problems and grade retention could reflect an increase in academic or behavioral problems, or they could be due to stricter academic and behavioral standards in their new schools, or discrimination by teachers or administrators.[37]

Other short-term findings suggested that children who moved out of public housing developments were less involved with their schools and neighbors. For example, in one city, children in the Section 8 group were less likely to participate in student–government groups than those in the control group. In another city, girls who moved to middle-class neighborhoods participated in fewer after school activities.[38] In addition, girls in the Section 8 group were less likely to have a friend in the neighborhood compared to girls in the control group. While earlier short-term impact studies found a mix of positive and negative results for educational outcomes, the 6-year interim evaluation revealed no significant effects on any measures of educational performance for children who moved to low-poverty neighborhoods across all MTO sites.[39]

Delinquency and Problem Behavior

It is thought that youth behavior can be shaped by neighborhoods in a number of ways: through neighborhood resources such as schools, after school programs and jobs, as well as peers, adult role models, and exposure to crime and violence.[40] Research has found significant differences in a number of outcomes for children who moved out of public housing developments through the MTO program, though not always in the direction expected. One early study found that although delinquency did not significantly decline for youth in the MTO program 3 years after implementation, youth in the Section 8 group had the lowest rates of delinquency, and youth in the experimental group were least likely to trespass, steal, or spray-paint graffiti.[41] However, the youth in the experimental group were more likely to hit someone or destroy property than youth in the other groups. Early research on the Boston site found a decline in problem behavior among boys aged 8–14 in the experimental group.[42] A study of the MTO Baltimore site found a decline in violent crime arrest among teenagers in the experimental group, but an increase in property crime arrests. Greater law-enforcement in low-poverty communities could explain some of the increase in property crimes.[43]

While short-term research suggested a mix of positive and negative impacts on problem behavior, the interim impact evaluation revealed negative impacts for boys and positive impacts for girls. The study found significant increases in behavior problems among boys aged 12–19 in both the experimental and Section 8 groups. There were large significant increases in the proportion of boys in the experimental group that were ever arrested and in the frequency of property crime arrests. In addition, there were significant increases in smoking among experimental and Section 8 group boys. However, for girls aged 15–19 in the experimental group, there were reductions in marijuana use and smoking; and for girls in the Section 8 group, there were large reductions in the proportion who had been arrested for violent crimes.[44]

Child Health

Studies suggest that children in the families who moved through the MTO program are experiencing positive effects on their health. Data from the Boston site indicate that children who moved to lower-poverty neighborhoods experienced a decrease in nonsports-related injuries (injuries from falls, fights, or dangers such as glass and needles). In fact, injuries among the experimental group declined 74 percent compared to the control group.[45] In addition, asthma attacks that required medical attention declined 65 percent among youth in the experimental group compared to the control group. Data from the New York site similarly found improved mental and physical health outcomes among children in the experimental group.

While these early findings are encouraging, the interim impact evaluation indicates that health outcomes may differ for male and female youth. In their cross-site analysis of over 4,000 households, researchers found large positive effects for female youth in the experimental and Section 8 groups on mental health and risky behavior; and small positive effects on physical health.[46] There was a very large reduction in the incidence of generalized anxiety disorder among girls in both the experimental and Section 8 groups, a moderately large reduction in psychological distress for girls in the experimental group, and a substantial decrease in the incidence of depression among girls in the Section 8 group.[47] While relocating out of high-poverty public housing communities had positive effects for female youth, relocation appears to have had adverse effects for male youth. Male youth in the experimental and Section 8 groups were more likely to have an *increase* in nonsports-related accidents or injuries and behavioral problems than youth in the control group. However, the adverse effects for males did not manifest right after the initial relocation, but after several years.[48] This is interesting since it was expected that the effects of relocation on youth might be negative in the short-term due to the disruption of moving and the difficulty of adjusting to new communities and schools, and more positive in the longer-term as they become more adjusted.

Evidence indicates that the MTO program may have profoundly different effects on male youth compared to female youth. Clearly, male and female youth may respond and interact differently to changes in their neighborhood environments. Researchers suggest possible mechanisms that could explain the gender differences. For example, girls may have been more at risk for particular negative outcomes in their old neighborhoods, and relocation may have reduced these risks. Girls may disproportionately suffer from domestic violence and sexual abuse, and therefore MTO relocation may have reduced their exposure to such risks, resulting in benefits particularly relevant for girls. In addition, female youth were more likely to have more adult role models to whom they talked about their problems, which could explain some of the gender differences in education, behavior, and mental health outcomes. Girls may be more likely to respond positively to new higher-income communities and peer groups, whereas boys may be more likely to respond by withdrawing or rebelling. Other possibilities include that boys may visit their old neighborhoods more often and therefore may be exposed to negative influences through their old neighborhood and old peers. New neighborhoods may also lack the institutions that provide support for at-risk boys that might have been present in their old neighborhoods.[49]

Summary of MTO Findings

Findings indicate that the MTO program is showing short to mid-term successes in improving neighborhood and housing conditions, adult mental health, girls' mental health, and girls' behavior for those who relocated out of public housing developments with housing vouchers. These interim successes show promise for long-term improvements in child and family outcomes. The lack of dramatic improvements to date in other child outcomes (educational performance, delinquency) and adult outcomes (employment, welfare use, income) are disappointing, but do not mean that improvements in neighborhood will not lead to long-term improvements in individual life chances. The small program impacts (positive and negative) on some of the child outcomes may reflect the fact that relocation did not lead to substantial benefits for parents (in terms of employment, welfare use, income, parenting practices, and involvement with schools).[50] In addition, relocation did not lead children to attend high-performing schools.

Potential long-term impacts of living in safer, lower-poverty neighborhoods include further improvements to adult and youth mental health, parent and child physical health, child development and behavior, and adult self-sufficiency. It is certainly possible that program impacts may be greatest for both parents and children in the long-term. Reducing exposure to violence and danger could improve child development, and perhaps, allow adults more freedom to pursue employment and education.[51] The positive impact on the mental health of mothers and female youth is promising. Sustained improvements in mental health could certainly lead to other improvements for families and children down the road.

THE HOPE VI PROGRAM

The HOPE VI program is another housing policy that seeks to deconcentrate poverty in public housing and improve the lives of low-income tenants. Passed by Congress in 1993, the HOPE VI program differs from dispersal initiatives like MTO because rather than strictly dispersing residents into different communities, it attempts to revitalize the public housing community itself. The HOPE VI program is aimed at redeveloping the "most severely distressed" housing projects throughout the country. These include developments that suffer not only from physical deterioration, but also from isolation, inadequate services, crime, chronic unemployment, welfare dependency, and high concentrations of extremely poor families of color.[52] Recognizing the negative effects of the isolation and poverty concentration in older distressed projects, the HOPE VI policy focuses on mixing public and private funding to build sustainable mixed-income communities, deconcentrating poverty, and encouraging resident self-sufficiency.

In addition to transforming the physical structure of buildings, HOPE VI transforms the social and economic structure of public housing by bringing in new residents—those of higher incomes—to offset the concentration of poverty. The goal is to create mixed-income communities where low-income public housing residents live among higher-income families who pay market-rate rents. It is expected that attracting and retaining higher-income residents will require better quality management and maintenance and bring better services to the area. HOPE VI redevelopment entails the demolition of decaying housing developments and the construction of new housing that blends in with the larger community. HUD has allocated $5.6 billion in HOPE VI grants to redevelop 231 sites around the nation.[53]

HOPE VI reflects a shift away from past public housing programs because in some ways it considers more than just peoples' housing needs. Many of the problems associated with public housing developments have been attributed to a severe lack of social infrastructure; and HOPE VI seeks to fill this void by providing funds for social services. Services provided include a range of programs designed to help residents move toward self-sufficiency, such as case management, education, job training, and child care.[54] While the available funds may not be enough to realistically help residents achieve self-sufficiency, the program has been admired for the fact that social service money is built into a public housing policy, representing a shift toward a more comprehensive housing program.

HOPE VI has received praise for recognizing the negative effects of concentrating extremely poor residents in disadvantaged housing developments and for bringing a more innovative approach to public housing. However, the program has received much criticism for its major drawbacks, including that it dislocates many families and reduces the nation's public housing stock. Because HOPE VI demolishes more units than it rebuilds and reserves a proportion of the rebuilt units for higher-income families, many public housing units are lost. The program entails the construction of 95,100 replacement units, only 48,800 of which will be public housing units.[55] Thus, in order to deconcentrate poverty and make room for higher-income residents, HOPE VI displaces a substantial number of low-income families.

Policymakers suggest that HOPE VI can decrease social isolation and increase the social mobility of public housing residents by altering the social and economic composition of their communities. It is assumed that higher-income families will be good role models for the poor, and that low-income families will benefit from having close contact with working families (i.e., by diversifying their social networks). However, since not all original residents can return to the redeveloped sites, these proposed benefits would likely only reach a segment of the community.

Overall, research and evaluation of the program has been challenging due to the lack of consistent data across HOPE VI redevelopment sites.[56] This is, in part, because HUD did not require evaluations of HOPE VI programs until the year 2000; and there are no strict guidelines for current evaluations. Further, the program has been evolving and changing since it began and looks different from site to site due to the flexibility given to housing authorities. HUD initiated "baseline" and "interim" assessments,[57] but these were case studies focused more on the physical redevelopment of the sites, rather than the outcomes of original residents. Still, there are several informative longitudinal studies of small samples of HOPE VI sites as well as single-site studies that provide a sense of how families are affected by the program.

Due to the extended time it takes to redevelop sites, most research to date focuses on how families fare during the initial relocation period. Whereas residents in the MTO program have the option to relocate (for those assigned to the Section 8 and experimental groups), residents in the HOPE VI program must move whether or not they wish to do so. Residents who have to relocate for HOPE VI typically relocate to other public housing developments or move to the private market with Section 8 vouchers. Although relocation trends vary site to site, the *HOPE VI Resident Tracking Study*, a retrospective study of residents from eight sites, found that 19 percent were living in redeveloped HOPE VI communities, 29 percent were relocated to other public housing developments, 33 percent relocated with vouchers, and 18 percent had left public housing.[58]

Although many HOPE VI residents relocate temporarily (usually for a few years until redevelopment is complete), others must relocate permanently since there are never enough units for all original residents to return to the rebuilt communities. Many families relocate not knowing whether they will return to the redeveloped community. One study that assessed the relocation choices of residents at four HOPE VI sites found that residents made relocation choices "based on significant misinformation about Section 8 procedures, HOPE VI move-back criteria, and availability of relocation services."[59] Others indicate that relocation assistance is significantly lacking, especially for hard-to-house families, such as those with many children, chronic health problems, disabilities, problems with domestic violence, gang affiliation, or substance abuse.[60] It is feared that these residents may face increased housing instability and even homelessness since they are unlikely to be successful finding suitable units in the private market with vouchers, and they are unlikely to return to the rebuilt communities due to the restrictions in the number of units, the size of units, and the new eligibility criteria.[61]

In addition to the expected benefits for families who return to the rebuilt mixed-income communities, there is also the potential for positive impacts on families who relocate to lower-poverty neighborhoods with vouchers. Yet, studies have found that HOPE VI residents often have a difficult time finding replacement housing with vouchers because the availability of affordable housing is severely limited in many regions, many landlords are reluctant to accept vouchers, most residents are inexperienced with using vouchers, and discrimination against minorities and public housing residents continues to be a problem.[62]

Neighborhood and Housing Quality

Despite these problems, studies show that similar to MTO relocation, HOPE VI relocation is improving the neighborhood conditions in which many residents live. For example, a study of five HOPE VI sites found that the average neighborhood poverty rate decreased from 40 percent to 28 percent.[63] For voucher holders, the average neighborhood poverty rate dropped from 60 percent to 27 percent.[64] However, about 40 percent of residents still reside in neighborhoods of concentrated poverty (over 30 %), and the majority still live in neighborhoods marked by extreme racial segregation.[65] In fact, 76 percent of relocated residents live in neighborhoods where 80 percent or more of the population is minority.[66] The families who end up relocating to other public housing developments or to other extremely poor, distressed, and racially segregated communities with or without vouchers are the families likely to fare the worst.

Many residents who relocated reported improvements in neighborhood safety, especially those who relocated with Section 8 vouchers. For example, while 67 percent of residents reported significant problems with shootings and violence in their old developments, only 20 percent had these problems in their new communities.[67] Many residents also experienced improvements in housing quality, with voucher holders experiencing the greatest gains. Although 75 percent said their units were better than the ones they left, the housing quality of all HOPE VI movers was still lower than other poor people nationwide.[68]

Reoccupancy by original residents varies from site to site and in many sites only a small portion of the original residents returned.[69] Overall, about 46 percent of original residents are expected to return to the newly redeveloped sites.[70] Many residents do not return to the redeveloped sites because stricter move-back criteria, such as employment requirements or criminal background checks, make them ineligible. Others may be eligible but decide not to return because they are comfortable in their new communities or do not want to move their families again. The fact that many original residents do not return to redeveloped HOPE VI communities is not necessarily a bad outcome if these families made informed decisions to relocate to better housing in better neighborhoods.

Self-Sufficiency

The combination of social services and increased proximity to higher income people (i.e., better job networks) is intended to help residents move toward self-sufficiency. Although self-sufficiency is a key goal of HOPE VI, baseline data suggest this may be a difficult goal to achieve.[71] Less than half of HOPE VI residents were employed, and the vast majority were living far below the poverty level.[72] The *HOPE VI Panel Study* found that employment rates did not change from baseline to follow up (a 2-year period) at five HOPE VI sites.[73] Many residents cycled in and out of employment, and significant barriers to getting or keeping a job included poor health, having young children, and a lack of jobs in the neighborhood.[74] There was a slight increase in incomes for working residents and a decrease in income for those not working. Welfare participation also declined, particularly for employed residents. There was an increase in the proportion of employed respondents who had been at their jobs for three or more years (45% versus 31% at baseline), and those who lived within a mile of their original public housing development were more likely to have been at their job three or more years. Only 1 percent of respondents reported that they had found a job through the HOPE VI program, compared to 16 percent at baseline. People continued to primarily use family and friends for job information, although social networks were more dispersed due to relocation. Others have found that residents are no more likely to find employment due to living in mixed income communities.[75] At one HOPE VI site, residents were using an array of new social services, but utilization was not related to employment, a key program outcome.[76] Overall, research does not show that the program is successful in preparing residents for or connecting them to the job market.

Although theory and policy suggest Section 8 movers may have the most to gain from relocation to lower-poverty neighborhoods, research indicates that relocation can sometimes have a negative impact on voucher users' financial stability. Studies have found that HOPE VI residents who relocated with Section 8 vouchers often experienced additional financial hardships due to the new responsibility of paying utility bills (families were not responsible for such bills as tenants of public housing).[77] The *HOPE VI Resident Tracking Study* found that residents who moved to private market housing with or without vouchers faced new challenges with economic stability.[78] About 50 percent said they were having difficulty affording enough food for their households, and 59 percent were having problems paying rent and utilities. One study of a Boston HOPE VI site found that Section 8 movers experienced more financial setbacks than others, and many continued to struggle paying their utility bills 2 years after relocation. The Section 8 movers were also much more likely to incur additional debt, obtain more credit cards, and have their telephone service and/or heat shut off for nonpayment during this same period.[79] The fact that many Section 8 movers were struggling to pay their utility bills 2 years following relocation raises questions about their likelihood of achieving long-term economic stability through this program.

Along with the increase in economic problems due to utility bills, studies have found that housing vouchers do not always bring housing stability, as some HOPE VI families make multiple moves with their vouchers.[80] Reasons for moving may include seeking a better quality unit, a unit in a different neighborhood, having problems with the landlord, or having a landlord who decides to sell the home or no longer accept the vouchers. In addition to the financial and housing instability multiple moves can cause, they also weaken the potential for positive "neighborhood effects." Relocating multiple times decreases the likelihood of families connecting with their neighbors and local social institutions and successfully adjusting to their new communities.

Health

Evidence indicates that the physical and mental health of residents residing in HOPE VI developments is substantially worse than other low-income Americans.[81] For example, 41 percent of HOPE VI residents reported being in fair or poor health, which is three times the national average. HOPE VI residents have alarmingly high rates of chronic health problems, including obesity, hypertension, diabetes, asthma, and arthritis. Mental health problems are also a significant problem, with 17 percent suffering a major depressive episode in the last year (nearly three times the national average). Rates of poor health are also significantly higher for HOPE VI children, with 25 percent suffering from asthma. Research indicates that many HOPE VI households are coping with multiple health problems while they are dealing with relocation.[82]

Many hope that relocation and redevelopment will lead to substantial improvements in both mental and physical health. Yet, chronic physical and mental health problems are unlikely to dissipate quickly and are likely to continue affecting residents' ability to become gainfully employed and successfully adjust in the new communities.[83] Research to date has not found changes in physical health for HOPE VI residents. One study found that Chicago residents who relocated for HOPE VI redevelopment experienced improvements in mental health, which researchers believe could have positive effects on employment and self-sufficiency in the long run.[84] Another study found that Section 8 movers were more likely to attribute improvements in emotional well-being to relocation than other movers. They cited better living conditions, more privacy, a new sense of dignity, and enhanced feelings of peacefulness from their new living situations.[85]

Social Capital

Another key issue explored by researchers is the impact of HOPE VI on residents' social networks and social interaction. While several previous studies and theoretical perspectives[86] suggested that programs like HOPE VI might help improve low-income residents' opportunities for social mobility by improving access to social capital and diversifying their social networks, HOPE VI research to date does not support this notion. In fact, the research supports previous work[87] that suggested that relocation might actually impose additional barriers to mobility by severing residents' strong social networks and weakening social capital building opportunities. HOPE VI researchers have found that relocation often breaks up strong social networks and results in a reduction in social support, which they suggest could lead to negative outcomes for families and communities.[88]

Although supportive social networks may be broken due to relocation, residents may rebuild networks in new neighborhoods. In addition, it is thought that residents who relocate to lower-poverty areas and to the rebuilt HOPE VI communities may be more likely to build ties to neighbors who are steadily employed and well-educated. Building these sorts of leveraging social ties may lead to improved opportunities for mobility.[89] Yet, research to date shows low levels of interaction among neighbors in redeveloped HOPE VI communities.[90] In addition, studies suggest that residents who relocate with vouchers also have little meaningful contact with their neighbors.[91]

Children

By improving distressed public housing communities and moving families to better neighborhoods, the HOPE VI program has the potential to improve children's life chances. About 39 percent of HOPE VI children changed schools due to relocation, and research indicates that relocated children are attending schools that are less poor, but still nearly all minority.[92] Voucher holders experienced the most improvements in school quality.[93] Parents who relocated with vouchers were less likely to report problems with school quality and more likely to perceive their children's schools as safe.[94] Children of voucher holders were also significantly less likely to be held back a grade than those still living in public housing (even those who changed schools).

Some parents also reported changes in children's behavioral problems after relocation. Parents who relocated with Section 8 vouchers were more likely to report improvements in behavioral problems, while public housing movers reported *increases* in behavioral problems among boys.[95] Clearly, relocation to other public housing developments means moving to other poor and often dangerous communities. Findings suggest that boys, in particular, may face more challenges in these new communities than those who relocate out of public housing with vouchers.

Although research found differences in child outcomes by relocation group, evidence indicates that certain parental characteristics play a key role. Parents who were more engaged with their children's education (attending meetings and after-school activities) and those who graduated high school or had a GED, were less likely to report behavioral problems or that their child was held back a grade and more likely to report that their child was very engaged in school.[96] On the other hand, parent suffering from depression were more likely to report child behavior problems. These parental affects hold true for children in all relocation groups, suggesting the importance of programs aimed at reducing parental stress and helping parents become more involved with their children's education.

Summary of HOPE VI research

In summary, the HOPE VI program has the potential to have major effects on the lives of low-income families. While some residents may benefit from better housing and better communities, others relocate to housing and communities similar to those they were forced to leave. Thus, HOPE VI deconcentrates poverty at the original public housing sites as intended, but reconcentrates poverty in other public housing developments and other poor communities to which many residents relocate. As for its intended economic and social effects, evidence to date does not suggest that HOPE VI is successful in helping families achieve social and economic mobility through the creation of economically integrated developments or through relocation to other communities. It is certainly plausible that the intended benefits of income mixing and relocation will take more time to generate. The gains in neighborhood and housing quality for some relocated residents may lead to longer-term benefits such as improved physical and emotional well-being and better job networks. Longitudinal studies examining impacted families before, during, and after HOPE VI relocation (including those who do not return to the redeveloped site) are still very much needed.[97]

CONCLUSION

MTO and HOPE VI research provide important insights into the short- and mid-term program impacts on low-income families. Research evidence indicates that people are not always affected by deconcentration and housing mobility programs as expected. For example, it was expected that children who relocated from high-poverty to low-poverty neighborhoods would show improvements in educational achievement, behavior, and delinquency. Yet research reveals that other factors including age, gender, parental characteristics, and school quality also play an important mediating role in determining outcomes. Likewise, it was expected that adults too would benefit from such moves by increasing employment opportunities and decreasing welfare participation. Yet, findings show minimal impacts, at least in the short to mid-term. It was also assumed that relocation to lower-poverty areas would lead to increases in resident engagement with higher-income neighbors, but research indicates this is not happening.

Both the MTO and HOPE VI programs appear to be producing both positive and negative effects on families. The most successful outcome of the MTO program appears to be the dramatic improvement in neighborhood quality for families who relocated with vouchers, but especially for those who relocated to low-poverty neighborhoods. Research indicates that relocating low-income families from high-poverty public housing developments to safer communities with greater social organization can lead to improvements in adults' and girls' mental health as well as girls' behavior. On the other hand, MTO relocation had little impact on the racial segregation of the neighborhoods in which families live. Further, these moves did not result in substantial gains in employment, earnings, welfare participation, or children's educational achievement. In addition, relocation from these communities appeared to have negative impacts on the behavior and health of boys.

Evidence from the HOPE VI program similarly suggests that relocation can improve housing and neighborhood quality, as well as adult mental health. Similar to the MTO findings, HOPE VI appears to have had very little impact on moving families to less segregated communities. HOPE VI research also found few positive economic or social effects. There is some evidence that relocating public housing residents to Section 8 housing may increase economic and housing instability. In addition, HOPE VI relocation often breaks up supportive social networks, which could thwart any positive effects from relocation.

Research evidence highlights key areas where the MTO and HOPE VI programs should be strengthened in order to achieve their full potential and improve the lives of low-income families.[98] First, while both programs show that providing vouchers to families living in distressed public housing enables families to relocate to better quality housing in better quality neighborhoods, the MTO program shows that providing people extra housing counseling and search assistance, as well as vouchers restricted to low-poverty areas, substantially improves outcomes. Based on the positive results from the MTO program, the HOPE VI program should provide more intensive counseling and assistance to families relocating through the program. Helping families consider the benefits and drawbacks of different neighborhoods and helping them assess where they will access services their families depend on (childcare, transportation, medical care) in new communities could lead to better outcomes and future housing and economic stability. In addition, both programs should encourage families to move to low-poverty and less-segregated communities. Housing authorities should work with landlords in a variety of neighborhoods to improve the selection of units and neighborhoods for residents using vouchers.

Intensive housing counseling and search assistance may be necessary to improve not only housing and neighborhood outcomes for families, but also their successful adjustment and integration into their new communities. More in-depth counseling could help minimize losses in social support and help movers rebuild social ties and access support and leverage in their new communities. In both programs, vulnerable families are moved from their communities and familiar support systems. The findings from the HOPE VI program, in particular, suggest a need for ongoing supportive services to help families access local services and successfully adjust to their new living arrangements. More extensive support could help reduce the stress of making an involuntary move, especially for those whose physical or mental health problems may be exacerbated by relocation. High rates of depression and chronic health problems, coupled with the challenges involved in making an involuntary move, warrant sustained support to help families successfully transition to their new communities.[99] Services targeted to youth, particularly male youth, could help decrease negative impacts and lead to future positive impacts.

Evidence suggests that further financial support is needed to help Section 8 movers cope with additional utility bills. Providing these movers supplemental support during the initial relocation years may improve families' long-term housing and economic stability. Finally, due to the severe lack of affordable housing and the growing need for subsidized housing around the nation, the HOPE VI program (and future housing programs) should do more to ensure public housing units are not lost due to redevelopment. This may entail rebuilding lower-density mixed-income communities at the original public housing sites, as well as building or acquiring units at other sites to make up for those lost. The benefits of relocating families with vouchers and building higher quality mixed-income communities should not mask the costs of reducing the nation's public housing stock (units with deep, long-term federal funding) for the lowest income families.[100] Lastly, the children of relocated families may ultimately be the ones most affected by housing mobility programs. Future MTO and HOPE VI research is needed to assess whether the negative interim impacts last over time and whether the positive interim impacts lead to greater long-term impacts. Understanding the long-term effects of housing programs like MTO and HOPE VI is critical to building an urban housing policy that helps improve the lives of low-income families.

NOTES

1. William O'Hare and Mark Mather, "The Growing Number of Kids in Severely Distressed Neighborhoods: Evidence from the 2000 Census." *The Annie E. Casey Foundation and the Population Reference Bureau* (2003).

2. Prudence Brown and Harold Richman, "Neighborhood Effects and State and Local Policy." In *Neighborhood Poverty Volume II: Policy Implications in Studying Neighborhoods*, ed. Jeanne Brooks-Gunn, Greg Duncan and Lawrence Aber (New York: Russell Sage Foundation, 1997); Tama Leventhal, Jeanne Brooks-Gunn, and Sheila Kamerman, "Communities as Place, Face, and Space: Provisions of Services to Poor, Urban Children and Their Families." In *Neighborhood Poverty Volume II: Policy Implications in Studying Neighborhoods*, ed. Jeanne Brooks-Gunn, Greg Duncan and Lawrence Aber (New York: Russell Sage Foundation, 1997).

3. Douglas Massey and Nancy Denton. *American Apartheid: Segregation and the Making of the Underclass* (Cambridge, MA: Harvard University Press, 1993). Also see: Larry Spence, "Rethinking the Social Role of Public Housing." *Housing Policy Debate*, 4(3) (1993): 355–368; Lawrence Vale. *Reclaiming Public Housing* (Cambridge, MA: Harvard University Press, 2002).

4. U.S. Department of Housing and Urban Development (HUD). *Section 8 Rental Voucher Program.* 2004. Available at http://www.hud.gov.

5. James Rosenbaum, Linda Stroh, and Cathy Flynn. "Lake Parc Place: A Study of Mixed-Income Housing." *Housing Policy Debate*, 9(4) (1998): 703–740.

6. James Rosenbaum and Susan Popkin. "Employment and Earnings of Low-Income Blacks Who Move to Middle-Income Suburbs." In *The Urban Underclass*, ed. Christopher Jenks and Paul Peterson, 342–365 (Washington, DC: Brookings Institution, 1991).

7. Larry Orr, Judith Feins, Robin Jacob, Erik Beecroft, Lisa Sanbonmatsu, Lawrence Katz, Jeffrey Leibman, and Jeffrey Kling, "Moving to Opportunity Interim Impacts Evaluation" (Washington, DC: HUD, 2003).

8. Leventhal, Brooks-Gunn, and Kamerman, *Neighborhood Poverty Volume II*; Lisa Sanbonmatsu, Jeffrey Kling, Greg Duncan, and Jeanne Brooks-Gunn, "Neighborhoods and Academic Achievement: Results from the Moving To Opportunity Experiment." *Princeton IRS Working Paper 492* (August 2004): 1–41.

9. Orr et al., "Moving to Opportunity Interim Impacts Evaluation"; John Goering, and Judith Feins, *Choosing a Better Life? Evaluating the Moving To Opportunities Experiment* (Washington, DC: Urban Institute, 2003).

10. Becky Pettit and Sara McLanahan, "Social Dimensions of Moving to Opportunity." *Poverty Research News*, 5.1(January 2001): 1–10; Orr et al., "Moving to Opportunity Interim Impacts Evaluation."

11. Orr et al., "Moving to Opportunity Interim Impacts Evaluation."

12. Pettit and McLanahan, "Social Dimensions of Moving to Opportunity."

13. Some have suggested that it is affluent neighbors, rather than middle-income neighbors, that can have positive effects on families.

14. Orr et al., "Moving to Opportunity Interim Impacts Evaluation."

15. Sanbonmatsu et al., "Neighborhoods and Academic Achievement."

16. Alessandra Del Conte and Jeffrey Kling. "A Synthesis of MTO Research on Self-Sufficiency, Safety and Health, and Behavior and Delinquency." *Poverty Research News*, 5.1 (January 2001): 3–6.

17. Emily Rosenbaum, "The Social Context of New Neighborhoods Among MTO Chicago Families." *Poverty Research News*, 5.1 (January 2001): 16–19.

18. Orr et al., "Moving to Opportunity Interim Impacts Evaluation."

19. Rosenbaum, "The Social Context of New Neighborhoods Among MTO Chicago Families."

20. Robert Sampson and Jeffrey Morenoff, "Durable Inequality: Spatial Dynamics, Social Processes, and the Persistence of Poverty in Chicago Neighborhoods." In *Poverty Traps*, ed. Samuel Bowles, Steve Darlauf, and Karla Hoff (Princeton, NJ: Princeton University Press, 2004); Mario Small and Katherine Newman, "Urban Poverty After the Truly Disadvantaged: The Rediscovery of the Family, the Neighborhood, and Culture." *Annual Review of Sociology*, 27 (2001): 23–45.

21. Rosenbaum, "The Social Context of New Neighborhoods Among MTO Chicago Families."

22. Del Conte and Kling, "A Synthesis of MTO Research on Self-Sufficiency, Safety and Health, and Behavior and Delinquency."

23. Tama Leventhal and Jeanne Brooks-Gunn "Moving to Better Neighborhoods Improves Health and Family Life Among New York Families." *Poverty Research News*. Jan.–Feb. 2001; Del Conte and Kling, "A Synthesis of MTO Research on Self-Sufficiency, Safety and Health, and Behavior and Delinquency."

24. Orr et al., "Moving to Opportunity Interim Impacts Evaluation."; Jeffrey Kling, Jeffrey Liebman, and Lawrence Katz, "Experimental Analysis of Neighborhood Effects," Princeton University Working Paper (June 2005): 1–31.

25. Orr et al., "Moving to Opportunity Interim Impacts Evaluation."

26. William Julius Wilson. *The Truly Disadvantaged* (Chicago, IL: The University of Chicago Press, 1987).

27. Kathryn Edin and Laura Lein. *Making Ends Meet* (New York: Russell Sage Foundation, 1997); Elliot Liebow. *Tally's Corner: A Study of Negro Streetcorner Men* (Boston, MA: Little, Brown, 1967); Carol Stack. *All Our Kin: Strategies for Survival in a Black Community* (New York: Harper and Row, 1974); Vale, *Reclaiming Public Housing*.

28. Pettit and McLanahan, "Social Dimensions of Moving to Opportunity."

29. Kling, Liebman, and Katz, "Experimental Analysis of Neighborhood Effects."; Orr et al., "Moving to Opportunity Interim Impacts Evaluation."

30. Del Conte and Kling, "A Synthesis of MTO Research on Self-Sufficiency, Safety and Health, and Behavior and Delinquency."

31. Del Conte and Kling, "A Synthesis of MTO Research on Self-Sufficiency, Safety and Health, and Behavior and Delinquency."

32. Kling, Liebman, and Katz, "Experimental Analysis of Neighborhood Effects."

33. Orr, et al., "Moving to Opportunity Interim Impacts Evaluation."; Del Conte and Kling, "A Synthesis of MTO Research on Self-Sufficiency, Safety and Health, and Behavior and Delinquency."; Tama Leventhal and Jeanne Brooks-Gunn "Moving to Better Neighborhoods

Improves Health and Family Life Among New York Families." *Poverty Research News.* Jan.–Feb. 2001.

34. Kling, Liebman, and Katz, "Experimental Analysis of Neighborhood Effects."

35. Orr et al., "Moving to Opportunity Interim Impacts Evaluation."; Sanbonmatsu et al., "Neighborhoods and Academic Achievement." For example, only 16% of children in the experimental group were attending schools that ranked above the state median in test scores.

36. Jens Ludwig, Greg Duncan, and Helen Ladd, "The Effects of MTO on Baltimore Children's Educational Outcomes," *Poverty Research News*, 5.1 (January, 2001): 13–15.

37. Ludwig, Duncan, and Ladd, "The Effects of MTO on Baltimore Children's Educational Outcomes."

38. Pettit and McLanahan, "Social Dimensions of Moving to Opportunity."

39. Orr et al., "Moving to Opportunity Interim Impacts Evaluation."

40. Del Conte and Kling, "A Synthesis of MTO Research on Self-Sufficiency, Safety and Health, and Behavior and Delinquency."

41. Tama Leventhal and Jeanne Brooks-Gunn "Moving to Better Neighborhoods Improves Health and Family Life Among New York Families." *Poverty Research News.* Jan.–Feb. 2001.

42. Del Conte and Kling, "A Synthesis of MTO Research on Self-Sufficiency, Safety and Health, and Behavior and Delinquency."

43. Del Conte and Kling, "A Synthesis of MTO Research on Self-Sufficiency, Safety and Health, and Behavior and Delinquency."

44. Orr et al., "Moving to Opportunity Interim Impacts Evaluation."

45. Del Conte and Kling, "A Synthesis of MTO Research on Self-Sufficiency, Safety and Health, and Behavior and Delinquency."

46. Kling, Liebman, and Katz, "Experimental Analysis of Neighborhood Effects."

47. Orr et al., "Moving to Opportunity Interim Impacts Evaluation."

48. Kling, Liebman, and Katz, "Experimental Analysis of Neighborhood Effects."

49. Kling, Liebman, and Katz, "Experimental Analysis of Neighborhood Effects."

50. Sanbonmatsu et al., "Neighborhoods and Academic Achievement."

51. Jeffrey Kling, Jeffrey Liebman, and Lawrence Katz, "Bullets Don't Got No Name: Consequences of Fear in the Ghetto." *Joint Center for Poverty Research Working Paper 225* (2005).

52. U.S. Department of Housing and Urban Development (HUD). *HUD Awards $35 million Grant to Boston to Transform Public Housing, Help Residents.* No.01-084. Washington, DC (September 27, 2001).

53. The current administration proposed to eliminate HOPE VI funding in 2005 and 2006. Congress has resisted, but funding was dramatically reduced. Annual funding has dropped from $574 million in 2002 to $99 million in 2006. Congressional Quarterly Today, "Bush Making Progress in Efforts to End Public Housing Renewal Program," February 9, 2006. Retrieved from www.Knowledgeplex.org. Also see: U.S. Department of Housing and Urban Development (HUD). *About HOPE VI.* Available at http://www.hud.gov/offices/pih/programs/ph/hope6/about. Washington, DC (2003).

54. HOPE VI grantees in the years 1993–2001 had budgeted a total of $714 million for Community and Supportive Services programs (GAO, 2003a).

55. Mary Cunningham. *An Improved Living Environment? Relocation Outcomes for HOPE VI Relocatees.* (Washington DC: Urban Institute, 2004).

56. Susan Popkin, Bruce Katz, Mary Cunningham, Karen Brown, Jeremy Gustafson, and Margery Turner. *A Decade of HOPE VI: Research Findings and Policy Challenges.* (Washington DC: Urban Institute, 2004).

57. Linda Fosburg, Susan Popkin, and Gretchen Locke. *An Historical and Baseline Assessment of HOPE, Volume I* (Washington DC: Department of Housing and Urban Development, 1996).

58. Larry Buron, *An Improved Living Environment? Neighborhood Outcomes for HOPE VI Relocatees.*(Washington DC: Urban Institute, 2004); Larry Buron, Susan Popkin, Dianne Levy, Laura Harris, and Jill Khadduri. *The HOPE VI Resident Tracking Study.* (Washington, DC: Urban Institute, 2002).

59. Robin Smith. *Housing Choice for HOPE VI Relocatees* (Washington, DC: Urban Institute, 2002): 1.

60. Larry Keating. "Redeveloping Public Housing: Relearning Urban Renewal's Immutable Lessons." *Journal of the American Planning Association*, 66.4 (2000); Susan Popkin, Diane Levy, Laura Harris, Jennifer Comey, Mary Cunningham, Larry Buron, and W. Woodley. *HOPE VI Panel Study: Baseline Report.* Urban Institute (2002); Susan Popkin, Diane Levy, Laura Harris, Jennifer Comey, Mary Cunningham, and Larry Buron. (2004b). "The HOPE VI Program: What About the Residents?" *Housing Policy Debate*, 15(2): 385–414.

61. Popkin et al., "The HOPE VI Program: What About the Residents?"; *A Decade of HOPE VI: Research Findings and Policy Challenges* (Washington DC: Urban Institute, 2004)

62. Finkel, A.E., Lennon, K.A., & Eisenstadt, E.R. (2000). HOPE VI: A Promising Vintage?" *Policy Studies Review*, 17, 104–119.

63. Buron, *An Improved Living Environment?*

64. This figure is for the eight sites studied in the HOPE VI Resident Tracking Study; Buron et al., *The HOPE VI Resident Tracking Study.*

65. Buron, *An Improved Living Environment?*; Buron et al., *The HOPE VI Resident Tracking Study.*

66. Buron, *An Improved Living Environment?*

67. Buron, *An Improved Living Environment?*

68. Jennifer Comey. *An Improved Living Environment? Housing Quality Outcomes for HOPE VI Relocatees.* (Washington DC: Urban Institute, 2004).

69. National Housing Law Project, *False HOPE: A Critical Assessment of the HOPE VI Public Housing Redevelopment Program.* Available at http://www.nhlp.org. (2002); Keating, "Redeveloping Public Housing."

70. For example, at 39 sites where reoccupancy was complete, less than 25 percent of original residents returned to 17 sites, and 75 percent or more returned to 7 sites. U.S. General Accounting Office (GAO). *Public Housing: HUD's Oversight of HOPE VI Sites Needs to be More Consistent.* GAO-03-555 (Washington, DC May 30, 2003); Popkin et al., "The HOPE VI Program: What About the Residents?"; *A Decade of HOPE VI: Research Findings and Policy Challenges.* (Washington DC: Urban Institute, 2004)

71. Diane Levy and Deborah Kaye, "How are HOPE VI Families Faring? Income and Employment.". (Washington, DC: Urban Institute, 2004).

72. And 35% reported incomes less than $5,000. Levy and Kaye, "How are HOPE VI Families Faring? Income and Employment."

73. Levy and Kaye, "How are HOPE VI Families Faring? Income and Employment."

74. While less than half of the respondents were working at baseline or follow-up, 60% were working either at baseline or follow-up. Levy and Kaye, "How are HOPE VI Families Faring? Income and Employment."

75. Rosenbaum, Stroh, and Flynn, "Lake Parc Place."

76. Mary Collins, Alexandra Curley, Cassandra Clay, and Rita Lara, "Evaluation of Social Services in a Mixed Income Housing Development." *Evaluation and Program Planning*, 28 (1), (2004): 47–59.

77. Buron et al., *The HOPE VI Resident Tracking Study*; Center for Community Change. *A HOPE Unseen: Voices from the Other Side of HOPE VI*. (Washington, DC: Center for Community Change, 2003); Alexandra Curley, "Hope and Housing: The Effects of Relocation on movers' Economic Stability, Social Networks, and Health," Boston University, Dissertation, (2006): 1–203.

78. Buron et al., *The HOPE VI Resident Tracking Study*.

79. Curley, "Hope and Housing."

80. Center for Community Change, *A HOPE Unseen*; Curley, "Hope and Housing."

81. Laura Harris and Diane Kaye, *How Are HOPE VI Families Faring? Health*. (Washington, DC: Urban Institute, 2004); Susan Popkin et al., *HOPE VI Panel Study*.

82. For example, 45% have at least one household member (adult or child) in fair or poor health. Harris and Kaye, *How Are HOPE VI Families Faring? Health*.

83. 28% of 18- to 44-year-olds who were not employed reported health barriers to employment; 59% of 45- to 64-year-olds reported health barriers to employment. Harris and Kaye, *How Are HOPE VI Families Faring? Health*, p. 5.

84. Susan Popkin and Mary Cunningham, *CHA Relocation Counseling Assessment: Final Report*. (Washington DC: Urban Institute, 2002).

85. Curley, "Hope and Housing."

86. For example, see Xavier de Souza Briggs, "Brown Kids in White Suburbs: Housing Mobility and the Many Faces of Social Capital. *Housing Policy Debate*, 9(1) (1998): 177–213.; Mark Granovetter, *Getting a Job: A Study of Contacts and Careers* (Cambridge, MA: Harvard University Press, 1974); Wilson, *The Truly Disadvantaged*.

87. For example, see Edin and Lein, *Making Ends Meet*; Robert Putnam. *Bowling alone* (New York: Simon & Schuster, 2000); Stack *All Our Kin*; Vale, *Reclaiming Public Housing*.

88. Susan Saegert and Gary Winkel, "Social Capital and the Revitalization of New York City's Distressed Inner-City Housing." *Housing Policy Debate*, 9(1), (1998): 17–60; Susan Greenbaum, "Social Capital and Deconcentration: Theoretical and Policy Paradoxes of the HOPE VI Program." Paper presented at the Conference on Social Justice, Windsor, Canada. May 5, 2002; Popkin et al., "The HOPE VI Program: What About the Residents?"; Susan Clampet-Lundquist, "HOPE VI Relocation: Moving to New Neighborhoods and Building New Ties." *Housing Policy Debate*, 15(2), (2004): 415–447; Curley, "Hope and Housing."; Edward Goetz, *Clearing the Way: Deconcentrating the Poor in Urban America* (Washington, DC: Urban Institute Press, 2003).

89. See Xavier de Souza Briggs, "Brown Kids in White Suburbs: Housing Mobility and the Many Faces of Social Capital."; Tama Leventhal and Jeanne Brooks-Gunn "Moving to Better Neighborhoods Improves Health and Family Life Among New York Families." *Poverty Research News*. Jan.–Feb. 2001.

90. Paul Brophy and Rhonda Smith, "Mixed-Income Housing: Factors for Success," *Cityscape: A Journal of Policy Development and Research*, 3.2 (1997): 3–31; Buron et al., *The HOPE VI Resident Tracking Study*; Smith, *Housing Choice for HOPE VI Relocatees*.

91. Curley, "Hope and Housing."

92. Susan Popkin, Michael Eiseman, and Elizabeth Cove, *How are HOPE VI Families Faring? Children*. (Washington, DC: Urban Institute, 2004).

93. For instance, an average of 68% of students qualify for free school lunch in their new schools, compared to 85% in their old schools. Popkin, Eiseman, and Cove, *How are HOPE VI Families Faring? Children.*

94. Voucher holders reported fewer problems with violence in schools than families still living in public housing (20% vs. 30%). In addition, only 21% of voucher holders reported school quality as a problem compared with more than 50% at baseline. See Popkin, Eiseman, and Cove, *How are HOPE VI Families Faring? Children.*

95. At baseline about two-thirds of children had one or more behavioral problems and about half had two or more. Boys who relocated with vouchers were more likely to have two or more behavioral problems at baseline compared to all boys (67% vs. 61%). But their behavior improved at follow-up and they were no more likely to have two or more behavioral problems than other boys. In contrast, boys who moved to other public housing developments were less likely to have behavioral problems at baseline (43%) but more likely to have behavior problems after relocation two years later (62%). Popkin, Eiseman, and Cove, *How are HOPE VI Families Faring? Children.*

96. Popkin, Eiseman, and Cove, *How are HOPE VI Families Faring? Children.*

97. Popkin et al., *HOPE VI Panel Study.*

98. For example, see Popkin et al., *A Decade of HOPE VI.*

99. Harris and Kaye, *How Are HOPE VI Families Faring? Health.*

100 Popkin et al., *A Decade of HOPE VI.*

CHAPTER 6

PROVIDING EDUCATIONAL OPPORTUNITIES FOR CHILDREN LIVING IN POVERTY

Hassan Tajalli

The history of public education policies in the United States is the history of shifting goals and orientations. The challenge of providing educational opportunities for poor children is shaped by a multitude of players with varying degrees of power and a bundle of ideological issues. Parents, living environment, schools, local school districts, state government, the federal government, and increasingly the courts directly affect the educational opportunities of poor children. There is also ongoing debate over the appropriate division of power and responsibility of schools, parents, and the various levels of government. But at the heart of the challenge lies fundamental ideological issues that the United States has been facing since its inception. The competing values of market competition and social justice, in particular, have shaped the vacillating educational policies toward disadvantaged children. The paramount values of the former are individualism, competition, and liberty. A market free of government interference is expected to create a self-regulating, self-correcting social system that promotes prosperity. To the advocates of the free market, education, like any other commodity, is an individual good that should be subject to the forces of the market. On the other hand, there are those who view the market to be irrational and self-destructive. If left unrestrained, they argue, market competition will not only undermine prosperity but will also lead to social injustice and an immense inequality of wealth and power that stifle liberty. To these advocates, education is a public good that can benefit both individuals as well as the entire society. Public education, therefore, should be protected from the inequalities that market promotes.

The purpose of this chapter is to show how these competing views and values have shaped the educational policies of the United States toward poor children. We will start our discussion by looking at the devastating impact of poverty on the educational performance of students and the current demographic distribution of these students in the United States. The ideological roots of education policies and the role that race and poverty have played in shaping these policies are examined. Inequality in public education, to a large degree, is related to the way public schools are financed in the United States. We will examine this issue to show how property-based public school financing has undermined educational opportunities of the poor. It is also argued that the current shift to performance-based education has failed to solve the educational problems of the disadvantaged students. Suggestions for improving educational opportunities of disadvantaged students are offered in the concluding section.

PROBLEMS OF POVERTY FOR STUDENTS

For most of its history, public education in the United States has not provided disadvantaged children a real chance to break out of the cycle of poverty. Currently, over 40 percent of school children in the United States lack the type of educational opportunities that are available to other children. This means that what they are taught is inadequate, their access to higher levels of education is limited, and the educational system does not equip them with the means to improve their chances in life. The problem is caused not only by the schools themselves and the educational policies of the various levels of government and the courts, but more importantly, by the physical, emotional, and behavioral scars that poor children bring to school everyday. The public educational system has been largely unable to compensate for these liabilities of poverty while at the same time narrowing opportunity gaps for these children.

The burden of poverty, weighs on the shoulders of poor children before, during, and after their school day. What children bring to school with them has a profound impact on how they perform at school. There is a large body of research on the antecedents of low academic performance by poor children. The search for the root causes of the problem has taken researchers as far back as the mother's prenatal care, care after birth,[1-3] and preschool education[4] of the children. The findings show that poor students suffer from every form of childhood deficiency, ranging from gross malnutrition, recurrent and untreated health problems, emotional and physical stress, to child abuse, and learning disabilities.[5] The physical and emotional scars that children of poor families bring with them to school impede their cognitive development. There is also widespread consensus that children enter school with a range of prior knowledge, skills, beliefs, and concepts that significantly influence what they notice about the environment and how they organize and interpret it.[6] Poor children enter schools with abilities and a mindset that places them at a competitive disadvantage. It is then no surprise that the academic achievement of poor students is not up to par with that of other students, even when they are placed in the same school environment as nonpoor children.

Poor children have persistently shown lower levels of performance on every indicator of educational achievement. The test scores, graduation rates, and college entrance/completion rates of low-income students have been significantly lower than those of their nonpoor peers. High school students living in low-income families are six times as likely as their peers from high-income families to drop out of high school.[7] Non-Hispanic whites between the ages of 25–29 in 2003 were more likely to have earned at least a bachelor's degree (32%) than their black (18%) and Hispanic (12%) peers who are predominantly low-income.[8]

These achievement gaps between poor and nonpoor are present in every kind of school district.[9] If fact, the disparity can be traced to preschools. For example, in a thorough investigation of educational gaps between white and black kindergartners, Lee and Burkam[10] found that black kindergartners are 34 percentile points below the levels of white kindergartners—roughly the same gap that exist in elementary and secondary schools.

Why has this problem persisted for so long, even in the face of many educational reforms and even when students are placed in similar educational conditions as the nonpoor? At times, the blame has been placed on the children themselves, their parents, or their ethnic community. Others have blamed the skills and expectations of schoolteachers and administrators. Still others have placed the blame on inadequate school funding.

The liabilities of poverty adversely affect the functioning and learning abilities of children. Schools, however, have powerful opportunities to compensate for these liabilities.[11] School management and accountability, financial resources and teachers can all positively influence students who are handicapped by their circumstances. However, an argument can be made that even schools and teachers who cater to poor children are directly and indirectly victimized by poverty. These schools lack resources, qualified teaching staffs, and administrations accountable to the parents of poor students. The teachers and administrators of these schools also have low standards and expectations of student performance. In fact, poor children who need the most help to catch up with their peers are the least attended to by the educational system. In an extensive survey of the literature, Paul Barton[12] found 14 factors associated with educational attainments that differentiate the performance of low-income and minority students from that of their nonpoor peers. The findings clearly show that educational achievement is associated with home, school, and societal factors. Almost all of these factors are determined by the underlying socioeconomic status of parents. In short, the ultimate solution for enhancing the educational opportunities of disadvantaged children lies in the enhancement of wide ranging educational policies and combating poverty in society.

WHO ARE THE POOR STUDENTS?

The burden of poverty on the academic achievement of disadvantaged children is well documented. But who are the poor children of the United States? What are the demographic characteristics of these children? How large is their population? These types of questions and their answers will ultimately shape our understanding of the problem and how to solve it.

Nationwide, about 40 percent of children in the United States live in low-income families, while about 18 percent live in families whose income falls below the federal poverty line. With over 60 percent of black and Hispanic students living in low-income families, poverty and race have become two sides of the same coin in the lexicon of educational reforms. The 2004 statistics show that 55 percent of low-income children live in families with at least one parent working full-time, year-round. Low-income children are mostly black or Hispanic and come from single-parent families with low levels of education. About 61 percent of black children and 63 percent of the Hispanic children are low-income. Nearly 51 percent of the children who live in a single-parent family live in low-income conditions, while 84 percent of the children whose parental education is less than high school live in the same conditions. Low-income children are mostly concentrated in urban (52%) and rural (47%) areas. The South (43%) and West (42%) have the highest concentration of low-income children. The Northeast has the lowest concentration of low-income children (33%).[13]

THE IDEOLOGICAL ROOTS OF PUBLIC EDUCATION

For nearly 200 years, the hallmark of American politics has been a struggle to balance individual liberty and social justice. However, there has been a sharp disagreement on what exactly these terms mean, how to bring into balance these competing values, how best to achieve them, and who should be the recipients of these values. The disagreements are best represented by two ideologies that share the two fundamental values of liberty and social justice. They are conservatism and welfare liberalism. For the most part, early Americans defined social justice in terms of liberty. They perceived liberty as the greater of the two values. However, their narrow conception of liberty served the privileged segment of society. Liberty to most early Americans was nothing more than the absence of restraint from government. They viewed government as an impediment to the free growth and development of the individual. Individuals could be free only when the tentacles of government left them alone. Unrestricted market competition was believed to be the best means of achieving freedom. Whatever resulted from free market competition was perceived to be just and fair. Early Americans, as a result, treated education like any other commodity that was available only to those who could pay for it. Poor children, for the most part, did not receive formal education; if they did, it was either an act of charity or an attempt to convert the slaves to Christianity. The Southern states opposed the education of blacks altogether. It was not until after President Abraham Lincoln issued the Emancipation Proclamation in 1863 that blacks were given the opportunity to receive education.

Some early pioneers, however, did not view education as another commodity that should be subject to market forces. Notable among them were Thomas Jefferson and George Washington who advocated the creation of a public school system for all American children, regardless of their socioeconomic background. They viewed free universal public education not only as morally right but also as socially beneficial for the new country. The progressive idea of free universal education, however, could not materialize in the wake of the enormous political, social, and economic issues facing the new nation.

By the mid-1800s, a new understanding of liberty and the role of government began to emerge in England. The new generation of liberals, known as welfare liberals, expanded our understanding of liberty, social justice, and equality. They argued that in the face of ignorance, poverty, illness, and prejudice, freedom and opportunity could not be realized without the active participation of government. A child born and trapped in poverty has no true chance of becoming free to grow and develop to the full extent of his or her abilities. Welfare liberals argued that the absence of government interference would not provide an opportunity for the poor to enhance their chances in life. The chains of ignorance and poverty are more insidious than any other hindrance to liberty and opportunity. The poor and the disadvantaged need to be empowered to be free. It is, therefore, the moral responsibility of the state to use its power to empower people—not only to fulfill the promises of liberty for all, but also for the common good of society. The power of the state, it was argued, needs to be used to overcome the obstacles to freedom and opportunity. The common good is served when society, acting through government, establishes, among other things, free public schools for the children of the needy.

The welfare liberal ideas that began in England in the mid-1800s soon found their way to the new world. Until the 1840s, the education system in America primarily served the children of white middle-class and wealthy families. Pioneer reformers such as Horace Mann of Massachusetts and Henry Barnard of Connecticut campaigned tirelessly to promote the new welfare liberal ideas on education. Mann started the publication of the Common School Journal. In his journal, Mann continuously argued that free common schooling is a public good that has social, political, and economic benefits for all. It was to promote good citizenship, unite society, and prevent crime and poverty. By the end of the nineteenth century many states were convinced by the argument and had adopted free education for all children, including the poor. In 1852, Massachusetts was the first state to pass such a law, followed by New York in 1853. By 1920, the remaining states had joined to mandate free compulsory elementary education for all children. Soon after, most states enacted legislation extending compulsory education to age 16.

The United States federal government did not play any noticeable role in public education until the onset of the Depression in the early 1930s. The Depression marked the ascendancy of welfare liberal ideology over the individualistic laissez-faire ideology of the past. The Depression convinced many Americans that poverty is not necessarily caused by laziness or character flaws, but rather by structural problems beyond the control of any individual. They were convinced that economic recovery was possible only through the active participation of government. Keynesian economics and its success in overcoming the Depression was a further proof to many that government policies can cure social problems such as poverty. For two generations since then, Americans came to believe that government could play a positive role in building a more decent and just society. Both Democratic and Republican administrations in this period were convinced that they could use the power of the federal government for achieving the common good. This belief in the positive power of government was the foundation of the New Deal, the Fair Deal, the New Frontier, and the Great Society programs, spanning presidents from Franklin Roosevelt to Lyndon Johnson. The same belief permeated many of the domestic policies of the Nixon, Ford, and Carter administrations.[14]

Massive federal government involvement in public education began in the 1960s under the most activist administration and Congress in the history of the United States. The major focus of federal reforms was the problem of equity for minority citizens. The new educational programs were aimed at schools with high concentration of poor children. As part of his "War on Poverty," President Lyndon Johnson launched a series of educational policies including the preschool program of Head Start, health programs, and massive federal aid known as Title I. Other federal acts that addressed educational issues were the National Defense Education Act of 1958, the Vocational Education Act of 1963, the Manpower Development and Training Act of 1963, and the Elementary and Secondary Education Act of 1965. All these programs sought to enhance the opportunities of economically and socially disadvantaged children.

Although federal spending on the education of needy students was only about 10 percent of total public school spending, the government used its regulatory power and enforced desegregation mandates to achieve its goal of equity for low-income students. Enforcement of civil rights as well as the antipoverty policies of this era tremendously enhanced the lot of poor students. Collectively, these programs resulted in "major increases of high school completion and college access, particularly for blacks. Southern blacks made the largest educational achievement gains, and the racial gaps in completion and achievement scores narrowed significantly."[15]

Historically, individual states, rather than the federal government, have had primary authority over public education. Individual states, in turn, have delegated most of their responsibilities to local school districts to collect taxes and run the day-to-day operation of their campuses. Public schools are heavily subsidized by local property taxes that are controlled by school districts. As a result, public schools in the United States have become a microcosm of their socioeconomic environment where wealthy communities have rich school districts that have both the financial resources to buy whatever money can buy and an environment that is conducive to learning. Poor school districts, on the other hand, are handicapped by all the misfortunes that poverty can bring.

Concerned with the gross inequalities among school districts, states have, since the 1930s, tried to narrow the gap between the haves and the have-not school districts. In the hope of narrowing the gap, states have consolidated many school districts into larger units and have begun spending more money on public education. In 1940, for example, there were over 117,000 school districts in the United States, but by 2004 the number had dropped to 14,383. Similarly, in 1940 local property taxes financed 68 percent of public school expenses. This number had decreased to about 43 percent in 2002.[16]

RACE AND INEQUALITY

In the United States, there has always been a racial and ethnic bias in the distribution of wealth. The wealth of a school district is often determined by the racial composition of its residents. Wealthier districts tend to be populated mostly by white non-Hispanic residents while African Americans and Hispanics mainly populate the poorer districts. Until the early 1950s, blacks were segregated from whites and the system was sanctioned by the Supreme Court of the United States in *Plessy v. Ferguson* (1896). Segregation created an inferior level of education for blacks. In 1940, for example, public spending per pupil in southern black schools was only 45 percent of what was spent on white pupils. The black schools had overcrowded and dilapidated facilities, staffed by less qualified teachers who were not paid adequately and students had to walk miles to and from school. In short, the issue of segregation in the United States is of the outmost importance because it is so strongly linked to poverty. Poverty matters because it denies individuals equal opportunities in life. The lack of equal opportunities, in turn, undermines the foundations of liberalism and democracy.

Since the early 1950s, the courts have played an important role in addressing the interrelated issues of race, poverty, equality, and freedom. Depending on the ideological mood of the nation and the composition of the Supreme Court, the decisions of the Court have favored either race and equality, or freedom of choice. For nearly 20 years since 1954, the Court's decisions favored desegregation, the rights of previously oppressed racial/ethnic groups, and the reduction of inequality for poor schoolchildren. Since a 1974 Supreme Court case, however, the tide of welfare liberalism has shifted back in favor of conservatives. Since then, the Court has shown less concern with racial segregation and educational opportunities for poor students.

A landmark Supreme Court decision that broke with the conservative tradition that had been set by the Plessy court was *Brown v. Board of Education of Topeka* (1954). The Brown court overruled the Plessy decision and declared that racial segregation in public schools was unconstitutional. The Brown ruling stated, "in the field of public education the doctrine of 'separate but equal' has no place. Separate educational facilities are inherently unequal." In line with the prevailing welfare liberal ideas, the Court stressed the fundamental importance of equal opportunities and the rights of individuals. It declared that "education is ... the very foundation of good citizenship.... it is a right which must be made available to all on equal terms (*Brown v. Board of Education 1954*)."

Three successive rulings expanded the mandates of the Brown decision. In *Cooper v. Aaron* (1958) the court prevented state governments from blocking desegregation on the claim that it would produce violence. In 1971 the Court ruled that the existence of all-white or all-black schools must be shown not to result from segregation policies and that busing could be used in efforts to correct racial imbalances (*Swann v. Charlotte-Mecklenberg Board of Education 1971*). In *Keyes v. Denver School District* (1973) the Court held school districts responsible for their racial policies. More importantly, it recognized Latinos' right to desegregation, as well as that of African Americans.

Under pressure from the federal government and the courts, reluctant Southern states gradually agreed to desegregate their public schools. Brown succeeded in dismantling legal segregation. For the two decades of the 1960s and 1970s, the Southern states made slow but significant progress in desegregating their public schools despite the massive exodus of the white population to suburban areas. Various Supreme Court decisions in the early 1970s, however, heralded a new era in the history of public education in the United States—an era that rejected the ideological underpinnings of the previous 50 years. This ideological shift was a reflection of profound changes that were taking place in society. By the early-1970s, a whole litany of political, social, and economic problems arose causing disillusionment of Americans with their government and its social and economic policies. While the Vietnam War undermined the legitimacy of government, double-digit inflation and high unemployment brought into question the wisdom of an activist government. American people came to believe that the past social policies were costly and counterproductive and that the antipoverty programs of the past not only were ineffective in reducing poverty but trapped the poor and their children in a cycle of welfare dependency.

The shift of attitude in the general public cast its shadow over the composition and the decisions of the Supreme Court. Beginning with the Milliken decision in 1974, the Supreme Court's support for desegregation began to fade as the national mood shifted back to the conservative ideas of the past and the Court lost its liberal majority. The Milliken decision effectively blocked interdistrict and city-suburban desegregation plans (*Milliken v. Bradley 1974*). The decision turned down the interdistrict busing that could remove the de facto segregation that existed between urban and suburban areas. It protected and exacerbated white flight to suburbia by confining integration to specified areas within cities. The ruling was encouraged by Richard Nixon and others who wanted an end to desegregation.[17, 18] The tide of desegregation was reversed in the Supreme Court case of *Board of Education of Oklahoma v. Dowell* in 1991 when the Court ruled in favor of dismantling desegregation plans. As a result, many school districts ended their desegregation plans. Subsequent decisions allowed piecemeal termination of school desegregation (*Freeman v. Pitts 1992*) and the termination of court supervision of desegregation cases (*Missouri v. Jenkins 1995*). The Dowell case, in particular, encouraged the resegregation of public schools. Since then, there has been a significant reversal toward segregation in most of the states that were highly desegregated before. Segregation is now present in a severe form in central cities of large metropolitan areas, smaller central cities and suburban rings of large metropolitan areas. Except in the South and Southwest, most white students have little contact with minority students. By the late 1990s, the segregation of black students surpassed that of the 1960s.[19]

Sadly, the process of racial resegregation has intensified the segregation of poor and wealthy schools. Segregated minority schools are often poverty-stricken schools that cannot provide equal educational opportunities for their students. Today black and Hispanic students in public schools are not segregated by law but by wealth. Government statistics show that as the proportion of black and Hispanic students increase, so does the proportion of students in the schools eligible for the school lunch program. In 2003, for example, about 71 percent of black and 73 percent of Hispanic fourth graders were in high-poverty schools (schools with more than 50% of students eligible for the school lunch program) compared to 21 percent of white students. The concentration of poor black and Hispanic students is even more severe in central cities. In 2003, within central city schools, 61 percent of black and 64 percent of Hispanic fourth graders were concentrated in the highest-poverty schools (schools with more than 75% of students eligible for the school lunch program) compared to 12 percent of white students.[20] In other words, black and Hispanic students are more likely than white students to attend schools with a majority of students from poor families.

PUBLIC SCHOOL FINANCE AND INEQUALITY

For many reformers who have not abandoned the welfare liberal ideals of equal opportunity, the de-facto segregation of public schools is unacceptable. Since the early 1970s, these reformers have turned their attention toward the unequal distribution of resources between poor and wealthy school districts. The underlying assumption, however, has always been that minority students will be the primary beneficiaries of the equitable distribution of resources. By shifting the focus of equity on the difference between poor and wealthy school districts, reformers significantly enhanced their chance of mobilizing support and success.

For most states, school finances are linked to their local real property taxes. Differences in real property values have created a significant disparity in educational opportunities for students who attend wealthy school districts and for those students who live in poor districts. While wealthy school districts can generate more money with less tax effort, poor school districts tax their residents at a higher rate and still generate less income for their school districts. During the 1985–1986 school year, for example, the wealthiest school district in Texas had $14 million in taxable property per student while the poorest district had $20,000 in taxable property per student. The white Independent School District in the Texas Panhandle taxed its property owners at 30 cents per $100 of value and spent $9,646 per student. Neighboring Morton I.S.D., on the other hand, taxed its property owners at 96 cents per $100 of value but was able to spend only $3,959 per student.[21]

Such discrepancies in school spending have been the basis of much litigation throughout the country. But the highest national court has become less activist since the Brown case.

In *Milliken v. Bradley* (1974), the Supreme Court showed its lack of enthusiasm for desegregation when it did not support interdistrict and city-suburban desegregation. In effect, the Milliken court exempted white suburban school districts from participating in real desegregation programs. This ruling was not unexpected given its milestone decision in the previous year. In a landmark decision in 1973, the U.S. Supreme Court took a step back in protecting disadvantaged school districts. In *San Antonio School District v. Rodriguez*, the court ruled that education is not a fundamental right protected by the U.S. Constitution and consequently gross inequalities in school finances are not necessarily unconstitutional. This ruling tossed the issue into the state court systems. For more than three decades, lawsuits to equalize school funding have been finding their way through the courts in 44 states. So far, the plaintiffs have scored victories in about half the states, forcing legislatures to increase funding for poor schools. The supreme courts of states such as Kentucky, Texas, Vermont, and New Hampshire have forced policymakers to accept some degree of wealth equalization among their school districts. The core argument of the litigants has been that inequality in the distribution of educational resources denies equal educational opportunities to students of poor school districts. They blame the lower academic performance of poor students on inequitable distribution of educational resources. They point out that had there been a more equitable distribution of school resources, poor students would not have been seven times less likely to earn a college degree than well-to do students.[22]

FROM EQUITY TO PERFORMANCE

The economic and political turmoil of the 1970s brought into question the tenets of welfare liberal ideology. The public's disillusionment with government and its polices culminated in the election of President Ronald Reagan—a man who completely rejected the ideological tenets of welfare liberalism. Since the presidency of Reagan, public education in the United States, for the most part, has been operating under the ideological principles of neoconservativism. Contrary to the earlier ideology of welfare liberalism that was directed toward social justice and equality, the neoconservative ideology embraces principles of the market and individual liberty as paramount social values. What results from market competition is thought to be necessarily good and able to resolve many of the present social ills such as poverty. For the free market to operate properly, the new ideology holds, individuals need to be free from the tentacles of government and take responsibility for their own destiny. The sharp edge of this ideology is directed toward the government's antipoverty programs. Overcoming poverty is not considered the responsibility of government but of the poor themselves. The focus is more on individual responsibility and freedom than the type of social justice and equality that were promoted by welfare liberals.

Beginning with the presidency of Reagan and extending through the Clinton and George W. Bush administrations, the focus of public education has shifted from being an instrument of opportunity to the "quality" of education. The Reagan administration's 1983 report on *A Nation at Risk* crystallized the necessity of this shift. The paramount educational values are no longer rights and equality but rather the market mechanisms of performance appraisal, competition, and rewards and punishment. Neoconservatives believe that solutions to educational problems cannot be found in poverty, inequality, and segregation but rather within the confinements of schools. Teachers and school administrators are responsible for the failure of poor students rather than inadequate school funding or the socioeconomic status of the parents. It is believed that a performance-based-educational system can resolve many of the existing educational problems of disadvantaged children. Under this system, measurable performance standards need to be set, students need to be regularly tested, and schools need to be held responsible for achieving the standards. Schools that fail to achieve the standards should be punished and those who achieve them should be rewarded. More testing, more course work, and rewards and punishment are, therefore, the tools of choice for improving the quality of education among disadvantaged children and preparing the next generation of workers for the coming global market competition.

The emphasis on performance, however, is predicated on questionable assumptions. First, the heightened concerns about the relatively low-average scores of American students on international tests ignore the fact that wealthy American schools do not have this problem. The problem of low performance is the problem of poverty in America. The main culprits for low-average score on international tests are not the rich schools that are populated by white students, but rather the poor schools catering to black and Hispanic students. The second questionable assumption is that low performance is the result of the laziness of students, teachers, and administrators and it can be improved if students and schools are held accountable. Test scores are to be considered impartial measures of student and school performance. There is virtually no discussion of the 800-pound gorilla of poverty in the middle of the room. No attention is paid to 40 years of research findings showing that test scores are strongly linked to nonschool forces in the lives of students. Since the publication of the groundbreaking Coleman[23] report in 1966, research has repeatedly shown that the socioeconomic background of parents, more than anything else, determines the academic performance of students. The new emphasis on performance, therefore, has brought into question whether it is a ploy to redirect attention from the real problem—namely inequality of resources and the wider problem of poverty.

The questionable assumptions of performance-based educational policies have produced questionable outcomes. Thirty years of data do not support the educational claims of neoconservatives. To evaluate the soundness of performance-based educational policy, it is important to compare the achievement gains of the current period with the reforms of the 1960s and the early 1970s. The comparison of the achievement results should humble the supporters of the current reforms. When the focus of U.S. educational policies was centered on the issues of desegregation and equal opportunity, in the 1960s and part of the 1970s, disadvantaged children achieved major academic gains as measured by increased high school graduation rates, college enrollment, and lowering gaps in academic achievement between the races. Black students made the largest educational achievement gains, particularly in the states that had traditionally excluded them.[24]

On the other hand, reviews of U.S. Department of Education's statistics reveal disappointing results in the educational gains of students since the end of the equity-driven educational reforms of the 1960s and early 1970s. Apart from some gains in mathematics achievement between 1973 and 1999, other indicators of achievement are unacceptable. There was no measurable difference in the reading proficiency scores of 17-year-olds in 1999 compared to 1971. Overall, grade 11 writing performance declined between 1984 and 1996. The biggest decline has been in the area of science.

The average science scores of 17-year-olds in 1999 remained 10 points lower than in 1969.[25] So long as the underlying problem of poverty among children is not addressed, one cannot expect any better results than what we have seen within the last 3 decades.

The latest educational reform of the neoconservatives is called 'No Child Left Behind' (NCLB). NCLB is a prime example of how a performance-based educational system of neoconservatives has exacerbated rather than alleviated the problems of public education in the United States. President George W. Bush signed the NCLB into a law in early 2002. The aim of the program, as was declared by President Bush, is to end "the soft bigotry of low performance." Under this program, federal educational funds are distributed not on the basis of need but successful results. The program measures success in terms of annual test scores of students. A strict system of reward and punishment is tied to the outcomes of test scores in order to enforce accountability among school officials. Low-performing schools are threatened with the loss of funds and, ultimately, closure. Like earlier performance-based educational approaches, NCLB ignores the fact that academic performance in the United States is ultimately attributed to the demographics of students. In fact, the system of reward and punishment that is built into the NCLB inadvertently exacerbates the problems of inequality, dropout, and achievement gaps for those children who need the most help.

Historically, failing schools have been racially segregated and poor. Successful schools, on the other hand, are the wealthy schools that serve primarily white students. Student test scores, more than anything else, reflect the differences in student background. Withholding funds from failing schools and funneling the funds to successful schools is tantamount to punishing poor students for being poor and rewarding rich students for having wealthy parents. The system ignores the fact that poverty and its by-product of inadequate school financial resources are the main causes of poor performance. Withholding more financial resources from these schools will not solve the problem of low performance. The system of reward and punishment that is promoted by the NCLB only widens and perpetuates the pervasive inequalities that exist in the American public education system.

The performance-based "No Child Left Behind" has had another perverse impact on the educational opportunities of disadvantaged students. The system encourages low-performing poor minority students to drop out of school or at best encourages them to pursue a GED outside formal public schooling. A joint research by Harvard University and The Urban Institute concluded that, "[t]he overwhelming focus of many states and school districts aiming to avoid test-driven accountability sanctions has led to increased reports across the nation of schools that "push out" low achieving students . . . in order to help raise their overall test scores."[26] The report indicates that racial and ethnic minority students are more likely to be pressured to leave the educational system. Dropout rates have also increased because of change in teaching methods. Public schools, particularly poor schools, feel increased pressure to narrow their curriculum and teach to the test. These changes discourage poor students who cannot see any value in the limited courses that are offered and the drilling methods that are used. All of these problems will exacerbate the cruel realities of inequality that are already present in the educational system.

In short, the neoconservative market-oriented approach to public education not only has exacerbated the twin problems of de facto segregation and inequality of educational opportunities, it has failed to improve the quality of education to any noticeable degree. The laissez faire market-oriented approach to public education has entrapped poor students in segregated and inferior school districts while protecting rich districts from opening up to students from less fortunate districts. The over emphasis of neoconservatives on individual liberty and responsibility, and their lack of attention to issues of social justice, has denied 40 percent of public school children equality of educational opportunity. The neoconservatives concern over the quality of education in the United States is also misguided. The problem of low educational performance is the problem of poverty. Research for the last several decades has repeatedly reminded us that the socioeconomic status of parents is the primary determinant of students' performance. As a result, a solution to low educational performance should go beyond schools and teachers accountability.

CONCLUSION

A market-based educational system ignores the root cause of the problems facing public education. Quality of education, equitable educational opportunities and real life opportunities for disadvantaged students can be greatly improved if the following are recognized. First, it should be recognized that the core problem of public education in the United States stems from poverty. Rich school districts, for example, are not facing the problems of poor quality of education, low student performance, excessive dropouts, and low college admission of their students. Nor are the graduates of these schools denied life opportunities. School districts populated with low-income students are the ones facing all of these problems.

Second, the focus of public education should shift to the needs of low-income students. A need-oriented public education system can greatly benefit the poor without lowering the quality of education for others. Under this system, resources would be distributed based on the needs of students and schools. The scars of poverty and the lack of preparedness of poor students place them in a competitive disadvantage when they enter the public schools. The physical, psychological, and cognitive needs of these students demand more attention and resources for preparing them for the challenges of schoolwork. More resources are also needed for recruiting skilled teachers and administrators, maintaining decent and acceptable school facilities and equipment. A need-based distribution of resources will not resolve problems such as parental involvement and the cues these students will receive from the environment that they live in, but it will alleviate some of the gross inequalities that exist under the current market-oriented system.

Third, it should be remembered that the root causes of the educational problems are outside of schools. More school resources, while crucial, will not necessarily rescue poor students from school failure or the vicious cycle of poverty. A real positive impact on educational achievements of poor students demands social policies that go beyond the school life of students. To begin with, the current market-driven social and economic policies that are in place and have entrapped the poor, need to be revised. Decent minimum wages, universal health insurance, restructuring of tax codes, and work incentives, are only a few public policies that can alleviate the problem of poverty. There must also be a recognition that the students' educational achievement is affected by many factors that occurred before they enter public schools. To improve the educational achievements of poor students, a number of protective policies such as prenatal care, early childcare, and preschool care and education need to be in place. Without these early protective policies, the chances of disadvantaged students to succeed in their educational career are greatly diminished.

Finally, improving the quality of education of low-income students will not necessarily enhance their life opportunities. As Reimers[27] has aptly pointed out, improving the educational achievements and capabilities of the poor will not necessarily change their status in life. Educational achievements, capabilities, and income of the poor may be improved without changing their relative standing in society because the nonpoor also would have increased their education. A narrow focus on enhancing the educational quality for the poor, in absolute terms, disregards the existing social distance between the poor and the nonpoor. Educational policies not only need to improve the capabilities of the poor but most importantly must be geared also toward closing the social and economic distance that eliminate the positive effects of more and better schooling. Reducing the social distance demands a change of attitude from market-oriented to social justice-oriented public policies. The promises of liberty and equality, the two bedrocks of a liberal democracy, cannot be realized if 40 percent of students in a society have no real chance of changing their social station to a higher ground.

NOTES

1. W. Steven Barnett and Colette M. Escobar. 1987. The Economics of Early Educational Intervention: A Review. *Review of Educational Research* 57(4): 387–414.

2. Robert E. Slavin, Nancy L. Karweit, and Barbara A. Wasik (Eds.). 1993. *Preventing Early School Failure: Research, Policy, and Practice*. Boston, MA: Allyn and Bacon.

3. Ruth H. McKey, Larry Condelli, Harriet Ganson, Barbara J. Barrett, Catherine McConkey, and Margaret C. Plantz. 1985. *The Impact of Head Start on Children, Families, and Communities*. Washington, DC: CSR, Inc.

4. W. Steven Barnett, J. W. Young, and L. J. Schweinhart. 1998. How Preschool Education Influences Long-Term cognitive Development and School Success: A Causal Model. In *Early Care and Education for Children in Poverty: Promises, Programs, and Long-Term Results*, ed. W. Steven Barnett and Sarane Spence Boocock, 167–184. Albany, NY: State University of New York Press.

5. Committee for Economic Development. Research and Policy Committee. 1987. *Children In Need: Investment Strategies for the Educationally Disadvantaged*.

6. J. D. Bransford, A. L. Brown, and R. R. Cocking (Eds.). 1999. *How People Learn: Brain, Mind, Experience, and School*. Washington, DC: National Academy Press; National Center for

Children in Poverty. 2006. *Low-Income Children in the United States: National and State Trend Data, 1994–2004.* New York: Columbia University, Mailman School of Public Health.

7. National Center for Education Statistics. 2004. *Dropout Rates in the United States: 2001.* Washington, DC: U.S. Department of Education, Office of Educational Research and Improvement, National Center for Education Statistics, Government Printing Office.

8. Federal Interagency Forum on Child and Family Statistics. 2005. America's Children: Key National Indicators of Children's Well-Being 2005. Available at *www.childstats.gov/americaschildren/index.asp.*

9. J. J. D'Amico. 2001. *A Closer Look at the Minority Achievement Gap. ERS Spectrum,* 19(2), 4–10.

10. Valerie E. Lee and David T. Burkam. 2002. *Inequality at the Starting Gate: Social Background Differences in Achievement as Children Begin School.* Washington, DC: Economic Policy Institute.

11. Belinda Williams (Ed.). 2003. *Closing the Achievement Gap: A Vision for Changing Beliefs and Practices.* 2nd Edition. Alexandria, VA: Association for Supervision and Curriculum Development.

12. Paul E. Barton. 2003. *Parsing the Achievement Gap: Baselines for Tracking Progress.* Princeton, NJ: Policy Information Center, Educational Testing Service.

13. National Center for Children in Poverty, *Low-Income Children in the United States.*

14. John E. Schwarz. 1988. *America's Hidden Success: A Reassessment of Public Policy from Kennedy to Reagan.* New York: W. W. Norton & Company.

15. Gary Orfield. 2000. Policy and Equity: Lessons of a Third of a Century of Educational Reform in the United States. In Fernando Reimers, ed., *Unequal Schools, Unequal Chances: The Challenges to Equal Opportunity in the Americas.* Cambridge, MA: Harvard University, David Rockefeller Center for Latin American Studies.

16. National Center for Education Statistics. *2005. Societal Support for Learning.* Washington, DC: U.S. Department of Education, Office of Educational Research and Improvement, National Center for Education Statistics, Government Printing Office.

17. Julie Kailin. 2002. *Antiracist Education: From Theory to Practice.* New York: Rowman & Littlefield.

18. George Lipsitz. 1998. *The Possessive Investment in Whiteness: How White People Profit from Identity Politics.* Philadelphia, PA: Temple University Press.

19. Gary Orfield and Chungmei Lee. 2004. *Brown At 50: King's Dream or Plessy's Nightmare?* Cambridge, MA: The Civil Rights Project at Harvard University.

20. National Center for Education Statistics. 2004. *The Condition of Education 2004: Indicator 5, Concentration of Enrollment by Race/Ethnicity and Poverty.* Washington, DC: U.S. Department of Education, Office of Educational Research and Improvement, National Center for Education Statistics, Government Printing Office.

21. Richard H. Kraemer, Charldean Newell, and David Prindle. 2002. *Texas Politics.* Belmont, CA: Wadsworth Publishing.

22. William C. Symonds. 2002. Closing the School Gap if no Child is to be Left Behind, We Must Overhaul Funding. *Business Week,* October 14: 124–24.

23. James S. Coleman. 1966. *Equality of Educational Opportunity.* Washington D.C.: U.S. Government Printing Office.

24. Orfield, *Unequal Schools, Unequal Chances.*

25. National Center for Education Statistics. 2004. *Digest of Education Statistics: 2003.* Washington, DC: U.S. Department of Education, Office of Educational Research and Improvement, National Center for Education Statistics, Government Printing Office.

26. Gary Orfield, Daniel Losen, Johanna Wald, and Christopher Swanson. 2004. *Losing Our Future: How Minority Youth are Being Left Behind by the Graduation Rate Crisis*, Cambridge, MA: The Civil Rights Project at Harvard University. Contributors: Advocates for Children of New York, The Civil Society Institute.

27. Fernando Reimers. 2000. Conclusions: Can Our Knowledge Change What Low-Income Children Learn? In Fernando Reimers, ed., *Unequal Schools, Unequal Chances: The Challenges to Equal Opportunity in the Americas*, 431–451. Harvard University Press, David Rockefeller Center for Latin American Studies.

CHAPTER 7

How Education Policy Continues to Leave Poor Children Behind

Roseanne L. Flores

"Not everything that counts can be counted, and not everything that can be counted counts."

—*Albert Einstein*

As we moved into the twenty-first century the gap between families living in poverty and those with adequate means to support themselves has widened. This trend began in 2000 and continues to rise.[1] According to the National Center for Children in Poverty many poor families face incredible hardships, such as the lack of affordable housing, inadequate food supplies, and lack of health insurance.[2] For many families these hardships imply that they are not living in safe and secure communities, that are supplied with adequate schools, libraries, or businesses, that in theory could provide them with secure gainful employment, or their children with a sufficient education. And on the off chance that poor families happen to live in more affluent communities that have ample resources, more often than not because of their economic status they will not have access to these resources. For example, poor families living in middle-class communities often do not have access to the same quality of health care as their middle-class peers. This lack of access to cultural and social capital prevents the majority of poor families from acquiring upward mobility, which is the American dream.

So why should we care about the impact of poverty on families? One very important reason is that poverty has the most deleterious effect on our youngest citizens, children, who are the future of America. If we don't invest positively in them today, we will invest negatively in them tomorrow.

According to the National Center for Children in Poverty, "Poverty is associated with negative outcomes for children. It can impede children's cognitive development and their ability to learn. It can contribute to behavioral, social and emotional problems. And poverty can lead to poor health among children." So what can be done? One of the most important solutions that has been put forth to address this social issue has been providing parents with adequate employment opportunities, and their children with better educational opportunities in order to break the cycle of poverty. Although parental employment has an indirect impact on children's development, that is, it can lead to a better home environment and better schools, this chapter will focus on the education of children.[3]

Since the birth of the nation it has been argued that education should function as the great equalizer, lifting people out of the burdens of their ignorance and circumstances.[4] If this notion was true over 200 years ago, it therefore stands to reason that in the twenty-first century education should also be able to provide children with the foundation needed to lead productive lives within American society. However this assertion will only hold true if all children receive an equal education; but what if they do not? The lack of access to equal educational opportunities has plagued America over the last several centuries and continues to plague us today. However not until recently has the federal government actually implemented a plan that would systematically change how America's children, attending public school would be educated. Given the introduction of this new educational reform at the federal level the question that arises is whether this it is actually working.

In 2001, in an attempt to address the inequalities within public education President Bush signed into law the No Child Left Behind Act. In his opening address to the nation, the president stated that a commitment had to be made that would ensure every child academic success, by guaranteeing that all American children would be able to read by the end of third grade. In order to ensure that this policy would succeed states and local school districts had to provide a licensed teacher for every classroom, schools needed to provide a rigorous curriculum based on scientific evidence, and children's skills needed to be assessed to make certain that they had mastered pertinent classroom information at grade level. To date, however, although the federal government boasts of success, (citing as evidence an increase in children's tests scores.) this commitment has not been fulfilled, due in part to inadequate funding and lack of support from local, state, and federal agencies. Once again the children who would have benefited most from the successful implementation of this program, America's poor children, the one's most at risk for under achievement and school failure, have been left behind. Given the enthusiastic tenets put forth by the No Child Left Behind Act (NCLB Act) how did this educational reform manage to leave poor children behind again?

This chapter begins by examining the history of American public education and its relationship to children reared in poverty. The second section examines public education in the current climate with the passing of the No Child left Behind Act. In this section I discuss the tenets of the No Child Left Behind and what they were meant to achieve. The final section focuses on how the No Child Left Behind policy has failed to be adequately implemented, and how this failure has led to the increased marginalization of poor children.

HISTORICAL OVERVIEW OF PUBLIC EDUCATION

Since the birth of the nation, education has been portrayed as one of the essential components necessary to build the strong foundation needed by children in order to succeed, and to ensure that as a country we continue to prosper and grow strong. As early as 1779, Thomas Jefferson proposed a plan that would provide free education for Virginia's children for 3 years to be supported by taxes.[5] Although his plan was never enacted, it prepared the groundwork for future discussions concerning the education of American's children. The American school system, as we now know it, originated with the Common School movement in the 1830s led by Horace Mann and Henry Bernard from New England, and the Jacksonian democrats and the Workingman's Association.[6] While both groups held opposing views, the purpose of the movement remained the same: to provide schools that could be attended by everyone, and that would be supported by public funds.[7] The overarching philosophy behind this movement was that education was the great equalizer among people, and therefore should be used to eradicate the majority of social ills, such as poverty and crime, while at the same time producing a common bond between diverse groups of people.[8] It was felt that by educating America's children the nation would continue to produce productive individuals while at the same time keeping the nation moving in a forward direction.

Given this vision, by the end of the nineteenth century, free public elementary education had become available to all children; however, because of the newness of the concept it was limited in scope and only addressed the needs of younger children. By the beginning of the twentieth century, America created the high school due, in part, to the fact that a large number of adolescents had voiced a desire to continue their education.[9] The goal of this new school was to provide a safe place where adolescents could continue to develop intellectually, obtain the skills necessary to acquire a job, and in some cases continue to further their education. In addition, the new high school also provided a place where those recently arriving to the nation could socialize and assimilate into mainstream society.[10]

Nevertheless, in spite of the original goals of the public education system, some groups of Americans were marginalized and left behind. In order to address these social inequalities the government enacted policies to ensure that equitable schools would be created for all Americans. However, because segregation existed in several communities, even this goal was thwarted.[11] In 1954 the federal government intervened and the Supreme Court ruled in the monumental case of *Brown v. the Board of Education* that segregation by race was illegal and "separate but equal" schooling was non-existent.[12] This ruling by the Supreme Court began the systematic integration of schools. It should be noted, however, that although the *Brown v. Board of Education* ruling led to the desegregation of schools and did much to make public education inclusive, the intent of the ruling was never fully recognized and discrimination continued to rear itself.

In 1965 Lyndon B. Johnson signed into law the Elementary and Secondary Education Act (ESEA) as part of his "War on Poverty." This act provided federal funds to help public schools meet the needs of "educationally deprived" low-income children.[13] In order to keep the federal government from usurping the responsibilities of the local governments and school districts, schools were given the flexibility to meet the educational needs of low-income children. While the goal of this legislation was laudatory, and some programs like Head Start were implemented that have supported and sustained educational change to this day, many interventions failed due to the lack of vision and consistency within the programs.[14]

In the 1980s the National Commission on Excellence in Education was charged by the Secretary of Education with the mission of evaluating America's educational system. As part of this evaluation the committee was mandated to examine the curricula, standards, and expectations of American schools across the nation, and to compare them to those of other advanced nations. As a follow-up, the members of this commission produced the now famous document "A Nation at Risk." In this report the commission outlined several limitations of the American educational system, some of which are described below. In general, they found that overall the curriculum was not rigorous, and did not measure up to that of other nations; that teachers were not prepared to teach math and science and many were ill-prepared to teach within their content areas; that children did not spend enough time engaged in educational activities; and finally, children lacked the technological skills necessary to keep pace with the ever-changing society. In response to these findings the commission recommended that changes be made to the content children were exposed to, with more of the curriculum covering core knowledge; that schools adapt higher academic and conduct standards; that more time be devoted to teaching the new core curriculum by using classroom time more efficiently, lengthening the school day, and the academic year; that teachers be prepared to meet the new goals through training, incentives, and career development; and, finally, that the local, state, and the federal government support these efforts with adequate leadership and funding. Although the report provided the framework for changing the underperforming American educational system, little was done to bring these reforms to fruition and, once again, the children who would have benefited most from these changes were left behind.

In 1994 Bill Clinton signed into law the *Improving America's Schools Act*. This was a reauthorization of the 1965 ESEA legislation. The goals of the reauthorization were (1) to ensure that each classroom met and maintained high standards; (2) to improve the quality of teachers and principles; (3) to provide flexibility to the states and school districts as to how they used federal funding, with the provision that schools, districts, and states would provide annual report cards; and (4) to ensure that children were provided with a safe and drug-free learning environment. Although this law pushed states and schools to regroup and provide all children, particularly disadvantaged children, with a better education it did not go far enough, with some states making more progress than others.

In 2001 George W. Bush introduced the No Child Left Behind Act that was signed into law in January of 2002. This legislation replaced the Elementary and Secondary Education Act of 1965. The purpose of the No Child Left Behind legislation was (1) to hold schools and local and state governments accountable for the performance of their students; (2) to give parents more flexibility in choosing where their children could attend school, if the schools were failing; (3) to have highly qualified teachers in every classroom; and (4) to ensure that children were reading by third grade. This law was a noble attempt on the part of the federal government to finally make happen what had been endorsed by many officials in the 1980s and 1990s.

TENETS OF THE NO CHILD LEFT BEHIND ACT

As part of the No Child Left Behind Act the federal government proposed several tenets that it felt needed to be met in order for the American education system to truly work and benefit all children. The policy called for no child in America to be left behind by (1) closing the achievement gap between disadvantaged children who were comprised primarily of low-income, minority, and immigrant children and their middle-class peers; (2) improving literacy; (3) expanding flexibility for states, local governments, and schools in terms of spending; (4) rewarding success and punishing failure; (5) providing parents with more choices; (6) improving the quality of teachers; and (7) making schools safe for the twenty-first century.

Equal Opportunity for All Children through High Standards and Increased Accountability

In order to close the achievement gap between disadvantaged children and their middle-class peers the No Child Left Behind policy proposed that states, local districts, and schools be held accountable for ensuring that all students achieved high academic standards. Moreover, it called for children to be assessed in math and reading to ensure that the academic achievement standards were met. The purpose of these assessments were (1) to provide the federal government with information concerning whether or not states, local governments, and schools were meeting the educational needs of the children, and (2) to provide parents with information concerning the satisfactory or unsatisfactory progress of their children's schools. Finally, a proposal was made to penalize schools if they failed to satisfactorily educate their disadvantaged students. For example, if schools continually failed to meet their Annual Yearly Progress (AYP), after 3 consecutive years, students could choose to leave the failing school with Title 1 funds used to make this move possible.

Improving Literacy

In order to improve literacy the No Child Left Behind policy proposed that schools focus on reading in the early grades, using reading curriculums based on scientific evidence for kindergarten through third grade. For states that adhered to this model, funding could be applied for under the Reading First Initiative. Moreover, for those states that participated in the Reading First Initiative funding would be made available from the Early Reading first program.

Greater Flexibility for States, School Districts, and Schools

Another goal of the No Child Left Behind Act was to reduce the duplication of spending across educational initiatives within the states. Given this provision, state and local governments were enabled to combine Title 1 funds with other local and state funds so as to benefit entire school programs. Under this provision, funds for technology and overlapping grants were allowed to be consolidated and sent to state, local, and school districts.

The Consequences of Success and Failure

Like most things in life, with greater freedom comes greater responsibility, and so along with the greater flexibility in controlling funding by the states, came greater accountability. Under the No Child Left Behind Act states that performed well in narrowing the achievement gap between low- and high-performing students were to be rewarded, and receive a one-time bonus based on their meeting the accountability criteria, with individual schools receiving bonuses for helping to improve disadvantaged children's performance. On the other hand, those states and schools that failed to meet the criteria would receive a reduction in their federal funding.

Greater Parental Choice and Involvement

Under the No Child Left Behind Act parents were to be given access to school reports so that they could make informed choices. If parents found that their child's school was on the list of failing schools they would be given the option to petition to their school district to have their child moved to a nonfailing public school, or to receive vouchers in order to pay for private school.

Enhancement of Quality Teachers

One of the major tenets of the No Child Left Behind Act was to ensure that there would be a qualified teacher in every classroom. How this was to come about was left to each state, but according to federal regulations each state would be held accountable for making it happen. In addition, states, local governments and school districts were to be held accountable for ensuring that professional development would be based on scientific research, and best classroom practices. Moreover, states were expected to strengthen their K-12 math and science programs by working closely with higher education institutions.

Safe and Drug Free Schools

Under the No Child Left Behind Act teachers were to be empowered to remove students from their classroom who posed a threat to themselves or others. Funds were to be made available for drug prevention and after-school programs. Children who were victims of school violence were to be removed and placed in a state school, with parents and the public being provided information concerning the safety of the school. And finally, schools were to be given additional funds to provide students with character education.

MOVING FROM THEORY TO PRACTICE: LIMITATIONS TO THE TENETS OF THE NO CHILD LEFT BEHIND ACT

Equal Opportunity for All Children through High Standards and Increased Accountability

Although the first tenet of the NCLB act has called for schools to provide lower achieving children with an education equal to that of their middle-class peers, in fact the opposite has occurred due to the stringent criteria imposed for meeting Annual Yearly Progress. According to the tenets put forth under the *NCLB* Act children were to be exposed to high academic standards in reading and math with all states mandated to create a set of standards and assessments to measure progress in these subject areas.[15] In general, this tenet is not new and therefore should not have been problematic. So why then has this tenet been difficult to achieve? If examined carefully, the problem is not in the actual tenet, but rather in the consensus concerning how standards for reading and math should be achieved, and ultimately assessed. Furthermore, not only is there a lack of consensus around the issue of standards and assessment but also a problem exists around the frequency with which the children should be tested. Under the current version of the No Child Left Behind Act states have been required to test children's skills every year as opposed to every 3 years, thus creating an additional burden for states and school districts.

So what will happen if this tenet is not met, and what have states and school districts done to avoid failure? The implications for not meeting this tenet are as follows: if a school fails to meet the criteria set by the state for passing a subject, they could be labeled as a failing school and be required to come up with a plan for improvement over the course of the following year, while simultaneously going on the list of schools which require improvement.[16] If, after 2 years, the school continues to fail, students could request a transfer to another school using the Title I funds allocated to the failing school to make the move possible.[17,18] Thus, in order to ensure that schools have not lost funds, states, schools, and teachers have felt increased pressure to make sure children perform adequately on tests, with this new focus on test performance having led to the watering down of the teaching of academic content.

While on the surface holding states and school districts accountable for their students' success appears to be a reasonable request, when one goes below the surface here is what in effect happens. According to the theory behind the NCLB Act, the curriculum and practices for disseminating the content of the curriculum are supposed to be based on scientific evidence and best classroom practices.[19] The problem is that the scientific evidence and best classroom practices tell us that testing is only one way to assess whether or not children have acquired knowledge. Moreover, previous work in the field of child development has demonstrated that true learning is not based on drill and practice, but rather on the ability to critically reason about the material disseminated in the classroom.[20] If children truly understand the conceptual material to which they are exposed, they will be able to take any test and pass it. Furthermore, the higher reasoning skills, which are required in upper mathematics and science courses, are based on the ability to reason abstractly and use the formulas. Scientists don't become scientists because they can produce a number of formulas in a specified amount of time, but rather because they are creative and can use those formulas to solve a problem—involving the ability to understand and analyze material beyond the surface level.

With the advent of the NCLB Act the focus on testing has caused schools to create an environment that has stifled learning. With the pressure for schools to perform and to meet AYP, teachers have begun to incorporate aspects of high-stakes tests into their curriculum spending more time on giving practices tests, rather than teaching the subject matter.[21] Although this has led to an improvement of AYP for some schools, it has also led to a narrower education for disadvantaged children, thus increasing the gap between these children and their middle-income peers.[22]

In addition, because states have been given the flexibility to set the standards for academic achievement, some states have created harder standards than others, making educational goals inconsistent across the nation. This imbalance across standards has led some states to have more failing schools than others and, as a result, states like Michigan, that once had a stringent passing rate on its English examination for high school students, has lowered it's criterion for passing.[23]

In short, given the number of problems that have surfaced due to the inconsistency in implementation of the NCLB Act across the states, it appears that the legislation in its present form is not working and is failing to provide an equal educational opportunity for all children.

Improving Literacy

Another major goal of the NCLB act was to put reading first. This initiative was based on the findings from the National Reading Panel which asserted that in order for reading instruction to be useful, it was necessary for children to have an understanding of phonemic awareness, phonics, and comprehension. In addition, the panel proposed that children should practice reading out loud and be given guided feedback.[24]

Again, in theory, the goal of this tenet is a laudable one, but, in reality, it has not been successfully implemented. In order to meet this initiative, schools needed to put in place reading programs that would allow children to become successful readers. For the most part, school districts have chosen what has been referred to as "off-the-shelf" programs because they are easier to implement, particularly when schools are lacking in expertise. But how effective are they?[25] In order to examine the effectiveness of different reading models on low-income children's reading ability, Tivnan and Hemphill examined the change in literacy skills of first grade children attending disadvantaged schools.[26] These authors found that, for the most part, in spite of their differing philosophical approaches, the programs adopted by the school districts had a similar effect on first grade children's reading ability, with children performing better on word reading and phonemic segmentation. However, although there was an increase in vocabulary, the children in this study still lagged behind the first grade reading norms on vocabulary and reading comprehension. In addition, this study found that programs that trained teachers to conduct reading groups, had students who were closer to grade level on reading comprehension at the end of the school year.

In general, many schools across the nation have adopted similar types of reading programs to meet the requirements of the NCLB Act. However, as the results of Tivnan and Hemphill study have demonstrated, children are not becoming effective readers, they are only learning a modicum of vocabulary and some word attack skills. According to previous research, vocabulary is one of the best predictors of reading achievement, which is usually acquired through the reading of text.[27] If the vast majority of reading programs are not exposing children to meaningful and challenging text, but only focusing on basic level reading skills, then they are failing poor children. Furthermore, if schools are not taking into account the beginning reading skills of their students when they are entering schools, as well as the expertise of their teachers, then they are also not providing the best environment for the success of their students. Because schools are required to assess the reading skills of their children at the end of the school year, teachers have taken to teaching to the test, rather than teaching reading. If this remains the model of choice, low-income children will be doomed to being poor readers, and the cycle will continue.

Greater Flexibility for States, Local Government and School Districts

Under the NCLB act states, local governments and school districts were given greater flexibility in the use of funding. According to this tenet, funds that were previously allocated for use by disadvantaged schools and students, could technically be transferred to a high-performing school and used to enhance the school overall. Again, given the principle of AYP and the removal of Title 1 funds from failing schools, the burden has fallen on impoverished, disadvantaged schools that disproportionately make up failing schools.[28, 29] Given the mandates of the NCLB Act, when a student transfers from a low-performing school to a high-performing school, part of the Title 1 funds transfer with them, with disadvantaged schools falling further behind. This transfer of funds hurts the low-performing school by leaving the students who remain in the school to suffer from the further draining of resources from an already impoverished base.[30] If the students who remain in the school that has been stripped of funding cannot find an alternative placement, they will be doomed to a fate bleaker than that of their peers who were able to transfer. Thus, the law that was to provide equal educational opportunities to poor and disadvantaged children is again failing them.

The Consequences of Success and Failure

Under the NCLB act, while some states and school districts have experienced success, many have not. Some failures have included schools that were once considered blue ribbon schools being designated as needing improvement, because of the failure of their special education students on math proficiency tests.[31] Other failures have occurred due to the labeling of teachers and schools as inadequate. Although school failures based on the loss of status due to the failing of a few students is troubling, even more disturbing are the devastating consequences the NCLB Act has had on the human psyche.

Ambrosio describes, in his article, one of the most severe consequences that the NCLB Act had on the teachers and students at the Roosevelt High School in Oregon, a school that served poor students of color.[32] According to the NCLB Act, there must be a qualified teacher in every classroom. A high-quality teacher is one who has certification, is proficient in an area, or has a bachelor's degree. The teachers at Roosevelt High School did not have any of these requirements and, therefore, were labeled as not being qualified. Because of their status, the teachers were asked to notify, by letter, their students and their students' parents, informing them that the school "needed improvement" and that their children could transfer to other schools if they wanted. Having the teachers participate in this process was demeaning, and not only demoralized the teachers, but made the students and parents feel terrible about the education the children were receiving. It was felt by everyone involved that this type of punitive action was not constructive. It did nothing to improve the school, but rather only caused humiliation for the teachers, students, and parents.

In addition to not being constructive, having teachers inform parents and students about their inadequacies was also in direct contradiction to one of the defining principles of the NCLB Act which was to provide children with character education. According to standard leadership and character building principles one of the major features of building a strong character is to have respect for self and others. If the goal of the NCLB Act is to create a learning environment where students want to succeed and value their education, then creating environments that provide win-win solutions rather than win-lose ones would be the objective. However, if students learn to view teachers as inadequate and incompetent, then it is doubtful that they will treat them with respect, which in some cases could lead to an increase of behavioral problems already rampart in some schools. Thus, given the previous example and under the current circumstances, the NCLB Act, in it's current form, can only lead to win-lose outcomes for everyone involved.

Greater Parental Choice and Involvement

According to the Merriam-Webster's Collegiate Dictionary the definition of the word "*choice*" implies having an option, and "*option*" implies a power to choose something that is specifically granted or guaranteed.[33] Under the tenets of the NCLB Act, parents were given the right to choose a better educational environment for their children. The question that arises, however, is what are the choices, and are the choices viable options?

According to the research reported by the Civil Rights project at Harvard University the options that parents have for their children who are attending low-performing schools are quite limited. In this research, the authors report that choices are limited, in part, because of the actual lack of options for transferring between schools. For example, in certain areas the schools available for students to transfer to are also low-performing schools, therefore making the *choice* nonexistent. In addition, the lack of funding necessary to support the No Child Left Behind Act also makes the option to choose less than optimal.[34] Moreover, although the tenets of the No Child Left Behind policy has called for all children to receive a "high quality" education, the policy does not explicitly define what features a high-quality education must have in order to be considered "high quality," making the definition somewhat relative.[35] So what constitutes a high-quality education? In order to address this question, one would have to examine the education of middle-class and affluent children. For the most part, children who are the recipients of a high-quality education not only have high-quality teachers, but are also exposed to many other cultural events and experiences that society deems necessary in order for a person to be considered educated. For example, children attending high-quality schools are exposed to foreign languages, have courses in math, reading, science, and social studies (that are challenging), receive music and art and have the opportunity to engage in several after-school activities, such as athletics, social clubs, theatre, and chorus to name but a few activities. Moreover, the parents of the children attending such schools expect that their children *will* learn, and when there is a problem, expect there to be a reasonable solution. Furthermore, the parents of children attending high-quality schools expect their children to have every advantage and opportunity so as to ensure their success not only in the present, but also in the future.

So where are these schools located and why aren't they viable *choices* for children attending low-performing schools? For the most part, the schools described above are located in middle-income and affluent suburban communities, with a few in urban environments that have been specially zoned so as to accommodate affluent children. However, according to the research most of these schools do not lie within the districts in which poor children live, making them not an option for poor families. Furthermore, because the No Child Left Behind Act does not provide incentives for wealthier districts to take students from low-performing schools, but instead often creates potential barriers, wealthier schools have become wary of reaching out and embracing this population. For example, if a number of students were admitted to a school in an affluent neighborhood and the students fail to adequately perform, the scores of the school could, in theory, drop the school from being a high-performing school to a low performing one. Then the school could easily be dropped from being a blue ribbon school because of a few scores. The fact that such an outcome is possible has caused most districts to abstain from actively pursuing low-performing children.[36]

So what about using the voucher system? According to the Center for Policy Alternatives vouchers do not adequately cover the cost of private school education, that often involves hidden costs, such as uniforms, transportation, payment for after-school care and the like.[37] And furthermore, because most private institutions will not take the face value of the voucher in lieu of the full tuition payment, parents would be forced to pay the out of pocket expenses on their own, that, for most parents, in this situation is not an option. Thus, once again, making the *alternative choice* is a less than optimal solution to the problem.

In addition to the lack of access to schools, lack of funding has also been cited as an impediment to local school districts adequately implementing the No Child Left Behind Act.[38] For example, states and school districts have reported feeling overburdened by the additional costs of administering tests, providing additional staff development in order to meet the mandates of the NCLB, (managing the data) all of which are not covered by the federal budget.[39] For some schools, these added stressors have led to low staff morale and anger on the part of parents, teachers, and students.

Enhancement of Quality Teachers

The No Child Left Behind Act states that there must be a qualified teacher in every classroom. According to the tenets of the law, qualified teachers must have at least a bachelor's degree, a full-state certification, and be competent in their subject area.[40] The problem lies not in the idea, but rather in the leeway that the federal government has given to defining what constitutes a high-quality teacher. For example, because of the flexibility in the standards, some states have chosen to follow the philosophy that anyone can be a teacher, with the requirements to become a teacher consisting of knowledge of the subject area and the completion of a few workshops on how to manage children. However, this philosophy flies in the face of educational research that argues qualified teachers need to know a great deal about child development in order to impart information to children in a developmentally appropriate manner. Understanding how children think, speak, and act is essential to providing them with a solid educational foundation and requires more than a 2-week training session. Having said this, when states introduce such lenient qualifications for individuals to become teachers it begs the question—would we allow a doctor to perform surgery after a few weeks of training dissecting rat pups? Or would we allow someone to build a bridge with a 2-week certification in engineering, arguing that the remainder of the skills could be learned on the job? If both of these examples appear to be ludicrous, how much more incredulous is it for us to believe that the skills required to help children not just pass tests—they can take a course focused on raising their test scores—but rather to be able to critically think and create new knowledge can be taught by just anyone after a few weeks of training and the passing of a multiple choice test? Why is such a proposal even entertained? One could only believe that the proposed model would be acceptable if we believed that the students attending low-performing schools need not aspire to becoming doctors, lawyers, philosophers or mathematicians, but rather that they be prepared to take on low-paying jobs that do not require many skills. If this is our a belief, then the model fits well. If not, then allowing states to set the bar so low for teacher qualifications (so that they can meet the requirements put forth under the No Child Left Behind Act), we are setting children up to fail. We are not providing them with the necessary skills that would allow them to eventually improve their economic plight, and to survive in our ever-changing global economy, therefore, we are just perpetuating the cycle of poverty for low-income children and future generations to come.

Safe and Drug-Free Schools

The final tenet that remains to be addressed in this chapter focuses on the safety of American schools. Are our schools safe? According to the NCLB law, children attending schools that are not safe have the right to transfer to a safer environment.[41] Again, the law allows flexibility in how the states define what is meant by "safety." Does safety only involve physical safety, or does it also involve sexual harassment, bullying, ridicule, and the like?[42]

Like the previous tenets, identifying schools as being unsafe, places schools in a somewhat precarious position because once listed, students and parents have the right to request a transfer. If this happens, schools run the risk of losing money and other resources. Thus, again, the fear of being penalized often leads teachers and administrators to underreport violent incidents.[43] Rather than creating safe and welcoming environments in which students learn, schools are engaging largely in record keeping so as to minimize the penalties imposed by the NCLB law and endangering the well-being of the nations children. So where do we go from here?

FUTURE DIRECTIONS FOR THE NO CHILD LEFT BEHIND ACT

America is currently the wealthiest nation in the world, yet so many of our children are not receiving an education that will allow them to succeed in the twenty-first century. In order for America to remain at the forefront in technology, science, math, and education, the nation must ensure that all of our youngest citizens receive the education that they need to compete in our ever-changing global economy. In an attempt to address this need, the federal government has instituted the No Child Left Behind Act. While at first glance the Act appeared as if it would help to eliminate the disparities that had been created between low-and high-performing schools over the last 30 years, in reality, it has widened the gap by not providing a mechanism that would allow the tenets of the law to be adequately implemented. States, local school districts, teachers, parents, and students have suffered. Schools have become more segregated, much needed resources have been taken from low-performing schools leaving the students who have remained behind worse off than they were initially, teachers have become disillusioned about their professions, states and school districts have looked for ways to meet the letter of the law, rather than the spirit of the law, and most importantly, poor students have been left behind.

Although children have learned in some cases to take tests, for the most part they have not learned to critically think which is the ultimate goal of education. If children are to become successful learners, then the NCLB Act needs to be overhauled. Research has shown that children learn in a variety of ways, and under a variety of conditions. If the goal is to produce educated children, then all of these circumstances need to be taken into account when designing methods to instruct children. Moreover, the goals, objectives, and time frame for how and when children are to progress through a curriculum in a developmentally appropriate manner need to be clearly specified, if we are to be able to assess whether or not children are mastering information. Once the goals and objectives are clear and have been implemented, then they can be systematically evaluated, retaining what works and revising or discarding what does not work. If the NCLB Act is patterning itself on the scientific method, then the authors of this Act must understand how science works, noting that the primary purpose of science is to confirm or reject theories based on hard evidence and replication. Given what we know to date concerning how states and local school districts have created and assessed standards, and based on the evidence obtained in support of the success of NCLB Act (that is, children's tests scores in reading, writing, and mathematics), one could argue that the children's tests scores, at best, provide inconclusive evidence concerning America's children's proficiency in reading, writing, and mathematics.

So what should be the goal of a valid education for America's children? The goal of a valid education should be to provide children with the skills necessary for learning. According to Piagetian theory learning occurs in two ways: "learning in the narrow sense" and "leaning in the broad sense."[44] For Piaget, when children learn in the narrow sense, they are learning a set of facts, for example, all of the capitals of the states. While this information is important and children need to learn it, it is also culturally specific, with children living in America learning information relevant to American culture and Canadian children learning information relevant to Canadian society.[45] On the other hand, learning in the broad sense requires that children develop ways of thinking that can be applied to many situations.[46] Again, this type of learning cannot be taught through direct instruction, but develops through active interaction with the environment.[47]

If learning in the broad sense cannot be acquired through instruction, why discuss it? According to Piaget, learning in the broad sense of development is a necessary precursor to learning in the narrow sense. If the cognitive structures do not develop and are not in place, then children will not benefit from instruction. Interaction with the environment leads to two types of knowledge: physical/observable knowledge and logicomathematical knowledge, which is essential for abstract reasoning. In the case of reasoning, if the child's experiences are limited, then the interactions will be somewhat impoverished and, therefore, the reasoning will be limited. These interactions can be impoverished either physically or socially.

Understanding child development and the theories of child development have a direct impact on how we view education, how children learn in general, and on No Child Left Behind Act specifically. First, at a very basic level, understanding how children learn and develop is crucial to educating them, and not to have this knowledge is irresponsible. To try and *make* people into teachers by giving them a few weeks of training is not only to devalue the profession, but also demeaning and unethical. Second, if it is understood that learning takes place on multiple levels and that standardize tests measure "learning in the narrow sense," but not necessarily "learning in the broader sense," then we must also acknowledge that when we use tests as the only measure of what children "know," we are sampling a very shallow level of knowledge. While standardized tests provide us with some information, they do not tap into the vast amount of knowledge that children may have, and, thus, to hold a child back, or fail a school based solely on one measure, is again inaccurate, and, at best, weak evidence for what children know and are learning. Finally, if we are really serious about educating children to think, then we must provide them with the physical and social environments that are conducive to such learning and development. Teachers must be free to allow their students to explore and question. They must not feel pressured to teach to a test, but rather to be empowered to provide children with experiences that will allow them to think. If teachers are not empowered to do this, then America's children may become the best multiple choice test takers in the world, but they certainly will not be the leaders of tomorrow in the sciences, arts, or humanities because either they will not have been exposed to them, or if they have, will not be able to think analytically about them.

In ending this chapter, I will leave you with one last thought. I wonder how Albert Einstein would have faired under the NCLB Act if he lived today. As a child he was slow to speak, abhorred high school because his success depended on him memorizing a list of facts, and failed his entrance examination for the Swiss Federal Institute of Technology.[48] Thank goodness the world will never know!

NOTES

1. National Center for Children in Poverty, "Who are America's Poor Children?"
2. National Center for Children in Poverty, "Basic Facts about Low-Income Children Birth to Age 18."
3. Huston, "Reforms and Child Development."
4. No Child Left Behind Act (2006).
5. No Child Left Behind Act (2006).
6. Cohen, "The American Common School."
7. Ibid.
8. Rippa, *Education in a Free Society*
9. No Child Left Behind Act (2006)
10. Ibid.
11. Nieto, "Public Education in the Twentieth Century and Beyond."
12. Ibid.
13. Rippa, *Education in a Free Society*
14. Bamberger Schorr, *Children in poverty.*
15. Beaver, "Can 'No Child Left Behind' work?"
16. Ambrosio, "No Child Left Behind."
17. Beaver, "Can 'No Child Left Behind' work?"
18. Ambrosio, "No Child Left Behind."
19. "No Child Left Behind."
20. Ginsburg and Opper, " Piaget's Theory of Intellectual Development."
21. Beaver, "Can 'No Child Left Behind' work?"
22. Ambrosio, "No Child Left Behind."
23. Beaver, "Can 'No Child Left Behind' work?"
24. National Reading Panel, Teaching Children to Read.

25. Tivnan and Hemphill, "Comparing Four Literacy Reform Models in High Poverty Schools."

26. Ibid.

27. Dickinson and Tabors, *Beginning Literacy with Language.*

28. Fusarelli, "The Potential Impact of the No Child Left Behind Act on Equity and Diversity in American Education."

29. Ambrosio, "No Child Left Behind."

30. Ibid.

31. Fusarelli, "The Potential Impact of the No Child Left Behind Act on Equity and Diversity in American Education."

32. Ambrosio, "No Child Left Behind."

33. *Merriam-Webster's collegiate dictionary* (10th ed.).

34. Kim and Sunderman, *Does NCLB provide good choices for students in low-performing schools?*

35. Ibid.

36. Ibid.

37. Center for Policy Alternatives, *School Vouchers.*

38. Center on Education Policy, From the capital to the classroom.

39. Ibid.

40. Berry, Mandy, and Hirsch, "NCLB Highly Qualified Teachers."

41. Bucher and Manning, "Creating Safe Schools."

42. Ibid.

43. Ibid.

44. Ginsburg and Opper, *Piaget's Theory of Intellectual Development.*

45. Ibid.

46. Ibid.

47. Ibid.

48. American Institute of Physics: Center for History, A. Einstein Image and Impact. f

REFERENCES

A. Einstein Image and Impact. Retrieved on June 16, 2006 from the American Institute of Physics: Center for History of Physics. Web site: http://www.aip.org/history/einstein/index.html

Albert Einstein Quotes. Retrieved on June 16, 2006 from S.F. Heart Web site: http://sfheart.com/einstein.html

Ambrosio, J. (2004). No child left behind: The case of Roosevelt high school. *Phi Delta Kappan*, 85(9), 709–712.

Bamberger Schorr, L. (1991). Effective programs for children growing up in concentrated poverty. In A. C. Huston (ed.), *Children in poverty* (pp. 260–281). Cambridge, MA: Cambridge University Press.

Beaver, W. (2004). Can "No child left behind" work? *American Secondary Education*, 32(2), 3–18.

Berry, B., H. Mandy, and E. Hirsch. (2004). NCLB highly qualified teachers—The search for highly qualified teachers. *Phi Delta Kappan*, 85(9), 684–689.

Bucher, K. T. and M.L. Manning. (2005). Creating safe schools. *The Clearing House: A Journal of Educational Strategies: Issues and Ideas*, 79(1), 55–60.

Center on Education Policy. (2006). *From the capital to the classroom.* Washington, DC: Author.

Center for Policy Alternatives (2006). *School Vouchers.* Washington, DC: Author.

Cohen, D. K. (1984). The American common school. *Education and Urban Society,* 16(3), 253–261.

Dickinson, D. K. and P.O. Tabors (eds.). (2001). *Beginning literacy with language: Young children learning at home and school.* Baltimore, MD: Paul H. Brookes.

Executive summary of the No child left behind act of 2001. Retrieved on May 8, 2006 from http://www.ed.gov/print/nclb/overview/intro/execsumm.html

Fusarelli, L. D. (2004). The potential impact of the No Child Left Behind Act on equity and diversity in American education. *Educational Policy,* 18(1), 71–94.

Ginsburg, H.P. and S. Opper. (1988). *Piaget's theory of intellectual development* (3rd ed.). New Jersey: Prentice Hall.

Huston, A. C. (2000). Reforms and child development. *Future of Children,* 12(1), 59–77.

Kim, J., and G.L. Sunderman. (2004). *Does NCLB provide good choices for students in low-performing schools?* Cambridge, MA: The Civil Rights Project at Harvard University.

Merriam-Webster's collegiate dictionary (10th ed.). (1996). Springfield, MA: Merrriam-Webster.

National Center for Children in Poverty. (2005). *Who are America's poor children?* New York: Columbia University Mailman School of Public Health.

National Center for Children in Poverty. (2006). *Basic facts about low-income children: Birth to age 18.* New York: Columbia University Mailman School of Public Health.

National Reading Panel (2000). *Teaching children to read: An evidence based assessment of scientific research literature on reading and its implication for reading instruction.* Bethesda, MD: Author.

Nieto, S. (2005). Public education in the twentieth century and beyond: High hopes, broken promises and an uncertain future. *Harvard Educational Review,* 75(1), 43–64.

No Child Left Behind. (2003). Retrieved on June 6, 2006 from http://www.whitehouse.gov/news/reports/no-child-left-behind.html

No Child Left Behind Act (2006). Retrieved on June 1, 2006 from http://encarta.wikipedia.org/wiki/No_Child_ Left_Behind

Public Education in the United States. (2006). Retrieved on May 31, 2006 from http://encarta.msn.com/text/761571494___0/Public_Educacation _in the _United_States.html

Rippa, S.A. (1997). *Education in a free society: An American history.* New York: Longman, Inc.

Tivnan, T. and Hemphill, L. (2005). Comparing four literacy reform models in high poverty schools: Patterns of first-grade achievement. *The Elementary School Journal,* 105(5), 419–441.

U.S. Department of Education. (1996). *Improving America's Schools Act of 1994.* Retrieved in June 2006 from http://www.ed.gov/offices/OESE/archives/legislation/ESEA/brochure/iasa-bro.html

CHAPTER 8

THE EDUCATION OF BLACK CHILDREN LIVING IN POVERTY: A SYSTEMIC ANALYSIS

Garrett Albert Duncan and Gail E. Wolfe

The sociologist Loïc Wacquant surmises that we cannot understand mass incarceration in contemporary United States society without understanding the North American institution of slavery, both as an historic and an historical starting point and as a functional analogue. In fact, Wacquant argues that U.S. slavery, Jim Crow, urbanization, and imprisonment are all linked by their historical and contemporary *race making* functions. By this he means that these institutions did or do not simply reinforce color-coded social divisions but either produced, or coproduced with other systems, racial divisions anew out of inherited, received demarcations of group power.[1]

Following Wacquant, we suggest that public schools have also served a race making function in America, particularly from the Reconstruction period through contemporary post-civil rights society. Like prisons, public schools help to redefine what it means to be a citizen though constructing its corollary: a racialized superfluous population of urban—and rural and suburban—students that exists outside the social or economic mainstream. During the first several decades of the twentieth century, the race making function of schools was linked to preparing black youth for what James Anderson called "Negro jobs." Negro jobs, as Anderson explained, were by default those jobs that remained after full white employment.[2] We posit that post-civil rights schools are still in the race making business of preparing students for "Negro jobs" and that this function takes on new meanings in contemporary post-industrial society, especially for black children and youth living in poverty.

In this chapter, we conduct a systemic analysis that examines the disparate forces that have shaped and continue to shape the education of black children and the other societal systems that play powerful roles in organizing their lives. We do this by analyzing the structures, organization, and practices of various social systems to understand how their different parts create educational outcomes that chronically place black children living in poverty at a disadvantage in contemporary schools and society. Specifically, the systemic analysis provided in this chapter explicates the aforementioned mechanisms to inform educational policy and practice toward positioning black children living in poverty as change agents to eventually transform their communities in their best interests and in the better interests of the larger society.

THE POST-CIVIL RIGHTS EDUCATION OF BLACK CHILDREN LIVING IN POVERTY

Post-civil rights conventional wisdom is perhaps the greatest obstacle to systemic change from the ground up insofar that it holds that community and self-imposed factors mostly contribute to the academic underperformance of black children living in poverty. *Post-civil rights* refers to the era that began with the 1954 landmark *Brown* v. *Board of Education* ruling that abolished legal segregation in public institutions, such as education, housing, and the workplace. Prior to *Brown*, or the pre-civil rights era, schooling inequalities were explained as the outcomes of segregation and discrimination. However, *Brown* purportedly eradicated institutional obstructions to opportunity and, nowadays, the storyline that blames black people for their disadvantages in society has tremendous currency in popular explanations for contemporary racial inequalities in schools.

Contemporary educational inequalities, captured in the catch phrase "achievement gap," are evident in academic disparities between black and white students, where the latter group outperforms the former on various measures of academic attainment. Two of the more popular views hold that anti-intellectualism is prevalent in black communities[3] and that parents place little value on education, which accounts for why their children underachieve in schools.[4] Another common explanation is that black children have oppositional identities[5] and reject academic achievement for fears of "acting white."[6] Some scholars speculate that high-performing black students who identify with education succumb to pressures from their black peers to underachieve[7] or who, in integrated schools, become so caught up in how they believe others view them that their academic performance suffers as a consequence.[8]

Certainly, disparities in measures of academic attainment between black and white students continue to exist. Gaps began to narrow in the 1970s and 1980s but widened in the 1990s. The National Center for Education Statistics' 2002 National Assessment of Educational Progress, or the "nation's report card," shows contemporary racial disparities in academic performance (Table 8.1).

While we acknowledge the significance of racial disparities in shaping the life chances of black children living in poverty, we believe that widely accepted causes for them are dangerously misguided. In our view, contemporary explanations for racial disparities that blame children exclusively for their educational outcomes fail to account for the tug-of-war that has characterized the schooling of Americans of African descent for nearly 400 years.[9]

Table 8.1
NAEP National Reading Results for Grade 12—Public School Percentages of Students
at Each Achievement Level by Demographic Characteristics, 2002

Demographic Characteristics	Achievement Level			
	Advanced	Proficient	Basic	Below Basic
All Students	4%	30%	38%	28%
National School Lunch Program Eligible	1%	19%	38%	41%
National School Lunch Program Not Eligible	5%	33%	38%	24%
White	5%	35%	38%	22%
Black	1%	14%	37%	48%
Hispanic	1%	19%	39%	41%
Asian American/Pacific Islander	4%	29%	39%	28%
American Indian	(Reporting Standards Not Met)			

Source: National Center for Education Statistics, National Assessment of Educational Progress (NAEP),
2002 Reading Assessment.

On one end of the ideological and programmatic spectrum that has shaped education in struggling black communities has been the advocacy of an education to extend the practice of freedom and democracy to its residents. The quest for black liberation here has been realized through a two-pronged approach to education from its very inception in the universal system of schooling in the south. For example, upon emancipation, according to Anderson, "the short-range purpose of black schooling was to provide the masses of ex-slaves with basic literacy skills plus the rudiments of citizenship training for participation in a democratic society. The long-range purpose was the intellectual and moral development of a responsible leadership class that would organize the masses and lead them to freedom and equality."[10]

On the other end of the ideological and programmatic spectrum was the advocacy of an education for black students to ensure the maintenance of white supremacy in U.S. society. Such was especially true during the post-Reconstruction era when local and federal agencies intervened to take control over the education provided children in poor black communities. An observation made by W. E. B. Du Bois, reported in a 1918 issue of *The Crisis*, is typical of the second-class education provided to black students during this period. Here, Du Bois decried the material disparities he found in the education of black and white students in Butte, Montana public schools:

What, now, is the real difference between these two schemes [white and black] of education? The difference is that in the Butte schools for white pupils, a chance is held open for the pupil to go through high school and college and to advance at the rate which the modern curriculum demands; that in the colored, a program is being made out that will land the boy at the time he becomes self-conscious and aware of his own possibilities in an educational *impasse.* He cannot go on in the public schools even if he should move to a place where there are good public schools because he is too old. Even if he has done the elementary work in twice the time that a student is supposed to, it has been work of a kind that will not admit him to a northern high school. No matter, then, how gifted the boy may be, he is absolutely estopped from a higher education. This is not only unfair to the boy but it is grossly unfair to the Negro race.[11]

As we've suggested, black communities have long advocated for themselves an education for liberation, that is, one that promotes their full participation in the civic and economic life of the broader society or, when thwarted in this primary goal, that provides the means for self-sufficiency. Yet, as suggested by Du Bois' observation, the goals of black communities notwithstanding, white power interests have historically used the material and political resources at their disposal to exercise tremendous control over the direction of the education of black children and youth.

For the most part, the educational goals of black communities continue to be thwarted, even despite the *Brown* ruling.[12] Certainly, *Brown* contributed to unprecedented improvements in the education of black children and youth, especially for those living in poverty. However, the legal ruling did not and could not completely resolve the centuries-long struggle of black communities to obtain quality schooling in America. For instance, as a federal legal intervention into the education of black students, *Brown* never fully equalized the resources that they received, especially in terms of per student funding. In addition, the landmark court ruling contributed to the mass displacement of black educators who have played an historical role of advancing the intellectual and moral objectives of black communities. Reduced resources and the dearth of black educators that serve black children in poverty in contemporary schools contribute to disparities between these students and their peers, placing them further at risk in a society where the skills required of full citizenship have been dramatically redefined in our post-industrial, global society.

These factors aid post-civil rights era schools in their race making function by creating a superfluous population in whom society invests more on incarceration than on education.[13] In addition, the 2001 No Child Left Behind Act, arguably the greatest federal intervention into schooling since the *Brown* decision, has actually contributed to the educational problems that black children encounter in schools as opposed to ameliorating them, as intended by the law. In what follows, we discuss each of these matters in turn before turning to a discussion of the work of educators who meet the contemporary challenge of educating black children living in poverty as an unremarkable feature of their practice.

Funding Disparities in New Century Schools

Huge racial disparities in academic outcomes persist in public schools largely as a result of the ways they are funded in the United States. Most local funding typically derives from property taxes, where it follows that in wealthier white districts, property values and, hence, property taxes are much higher than those in less affluent and poor districts where black students are concentrated. In the 1990s this resulted in funding disparities in which New York State, for example, spent $38,572 per student in its richest school district, a sum which was seven times more than that of its poorest district, $5,423; the disparity was even greater in Texas where the wealthiest schools

Table 8.2
Average Funding Gaps between High-Minority and Low-Minority Districts, 2003

State	Low Minority Districts	High Minority Districts	Funding Gap
California	$6,682	$5,998	– $684
Florida	$6,008	$5,908	– $100
Missouri	$6,344	$6,764	$419
New York	$10,197	$7,778	– $2,419
Texas	$7,626	$6,018	– $1,608

Source: Education Trust 2005.

spent as much as ten times more on its students at $42,000 per pupil than those in its poorest district spent on its students at $3,098 per pupil.[14]

In the first decade of the twenty-first century, funding inequalities still persist between poor and wealthier districts and between schools with predominantly black student populations and those with mostly white student populations. Oftentimes, poverty and race overlap to further impact on the schooling opportunities of black children living in poverty. The significance here is that disadvantaged student populations require greater resources to account for dilapidated physical plants, underresourced facilities, and higher concentrations of special needs programs to equalize their life chances with those of their peers in wealthier districts. Most analyses of school funding apply a formula that indicates that students living in poverty require on average 40 percent more than their wealthier peers to level the field of resources and, hence, their future opportunities.[15]

However, with few exceptions, states spend approximately $900 less on districts with high concentrations of students living in poverty than they do on those with low concentrations of students living in poverty and $614 less on districts with large student of color populations than they do on those with predominantly white student populations. With the 40 percent adjustment, class-based disparities increase from $907 to $1,436 per student and race-based disparities increase from $614 to $964. Although, nationally, class-based inequalities are greater than race-based inequalities, more states (30) invest less in students of color compared to white students than states (27) that invest less in poor students compared to wealthier ones.[16] Table 8.2 provides 40 percent adjusted data that demonstrate the funding disparities in school districts in representative states with large concentrations of black children living in poverty.

We should point out that in 2003 the Missouri public K-12 school population was mostly white at 79 percent; black students, on the other hand, comprised only 17 percent of the pupil population, with Asian American, Latino, and Native American students together totaling 3 percent.[17] Significantly, in Missouri the majority of black students attend public schools with other black students in either St. Louis or Kansas City. Thus, the data reported above on the state's general investment in its public education system obscure how segregation contributes to the unequal distribution of educational resources as well as to disparate educational outcomes along racial lines. The quality of education in both cities is directly related to the effects

Table 8.3

Percentage of Secondary-Level Classes Taught by Teachers Lacking a Subject-Area Major or Minor, 1999–2000

	US	CA	FL	MO	NY	TX
Average	24%	27%	28%	24%	18%	30%
Low-poverty schools	19%	23%	14%	14%	18%	23%
High-poverty schools	34%	27%	47%	37%	15%	36%
Low-minority schools	21%	28%	18%	22%	16%	24%
High-minority schools	29%	26%	31%	39%	21%	30%

Note: "Low" denotes less than 15%; "high" denotes greater than 50%.
Source: Education Trust, *Education Watch—key education facts and figures* (the nation, CA, FL, MO, NY, and TX) 2004.

of white flight, restrictive covenants, and redlining in the region.[18] It should also be noted that students that attend St. Louis public schools are further isolated along the lines of race and class as a sizeable number of school-age students in the city, especially those from middle-class families, attend private schools.

Along with fewer material resources, black children living in poverty will most likely be taught by teachers who are less qualified than those who teach their white peers in more affluent schools. Table 8.3 shows the percentages of teachers who lack subject area college degrees in the middle and high school classes they teach.

Similarly, in our own research, we have found evidence that implicates teacher quality in the educational outcomes of the students at the urban schools we studied.[19] In one school, teachers typically subjected their students to dated curriculum and instruction, despite the availability of up-to-date resources. For example, from 1996 through 2000, students in a classroom at an elementary school in our study used model 186 and 286 personal computers, despite the fact that new, Internet-ready computers were available throughout the school, including in the room next door to where the older computers were housed. Some of these computers went unused over a span of 3 years. During this period the school was under scrutiny and was subsequently placed on the district's "school of opportunity" list, a designation that effectively placed the school on academic probation and at risk for being closed— which is precisely what happened to it in the summer of 2004.

At the same time, access to modern technologies, such as computers, does not mean that students will be allowed to use them in ways to promote the acquisition of the skills needed to succeed in the worlds of higher education and work in our high-tech society. These technologies are rarely exploited for their potential to promote academic achievement of black students but instead are typically used for drill and practice. For example, in 1998 more teachers reported using computers primarily for drill and practice with their black eighth grade students (42%) than they did with their white (35%), Asian American (35%), or Latino (35%) eighth graders. In contrast, fewer of these teachers reported simulations and applications or learning games as their primary computer use with black students (14 and 48 percent, respectively) than they did with their white (31 and 57%), Asian American (43 and 57%), and Latino (25 and 56%) students.[20] These findings reflect a timeworn pattern in which teachers routinely employ qualitatively different curricular and instructional strategies with their students in ways that sustain the race making function of schools in post-civil rights America. Such practices specifically place black students at a disadvantage in higher education and the workplace in a high-tech, digital socioeconomic order that requires of its participants innovation, creativity, intellectual dexterity, and initiative.

Culture and Power in Post-Civil Rights Schools

In the preceding section, we focused on the unequal distribution and use of resources, with the premise being that access to resources is a prerequisite to creating equitable outcomes for disadvantaged students. However, access to resources alone will not bring about changes in the education and the life chances of black children living in poverty. Matters related to decision making and the social division of power in schools also shape the education of these students. Along these lines, the absence of black educators in teaching and administrative positions in K-12 public schools also characterizes the post-civil rights education of black children,[21] leaving them having often to fend for themselves in hostile educational environments.

In the absence of black school leaders, black students often encounter second-generation discrimination and other challenges to obtain quality education.[22] Second-generation discrimination refers to unjust educational practices, such as the resegregation of students in previously desegregated schools and the disproportionate punishment of black students. These forms of injustice often stem from the failure of teachers and administrators to recognize or respect the self-determination of their black students; indeed, incidents of second-generation discrimination decrease in schools with black leadership.[23]

With respect to the first practice, resegregation in integrated schools counselors with the assistance and approval of teachers typically sort students into homogeneous subsets by ability groupings. This generally results in the concentration of white students in honors and gifted classes and of black and Latino students in lower tracks, remedial courses, and special education programs. Racial inequality is indicated by the statistically disproportionate distribution of students enrolled in the respective programs. Researchers apply a plus/minus 10 percent formula to determine if there is a disproportional placement of racial groups within a certain category of programs.[24] Table 8.4 indicates how students are distributed nationally across gifted and talented and remedial programs.

A proportional number of black students in any of the categories indicated in Table 8.4 relative to their school population would fall within the range of plus and minus 10 percent of 17 (i.e., 1.7) or roughly between 15 and 19 percent in any given program. Percentages that fall outside of this range are an indication that either too many or too few black students are represented in a program relative to their proportion within the broader student population.

Table 8.4

National Student Placement in Public School Programs by Race/Ethnicity, 2000

Race/Ethnicity	Public K-12 Enroll.	Gift. & Talent.	Remedial	Suspension
White	61%	74%	60%	48%
Black	17%	8%	22%	34%
Hispanic	16%	10%	15%	15%
Asian American/ Pacific Islander	4%	7%	2%	2%
American Indian	1%	1%	1%	1%
Total	47,018,606	2,926,034	3,908,226	3,053,449

Source: Education Trust, *Education Watch: The nation—key education facts and figures* 2004.

Table 8.4 also indicates a second feature of second-generation discrimination, that is, the racial disparities in the way that discipline is meted out in post-civil rights schools. These gaps increased in the late-1990s and the early 2000s as a result of the adoption by districts of "zero-tolerance" policies to curb real and imagined violence in American schools.[25] Widespread reports and highly publicized incidents of the expulsion of black students in the late 1990s refueled concerns in communities of color about educational justice and prompted the civil rights leader, the Reverend Jesse Jackson, to observe that, with increasing frequency, "school districts [are choosing] penal remedies over educational remedies when it comes to disciplining students."[26]

While, in general, poorer students are more likely to be suspended than wealthier students, researchers have found that black students from the wealthiest families were suspended at almost the same rate as white students from the poorest families.[27] Interestingly, a 2005 Yale study found that, nationally, prekindergarten students are expelled at three times the rate as are students in K-12 settings and, predictably, that black prekindergarten students are twice as likely to be expelled as are their white and Latino preschool classmates.[28]

The warehousing of black students in remedial programs as well as their exclusion from school is in many ways a form of racial profiling that delimits their opportunities in life. Racial profiling is a systemic feature of life for black children and youth in society and occurs systematically at various levels of the educational system, where policymakers, researchers, and educators often conflate "black" and "urban." For example, in his study of city schools, Pedro Noguera describes how policymakers and society talk about and respond to things designated as urban in ways that suggest that the appellation refers neither to geographical locations nor to spatial configurations. Rather, Noguera argues that urban is typically employed "as a social or cultural construct used to describe certain people and places."[29] This view of urban (re: black) schools results in policy decisions that pose difficulties for black students from impoverished areas to change their circumstances, either by entering into higher education[30] or into the workforce.[31]

With respect to the racial profiling in higher education admissions, two city students whom the first author recommended for admission to his university were placed on a waiting list. After he contacted the admissions office on their behalf, he received the following response from the officer in charge of their application:

> I want to thank you for your words of support for both Aaron and Margaret. I am SO sorry to inform you that we have all but finished with our waitlist for this year's class, so I see very little hope of them coming to [the university] as freshmen.
>
> Though not the ideal arrangement, if they REALLY want to be here, transferring is always an option. We work with many students each year to make this happen. If you think that this may be an option for either of them, please let me know, and I will do what I can to help. They both sound like exceptional individuals and people who would both contribute to and benefit from the [university] community. It is frustrating not to be able to give you better news. I do hope, though, that as you continue to meet students you believe to be good candidates, you bring them to the attention of our office. It is often because of information such as what you've provided here a student comes to our attention in ways he or she may not have otherwise.
>
> It is challenging to find and capture talented students from the [city] schools, so I am especially sad at not being able to be more helpful with Aaron and Margaret. So often, students who have their sights set on [the university] coming from the [city] have not been adequately academically prepared. Those who are well prepared/top students are often looking to go somewhere other than [here]—away from home—and do. . . . In any case, PLEASE keep those names of qualified students we should be looking at carefully coming![32]

The admissions officer's contradictory response suggests that the university viewed these students and the urban city district in which they were educated with sweeping generalizations indicative of profiling, despite the fact that the school from which they graduated consistently ranked first in the state on a broad array of academic indicators.[33] Similarly, in urban classrooms profiling inheres in what Ann Arnett Ferguson calls the adultification of black boys in the school that she studied. Adultification occurs as the behaviors of boys as young as eleven and twelve foreclose their futures in the eyes of adults who often identify them as headed for jail.[34] Similarly, in his study of school violence, Ronnie Casella found that urban school officials were prone to "punishing dangerousness"—punishing not the specific violent behavior of youth but the *possibility* of their violent behavior somewhere off in the future.[35]

With respect to the prospects of black youth entering the workforce, as government jobs are eliminated due to federal downsizing and automation, employers in private industries are loathe to hire black workers, especially younger ones.[36] Employers cite a variety of reasons, but two predominate: (1) young black women and men lack the prerequisite technical and social, or "hard," skills, and (2) skills notwithstanding, they lack the appropriate "cultural capital" (e.g., attitude, demeanor) and are a liability in a market that relies heavily on image, presentation, and perception. The first concern of employers is connected to the quality of education, mainly in urban schools, that prospective employees receive while the second concern is associated with yet another pedagogical institution, the media that disseminate stereotypical imagery of them. To be clear, the larger point that we are making here is that the concomitant effects of various institutions contribute to poor prospects for black children who will one day seek to enter the U.S. economy and larger American society as productive citizens.

The Resegregation of Public Schools in New Century America

Despite integration gains in the 1970s and 1980s, public schools have become more segregated in the 1990s and the early years of the twenty-first century, making it easier for them to sustain race making functions. Jonathan Kozol, a prominent critic of educational inequality, observed that schools were more segregated in 2006 than they were anytime since 1968.[37] Urban and fringe city school districts, for instance, are being populated by increasingly multicultural populations of students of color from working-class, poor, and immigrant families and more affluent suburban schools were being populated by homogeneous bodies of white students from middle-class families.[38]

The reversal of school integration is attributable both to failed attempts to integrate schools at the local level as well as to significant Supreme Court rulings such as *Milliken* v. *Bradley* (1974) that removed federal courts' powers to impose interdistrict remedies between cities and surrounding suburbs to desegregate city schools. In addition, the resegregation of schools in the 1990s and 2000s occurs within the broader political and economic context of changing public investments where states are increasingly spending more on criminal justice than they are on public education.[39] Indeed, during the opening years of the twenty-first century, states on average spent three times more on criminal justice than they did on education[40] and the same amount that they did on Temporary Assistance to Needy Families (TANF) and food stamps combined.[41] Such public policy decisions have resulted in what Kozol has called the "savage inequalities" that plague urban and rural schools, leaving them in the new millennium to provide their largely black student populations with what Robert Moses has called a "sharecropper's education."[42]

Moses' observation augurs poorly for black children living in poverty in contemporary society where access to and the manipulation of symbols and information define the economy, skills that require the support of much more than what a sharecropper's education can provide. Jeremy Rifkin brings the implications of a sharecropper's education in contemporary U.S. economy for the future of black children into bold relief: "Automation ha[s] made large numbers of black workers obsolete. The economic constraints that had traditionally kept black Americans 'in line' and passively dependent on the white power structure for their livelihoods, disappeared."[43] Along these lines, the Bureau of Labor Statistics anticipates that between 1998 and 2008, most of the 2.1 million jobs to be created in the United States will be related to information and service.[44] More recent projections indicate that the vast majority of jobs that will be created between 2002 and 2012 in the service-oriented, high-tech economy will require workers who have a firm grasp of mathematical, scientific, and computer skills,[45] the very skills that are compromised by a "sharecropper's" education.

No Child Left Behind and the Education of Black Children in Poverty

Amid growing concerns over schooling inequalities, the 2001 No Child Left Behind (NCLB) Act, the cornerstone of President George W. Bush's domestic policy during his first term, was passed with bipartisan support, marking the broadest expansion of the federal government into K-12 schooling since *Brown*. Although met with skepticism by those who saw the measure more as a political maneuver to position the President and his party in a positive light, NCLB includes remarkably explicit language to eliminate academic inequalities and to reduce educational disparities among children from different racial and economic backgrounds. Not since *Brown* had federal policy taken such strong measures to compel school districts across the nation to seriously educate all children.

No Child Left Behind's egalitarian rhetoric, however, has been betrayed by federal budget cuts that have severely undermined the capacity of public school officials to comply with the law's mandate. For example, federal cuts for the 2005 fiscal year eliminated more than $9 billion of promised funds from the NCLB budget. In addition, the government cut more than $7 billion from monies intended for Title I programs, the very programs directed at student populations especially at risk for failing in school, a population that is comprised largely of black children living in poverty (see Table 8.5 for selected school districts).

As Table 8.5 indicates, such cuts tremendously impact school districts with high concentrations of poor students as well as those with large black student populations. In Missouri alone, where we live and work, Kansas City and St. Louis city schools lost nearly $35 million, or 41 percent of their respective budgets, of promised Title I funds during the 2005 fiscal year. Larger public school districts lost even more. For instance, federal cuts eliminated nearly $300 million from the budgets of Title I programs in Los Angeles public schools, as indicated in Table 8.5, and downsized the budgets of those in the schools in the five New York City boroughs by 38 percent to the tune of $650 million.[46] These cuts resulted in a severe strain on teachers, resources, and educational programs that are necessary to ensure that no child is left behind in America's schools.

The budget cuts also exacerbate other conditions that place black children living in poverty at risk in school and society. For instance, although NCLB's sweeping provisions allow for multiple ways to assess learning, underfunding contributes to the over-reliance by schools on standardized testing to measure student achievement. The extensive use of testing has also resulted in promoting the very sort of curriculum and instruction in schools that further marginalize—academically and socially—those who are at the greatest disadvantage in society.

Further, the general abuse of testing occurs at a time when students complain that schools neither challenge them nor prepare them for the worlds of work and higher education. Similarly, employers and college and university administrators complain that high school graduates often come to them without the basic skills that they expect young people to gain in school. Whether entering the workforce or enrolling in college, young people need to be highly skilled to survive and flourish in our

Table 8.5
Bush Administration's Proposed Fiscal Year 2005 Budget for Title I versus Title I Funding Promised by No Child Left Behind

School District	Administration Proposed Title I Budget	Title I Funding Promised under NCLB (Estimate)	Difference ($)	Difference (%)
Los Angeles Unified	$452,705,000	$747,310,200	–$294,605,200	–39.42%
Dade County (Miami)	$138,857,300	$225,414,000	–$86,556,700	–38.40%
Kansas City (MO)	$16,836,500	$28,338,800	–$11,502,300	–40.59%
St. Louis City	$30,288,300	$53,341,100	–$23,052,800	–43.22%
Bronx County (NYC)	$252,754,800	$406,375,000	–$153,620,200	–37.80%
Dallas Independent	$79,963,600	$135,281,300	–$55,317,700	–40.89%
Houston Independent	$108,036,600	$186,107,200	–$78,070,600	–41.95%

Source: Children's Defense Fund 2005.

contemporary postindustrial society. Both colleges and universities require of the students they admit the same skills and knowledge base that employers demand of high school graduates they employ: innovation, creativity, intellectual dexterity, and initiative. These are the very skills that are compromised in the unbridled pursuit of increasing test scores and that prepare black children living in poverty for the "Negro jobs" that no longer exist in postindustrial society. To be certain, neither NCLB nor standardized testing can be blamed for creating all the problems that exist in our schools but federal budget cuts can be rightly criticized for having exacerbated them.

THE EDUCATION OF BLACK CHILDREN LIVING IN POVERTY IN NEW MILLENNIUM AMERICA: LESSONS FROM THE "GAP CLOSERS"

Echoing a view expressed by W. E. B. Du Bois at the beginning of the twentieth century, the eminent American historian John Hope Franklin noted that the problem of the color line also promises to be part of the legacy and burden of the twenty-first century.[47] What we've described thus far in this chapter would seem to give credence to Franklin's words. For sure, contemporary public schools appear to sustain their historical race-making function in society by providing black children and youth a sharecropper's education, or one that effectively prepares students for "Negro jobs" in post-civil rights society. Such an education has devastating implications for children living in poverty in a postindustrial society that is absent a full-employment economy: It implicates schools in the untenable role of contributing to the creation of a superfluous population, one for whom society is prone to invest more on incarceration than it does on education.[48]

However, we are optimists by moral necessity as well as by lived experience and are emboldened by the frontline educators across the nation who are responsible for realizing the promise of *Brown* some 50 years after its rendering. These educators routinely lay bear the institutional lie that we cannot educate black children living in poverty as to do so is normal, those educators whom Asa Hilliard calls *gap closers*.[49] Gap closers are teachers, principals, and programs that normally promote academic excellence among typically low-achieving black students. As Hilliard notes, gap closers are generally unacknowledged in debates on school reform and rarely influence the direction of teacher education and school leadership programs that prepare teachers and administrators to work in schools with low-achieving black students. Instead the vast majority of researchers, educators, and policymakers operate from the assumption that failure is inevitable when it comes to educating most black students and that the most we can hope to do is to assist these students in meeting minimum competency standards.

These beliefs prevail despite the presence of gap closers and gap-closing schools in diverse settings in every part of the country. For example, black children living in poverty have a long tradition of academic excellence at the high-powered, African-centered Marcus Garvey School in Los Angeles. They also fare extremely well in the public Central Park East Elementary and Secondary Schools of New York. These latter schools feature a fairly traditional but nonetheless rigorous curriculum with high-performance standards. In addition, an untold number of parochial schools and military academies also have had considerable success promoting high-academic achievement among black students. Despite their different ideological commitments, educators at these schools abide by the belief that, regardless of their backgrounds, all students can meet high standards. More importantly, though, these educators go about the business of educating black students as though such expectations are nothing out of the ordinary.

These seemingly disparate settings have in common certain philosophical principles when it comes to educating black children living in poverty. Theresa Perry captures these tenets in the following statement:

> African-American students will achieve in school environments that have a leveling culture, a culture of achievement that extends to all of its members and a strong sense of group membership, where the expectation that everyone achieve is explicit and is regularly communicated in public and group settings. African-American students will achieve in these environments, irrespective of class background, the cultural responsiveness of the setting or the prior level of preparation.[50]

In the above statement, Perry calls into question the common reasons that many educators and policymakers use to explain black student underachievement: Poverty, cultural difference, and educational history. In many ways, Perry suggests that when we are present with students and begin teaching where they are, as opposed to where they have been or should be, we can promote academic excellence. Similarly, Antonia Darder writes that the extent to which we embrace our students as integral beings is directly linked to our "willingness and ability to be fully present and in possession of the capacity to enter into dialogical relationships of solidarity with students, parents, and colleagues."[51]

Gap closers across America are largely comprised of educators who have entered into relationships of solidarity with students, parents, and colleagues and have made remarkable changes in previously struggling schools with large populations of children living in poverty. For example, in Texas, Jim Scheurich examined highly successful and loving, public elementary schools populated mainly by low-socioeconomic status children of color. In his research, Scheurich describes what the leaders of these schools have come to call the HiPass model of school reform; HiPass is an acronym for High Performance All Student Success Schools. As Scheurich explains, this model "did not come from the reform literature or from the leadership or organizational literatures."[52] In fact, as he reports, "those who developed the model were not self-consciously developing a model; in their view, they were just developing schools that were successful" for traditionally underserved working class and poor students of color, students whom they called "their children."[53] In addition to being academically engaged and civic minded, students at these schools typically achieve scores on high-stakes standardized tests that either match or exceed those of their peers at more affluent area suburban schools.

The schools in Scheurich's study are characterized by five core beliefs: (1) all children can achieve at high academic levels—no exceptions allowed; (2) work must be refocused on the needs of the child rather than on the demands of the bureaucracy; (3) all children must be treated with love, appreciation, care, and respect—no exceptions allowed; (4) the racial culture, including the first language of the child is always valued—no exceptions allowed; and (5) the school exists for and serves the community—there is little separation. These schools go further than affirming the Constitutional rights reasserted in the *Brown* ruling and support those critical rights affirmed by the Universal Declaration of Human Rights that are imperative to promoting the civic purpose of public schooling in multiracial, multicultural societies.

The organizational cultures of these schools are characterized by seven interwoven, mutually reinforced features, or "shared meanings," that are readily observable by anyone upon entering a site: (1) a strong, shared vision; (2) loving, caring environments for children and adults; (3) collaborative, family-like environments; (4) innovation, experimentation, and openness to new ideas; (5) hardworking but not burning out; (6) an appropriate conduct that is built into the organizational culture; and (7) a sense of shared responsibility in which the school staff as a whole hold themselves accountable for the success of all children.

Most remarkable about these schools in Scheurich's study is the fact that they had previous histories of chronic underachievement and were typically transformed in 3–5 years under the leadership of newly assigned principals. These principals guided the transformation of their schools from low-performing to high-achieving educational centers while keeping 80 to 90 percent of the teachers and without changing the general socioeconomic demographics of their student populations.

Research conducted on the urban secondary schools in New York report similar findings.[54] Guided by values and supported by organizational cultures similar to those found among the elementary schools in Texas, the schools in New York also demonstrate remarkable support for their largely black and student of color populations from working class and poor backgrounds. These schools promote among poor students of color the sort of capital by which they come to see themselves as responsible change agents in their school and in their communities. Like their younger peers in the Texas elementary schools, students in the New York high schools report that their teachers are academically and socially responsive. Also, these students' perceived sense of belonging in school contributes to a sense of academic press in which they are likely to feel more challenged and prepared for college than do their black peers in suburban settings.

These schools also defy academic prescriptions and popular conventions that overpredict the impact of poverty and parental education or family educational status on student aspirations, engagement, motivation, and achievement. In other words, in these schools, "parental education was not correlated with student level of engagement or aspirations for college."[55] These findings are consistent with research on schools that promote black student success in diverse settings around the country. Despite their different ideological commitments and programmatic features, educators at these schools abide by the belief that, regardless of their backgrounds, all students can meet high-performance standards. More importantly, though, these educators go about the business of educating black students as though such expectations are nothing out of the ordinary.

In our work in St. Louis, we have also encountered dedicated students and skilled gap closers from racially, economically, and linguistically diverse backgrounds in elementary and secondary schools throughout the city. These educators embrace radically humanistic values in the tradition of Jean-Jacques Rousseau, John Dewey, Septima Clark, and Paulo Freire and, most importantly, foster cultures of achievement in their schools or classrooms. These, like other gap closers around the nation, resist the idea that failure is inevitable when it comes to educating black students or poor students or immigrant students, or that the most we can hope to do is to assist these students in meeting minimum competency standards. They, like their gap-closing peers, know that the real achievement gap is the disparity between the widely reported underperformance of black students and the capacity of these students for excellence as opposed to differences in test scores between black and white students.[56] Most importantly, however, the values that these educators translate into school policy and classroom practices are theoretically and ethically consonant with the educational values that have inspired black children, youth, and adults of all backgrounds to invest themselves in schools, even when their goals and aspirations have been hijacked, either by judicial decree, state and federal mandates, coalition politics, or the decisions of those who are elected and charged to serve them.

CONCLUSION

As we conclude, we are mindful that, as the noted social theorist Anthony Giddens explains, the world in which we now live is much more complicated than the ones of the past. This is due to the proliferation of media and other forms of communicative technologies that allow for the unchecked dissemination of information, images, and symbols. This is a "runaway world," Giddens notes—one that is associated with drastic social and economic changes in both the United States and the broader international society.[57] These changes, attendant to postindustrialism and globalization, present individuals with a vast array of social, cultural, and economic opportunities.

At the same time, opportunities have not been available to all and, so far, both postindustrialism and globalization have reinforced patterns of racial dominance, both in the United States and abroad. As indicated previously, jobs in the United States for the foreseeable future will be divided between disproportionately high numbers of opportunities in low-paying, low-status, unstable positions and small numbers of high-paying, high-status, more secure ones. Poor black children and youth are generally destined to fill the former category as adults later in life and increasingly are being left out of both.

Thus, basic shifts in the U.S. economy in the past 20 or so years have altered both the technical function of public schools as institutions that develop socially recognizable skills among students and the moral imperatives of these places as sites that promote citizenship and social justice. To be clear, however, no one approach, philosophy, program, or political posture represents the magic formula to guarantee underserved children and youth educational settings that affirm human dignity, promote intellectual development, and foster a deepened sense of community. Yet, as history and the efforts of the gap closers discussed in the previous section have shown, black communities are the primary and most enduring resources in the education of their children and youth; any effort to promote educational excellence among underserved students must honor the voices that originate in these communities— both in and on their terms.

NOTES

1. Loïc Wacquant, "From slavery to mass incarceration: Rethinking the 'race question' in the U.S.," *New Left Review* 13 (2002): 41–60.

2. James D. Anderson, *The education of blacks in the south, 1860–1935* (Chapel Hill, North Carolina: University of North Carolina Press, 1988).

3. John H. McWhorter, *Losing the race: Self-sabotage in black America* (New York: Perennial, 2000).

4. Ruby K. Payne, *A framework for understanding poverty* (Highlands, TX: aha Process, Inc., 2003).

5. John Ogbu, *Black American students in an affluent suburb: A study of academic disengagement* (Mahwah, NJ: Lawrence Erlbaum Associates, 2003).

6. Signithia Fordham and John Ogbu, "Black students' school success: Coping with the 'burden of "Acting White"'," *The Urban Review* 18(3) (1986): 176–206.

7. Signithia Fordham, *Blacked out: Dilemmas of race, identity, and success at Capital High* (Chicago, IL: University of Chicago Press, 1996).

8. Claude Steele, "A threat in the air: How stereotypes shape the intellectual identity and performance of women and African Americans," *American Psychologist* 52 (1997): 613– 629.

9. Garrett Albert Duncan, "Race and education," in *Encyclopedia of education and human development*, vol. 1 (Armonk, NY: M. E. Sharpe, Inc., 2005); Garrett Albert Duncan, "Education in the United States," in *Encyclopedia of African-American culture and history: The black experience in America* (Farmington Hills, MI: Macmillan Reference USA, 2005).

10. Anderson, *The education of blacks in the south*, 31.

11. W. E. B. Du Bois, "Negro education," in *W. E. B. Du Bois: A reader*, ed. David Levering Lewis (New York: Henry Holt and Company, 1995), 263.

12. Derrick Bell, "Waiting on the promise of *Brown*," in *The courts, social science, and school desegregation*, ed. Betsy Levin and Willis D. Hawley (New Brunswick, NJ: Transaction Books, 1977), 341–373; Derrick Bell, "Serving two masters: Integration ideals and client interests in school desegregation litigation," in *Critical race theory: The cutting edge*, ed. Richard Delgado (Philadelphia, PA: Temple University Press, 1995), 228–238; Derrick Bell, *Silent covenants: Brown v. Board of Education and the unfulfilled hopes for racial reform* (New York: Oxford University Press, 2004).

13. Noam Chomsky, "Expanding the floor of the cage: An interview with Noam Chomsky," interview by David Barsamian, *Z Magazine* 10(3) (1997): 36–43; Jason Ziedenberg and Vincent Schiraldi, *Cellblocks or classrooms?: The funding of higher education and corrections and its impact on African American men* (Washington, DC: Justice Policy Institute, 2002).

14. Applied Research Center, *Education and race* (Oakland, CA: Applied Research Center, 1998).

15. Education Trust, *The funding gap 2005: Low-income and minority students shortchanged by most states* (Washington, DC: Education Trust, 2005).

16. Ibid.

17. Education Trust, *Education watch: Missouri—key education facts and figures; achievement, attainment and opportunity from elementary school through college* (Washington, DC: Education Trust, 2004).

18. Amy Stuart Wells and Robert L. Crain, *Stepping over the color line: Black students in suburban schools* (New Haven, CT: Yale University Press, 1997).

19. Garrett Albert Duncan, "Critical race ethnography in education: Narrative, inequality, and the problem of epistemology," *Race Ethnicity and Education* 8(1) (2005): 95–116.

20. Harold Wenglinsky, *Does it compute?: The relationship between educational technology and student achievement in mathematics* (Princeton, NJ: Educational Testing Service, 1998).

21. S. B. Ethridge, "Impact of the 1954 *Brown vs Topeka Board of Education* decision on black educators," *The Negro Educational Review* 30(4) (1979): 217–232.

22. Kenneth J. Meier, Joseph Stewart, Jr., and Robert E. England, *Race, class, and education: The politics of second-generation discrimination* (Madison, WI: University of Wisconsin Press, 1989).

23. Jeffrey R. Henig, Richard C. Hula, Marion Orr, and Desiree S. Pedescleaux, *The color of school reform: Race, politics, and the challenge of urban education* (Princeton, NJ: Princeton University Press, 2001).

24. Beth Harry and Mary Anderson, "The disproportionate placement of African American males in special education programs: A critique of the process," *Journal of Negro Education* 63(4) (1995): 602–619.

25. Applied Research Center, *Education and race* (Oakland, CA: Applied Research Center, 1998).

26. *Washington Post*, "Study: Racial disparity in school discipline," December 17, 1999, A3.

27. Applied Research Center, *Education and race*.

28. Walter S. Gilliam, *Prekindergarterners left behind: Expulsion rates in state prekindergarten systems* (New Haven, CT: Yale University Child Study Center, 2005).

29. Pedro Noguera, *City schools and the American dream: Reclaiming the promise of public education* (New York: Teachers College Press, 2003), 23.

30. Garrett Albert Duncan, "'At the Risk of Seeming Ridiculous': Toward an Ethic of Love in Researching and Schooling the Lives of Adolescent Black Males" (paper presentation, invited symposium, Annual Meeting of the American Educational Research Association, Division G, Section 4, New Orleans, LA, April 2, 2002).

31. Elijah Anderson, *Code of the street: Decency, violence, and the moral life of the inner city* (New York and London: W.W. Norton and Company, 1999); William Julius Wilson, *When work disappears: The world of the new urban poor* (New York: Alfred A. Knopf, 1996).

32. E-mail message to first author, June 21, 2001 (capitals in the original message).

33. Garrett Albert Duncan, "'At the Risk of Seeming Ridiculous'."

34. Ann Arnett Ferguson, *Bad boys: Public schools in the making of black masculinity* (Ann Arbor, MI: University of Michigan Press, 2000).

35. Ronnie Casella, "Punishing dangerousness through preventative detention: Examining the institutional link between schools and prisons" (paper presentation, The School to Prison

Pipeline: Charting Intervention Strategies of Prevention and Support for Minority Students, Northeastern University, Cambridge, MA, May 15, 16, 2003).

36. William Julius Wilson, *When work disappears: The world of the new urban poor* (New York: Alfred A. Knopf, 1996).

37. Jonathan Kozol, *The shame of the nation: The restoration of apartheid schooling in America* (New York: Crown Publishers, Inc., 2005).

38. Gary Orfield and John T. Yun, *Resegregation in American schools* (Cambridge, MA: The Civil Rights Project, Harvard University, 1999).

39. Jason Ziedenberg and Vincent Schiraldi, *Cellblocks or classrooms?: The funding of higher education and corrections and its impact on African American men* (Washington, DC: Justice Policy Institute, 2002).

40. Children's Defense Fund, *The state of America's children 2004* (Washington, DC: Children's Defense Fund, 2004).

41. Loïc Wacquant, "The great carceral leap backward: Imprisonment in America from Nixon to Clinton" in *The new punitiveness: Current trends, theories, perspectives*, ed. John Pratt et al. (London: Willan, 2005), 3–26.

42. Robert Moses and Charles E. Cobb, Jr., *Radical equations: Math literacy and civil rights* (Boston, MA: Beacon Press, 2001).

43. Jeremy Rifkin, *The end of work: The decline of the global labor force and the dawn of the post-market era* (New York: A Jeremy P. Tarcher/Putnam Book, 1995), 79.

44. Rolf Anderson, *Atlas of the American economy: An illustrated guide to industries and trends* (Washington, DC: Congressional Quarterly, 1994); Charles Bowman, "BLS projections to 2008: A summary," *Monthly Labor Review* (November 1999): 3, 4.

45. Michael Horrigan, "Employment projections to 2012: Concepts and context," *Monthly Labor Review* (February 2004): 3–22.

46. Children's Defense Fund, *Bush Administration's Fiscal Year 2005 proposed budget for Title I versus promised funding under the No Child Left Behind Act (for all US school districts)* (Washington, DC: Children's Defense Fund, 2005).

47. John Hope Franklin, *The color line: Legacy for the twenty-first century* (Columbia, MD and London: University of Missouri Press, 1993).

48. Garrett Albert Duncan, "Urban pedagogies and the celling of adolescents of color," *Social Justice* 27(3) (2000): 29–42; Jason Ziedenberg and Vincent Schiraldi, *Cellblocks or classrooms?: The funding of higher education and corrections and its impact on African American men* (Washington, DC: Justice Policy Institute, 2002).

49. Theresa Perry, Claude Steele, and Asa Hilliard, *Young, gifted, and black: Promoting high achievement among African-American students* (Boston, MA: Beacon Press, 2003).

50. Ibid., 107.

51. Antonia Darder, *Reinventing Paulo Freire: A pedagogy of love* (Boulder, CO: Westview Press, 2002), 98.

52. James Scheurich, "Highly successful and loving, public elementary schools populated mainly by low-ses children of color: Core beliefs and cultural characteristics," *Urban education* 33(4) (1998): 453.

53. Ibid.

54. Michele Fine, Janice Bloom, April Burns, Lori Chajet, Monique Guishard, Yasser Payne, Tiffany Perkins-Munn, and Maria Elena Torre, "Dear Zora: A letter to Zora Neale Hurston fifty years after *Brown*," *Teachers College Record* 107(3) (2005): 496–528.

55. Ibid., 520.

56. Theresa Perry, Claude Steele, and Asa Hilliard, *Young, gifted, and black: Promoting high achievement among African-American students* (Boston, MA: Beacon Press, 2003).

57. Anthony Giddens, *Runaway world: How globalization is reshaping our lives* (New York: Routledge, 2000).

CHAPTER 9

RESETTLING REFUGEE CHILDREN

Qingwen Xu and Denise Pearson

The United States is by far the largest of the 10 traditional resettlement countries, in that it has historically accepted more refugees for resettlement than all other countries combined. Every year, refugee men, women, and children enter the United States with hopes of finding a life better than the one they left. They come with the expectation to integrate into American society, in employment, education, community, and social settings. From 2001 to 2004, America resettled about 160 thousand refugees.[1] Among them, a substantial number are children. Worldwide, school-age children (age 5–17) represented about 49 percent of refugees received in 2002, according to the United Nations High Commissioner for Refugees (the UNHCR).[2] In the United States, from 1989 to 2001, there were approximately 400 thousand refugee children (age <19 years), accounting for 30 percent of refugees.[3] Refugee children are normally exposed to numerous risk factors resulting from settlement, including lack of formal education, exposure to violence, forced displacement, and multiple losses. In addition, refugee children frequently live in families that are financially poorer, have less educated parents (without English proficiency) than their counterparts in the host country, and endure substandard health and mental health conditions. Meanwhile, refugee children and their families are resettled in a society of which they know little; some of this knowledge, such as the knowledge of educational, social, and legal systems, is critical to successful resettlement and adjustment. Consequently, the lack of knowledge frequently sets refugee children apart from the mainstream community and causes further concerns for their overall development.

Unfortunately, researchers have not paid adequate attention to the plight of refugee children, in particular to their resettlement in the United States. Refugee children's special circumstances ask for appropriate response from both policymakers and social service practitioners. This chapter first examines systematic barriers to refugee children's successful resettlement, and the role of the U.S. child welfare system in the resettlement process. Then it introduces a Parenting Empowerment Program offered by a voluntary resettlement agency in Colorado. Last, based on the review of U.S. resettlement policies and service programs and empirical data from the Parenting Empowerment Program, this chapter offers recommendations for policy changes and for more effective practices in order to better address refugee children's needs so as to secure their future well-being.

REFUGEE CHILDREN AND THEIR JOURNEY TO THE UNITED STATES

Refugee Children and Their Special Journeys

Refugee children come to the United States via diverse journeys, and gain their legal status and rights to stay in the United States in diverse ways. The majority of children come to the United States under the protection of the UNHCR and in accordance with international arrangements, such as the Somali refugee program. Because of wars and armed conflicts, these children are classified by the UNHCR as refugees. They flee en masse, often by foot, from their home country into neighboring countries, and normally live in refugee camps operated by governmental entities. As one of the UNHCR's "durable solutions," rather than returning to their home country, some refugee children and their families are permanently transferred from refugee camps to the United States, where they can begin a new life. Because the UNHCR's ultimate goal is family reunification, refugee children are usually resettled in the United States together with their parents and/or extended families. A smaller number of children gain their refugee status and are eligible for resettlement as a result of reunification with their refugee families who are already in the United States. Between 1997 and 2002, approximately 93 percent of refugee children arrived in the United States in the company of biological or legally adoptive parents; others traveled to the United States to reunite with caregivers, or to join a relative who had been newly designated as their caregiver.[4] Normally, refugee children and their families receive a series of resettlement services before their departure, during travel to the host country, and after their arrival.

A special category of refugee children is "unaccompanied minors," who come to the United States without a parent or legal guardian. These children travel alone either voluntarily in hope of eventually joining their parents and relatives, or by force, fraud, and coercion. Children in this category are either identified by the Department of State (DOS) before their arrival, reclassified after arrival, or granted asylum. Over the last several years, the plight of unaccompanied children in federal custody pending immigration hearings has gained significant attention from the media, Congress, the legal community, and the public.[5] In November 2002, Congress acted to redress the plight in the Homeland Security Act by transferring basic care, custody, and placement functions from the Immigration and Neutralization Service (INS) to the Department of Health and Human Services (DHHS). DHHS thereafter retains the exclusive authority to place refugee children in state juvenile dependency proceedings and foster care, and provide services through its Unaccompanied Refugee Minor Program (URM), which was developed in the 1980s to address the needs of thousands of children from Southeast Asia without a parent or guardian to care for them. Since 1980, almost 12,000 minors have entered the URM program, according to the Administration for Children and Families (ACF).

Risk Factors to Refugee Children

Regardless of their different journeys to the United States, refugee children are exposed to multiple risk factors that can negatively affect their development. Economic, political, and social factors can affect refugee children's development as they resettle in a new country. Such factors are important in predicting their adjustment to their new circumstances as well as their physical and psychological well-being. The effects of war and trauma on children have been documented since World War II.[6] Subjected to the horror of war, dependent children's developing coping skills put them at risk for mental health disorders.[7] Researchers found that while children's physical health could recover rather quickly, children's social behavior was slower to improve, and some refugee children have persistent developmental issues.[8] Within the last decade there has been research examining refugee children's mental health. Indeed, a group of studies published in 1995 found that serious psychiatric disorders were present in 40–50 percent of refugee children.[9]

In addition to the effects of war and trauma, the literature also suggests that refugee children have experienced extra difficulties in the process of resettling in a new society and adjusting to a new social system. Refugee children and their families enter a new country; the process of gaining refugee status is not only complex and difficult but also emotionally draining. Most refugee children have lived in a condition of continual stress caused by uncertainty about their future, which compounds the trauma experienced in their home country. They are likely to live in temporary housing and attend substandard schools.[10] Once settled in a local community, however, refugee children's mental health does not improve much, because they face new challenges of achieving acceptance at school, developing a personal identity in a new society, and acting as "cultural brokers" for their parents at home.[11] Researchers have found that Indochinese refugee children who resettled in the United States reported significant mood disturbances and psychological distress within the first 2 years of resettlement.[12] Furthermore, living in a Western society as ethnic minorities, refugee children have experienced discrimination at schools and in the community, which creates high levels of stress and psychological distress.[13] Researchers have indicated that new life circumstances in their host communities, such as peer relationships and exposure to bullying, are of equal or even greater importance than previous exposure to war and violence, which affect refugee children's social adjustment and self-worth assessment.[14]

Unfortunately, unlike most other children, refugee children frequently lack the support and help from their parents and families to cope with the stress and psychological distress during their resettlement and adjustment. While it has been recognized that the family is the natural environment for the growth and well-being of children (as stated in the 1989 Hague Convention on the Rights of the Child), refugee children often lack such a healthy family environment; their parents and families are often suffering from high rates of depression and psychological distress as a result of adjustment.[15] Researchers have identified that stress in the family and exposure to war and violence are two equally weighted determinants of refugee children's poor mental health.[16] Certain aspects of the home environment highly correlate with children's cognitive development, including the manner in which the mother responds emotionally and verbally to the child, the mother's emotional well-being, the mothers' ability to cope with the stress of displacement, and the organization of the child's physical and temporal environment.[17] Also, because refugee children in the United States usually learn English and customs faster than their parents, they may find themselves mediating between their parents and the outside community[18] rather than receiving support from their parents.

In order to assess refugee children's needs and better support their development, researchers recommend services that facilitate the successful adaptation of refugee children, help refugee children and their families heal from their experiences, and begin integrating into the host society. Therefore, whether current resettlement services can meet these challenges and objectives, and what is the best practice to resettle refugee children become critical. This chapter, then, systematically evaluates present refugee children's resettlement programs and services in the United States, also the administrative structure, funding sources, and roles of social service institutions in the process of resettling refugee children.

SOCIAL SERVICES FOR REFUGEE CHILDREN IN THE UNITED STATES

Resettlement Program and Structure

Social services provided to refugee children and their families in the United States generally include two stages. For the first stage, services are provided mainly to assist in immediate resettlement efforts, that is, for the first 6 months upon refugee's arrival. The second stage includes long-term resettlement and integration programs and other mainstream social services such as Medicaid and Food Stamps. The initial resettlement service is administrated by the U.S. Refugee Resettlement Program and funded by the Department of State (DOS) Bureau of Population, Refugees and Migration (PRM). In fiscal year 2004, the DOS designated $132 million for refugee admissions and resettlement programs. The UNHCR is a designated partner in the U.S. refugee resettlement program, and is involved in the process of determining processing priorities, setting the annual cap for admission, and facilitating the refugee migration. The DOS distributed funds to a network of over 400 voluntary agencies (Volags) throughout the United States through what is called the Reception and Placement (R&P) grant. The DOS contracts with Volags to provide refugees with food, housing, employment, medical care, counseling, and other services to help refugees make a rapid transition to economic self-sufficiency. While the R&P grants are supposed to fund services to resettle refugees during their first 30 days in the United States, recipients of R&P grants are expected to augment funds with private cash and in-kind contributions, and provide services to refugees, including sponsorship, prearrival resettlement planning, reception upon arrival, basic needs support for at least 30 days, and case management and tracking for 90 to 180 days.

Domestic long-term refugee resettlement and integration programs are closely coordinated by the PRM but funded through the DHHS's Office of Refugee and Resettlement (ORR). Ongoing benefits for the newly arrived refugees include transitional cash assistance, health benefits, and a wide variety of other services. The primary focus is job placement, cultural orientation, English language acquisition, and health care access. Most services at this stage are provided up to the first 8 months after arrival; refugees are expected to become employed and self-sufficient by that time. Refugee Cash Assistance and Refugee Medical Assistance are only available for the first 8 months. After this period, unemployed and low-income single people and childless couples are not eligible for any cash assistance. Families with children (<18 years of age) then have to turn to mainstream welfare programs, such as the Temporary Assistance for Needy Families program, which assists poor families for 2 years, and Medicaid, which provides health benefits for unemployed and low-income families. Under the DHHS umbrella, additional services are offered, such as family strengthening programs, youth and elderly services, adjustment counseling and mental health services, aimed to further assist refugee families adjust to their new lives in the United States. However, social services provided through the refugee resettlement system, such as employability services under the State Formula Grant Programs, are available only for the first 5 years after arrival in the United States; the services, in reality, are structured to promote employment and self-sufficiency for much earlier than 5 years. Unfortunately, refugee children's needs and needs assessment are not specifically identified in the refugee resettlement program, as described above. Services are primarily designed for parents and families in hopes that a resettled family with at least one family member employed will assure refugee children's well-being and provide for their needs.

The program, in particular for refugee children, is for unaccompanied refugee minors who have not joined with parents and/or do not have a legal guardian. The URM program, under the direct administration of ACF, provides a comprehensive range of services for unaccompanied refugee minors and places them in culturally appropriate places. Currently, the URM program offers special foster care for these children in ten states, and has developed an array of services, such as shelter care, residential treatment care, and services for the young age, pregnant girls, or children with mental illness. The primary focus of the URM program is to reunite refugee children with their relatives whenever possible; therefore, refugee children in foster care are not available for adoption in accordance with standards of the UNHCR, and this leaves open the possibility of family reunification.

Discussion

Taking into account refugee children's special circumstance, a review of U.S. refugee resettlement programs suggests that refugee children's needs have been largely underserved. This situation can be explained by two policy objectives. First, the U.S. refugee resettlement programs and services focus primarily on the initial stage of resettlement. Primary resources and services are to address the refugees' most urgent needs once they reach the destination—food, shelter, health care, water and sanitation alike. Given the refugees' initial vulnerability, services are provided free of charge, and require little or no contribution from the recipients. Later on, education, skills training, psychosocial support, and other services are added to the mix, but at a minimal level. In the United States, the initial period of settlement is 6 months. In the longer term, since it is believed that a refugee's levels of vulnerability decrease, there is no systematic program available. Secondly, the primary focus of refugee resettlement services is employment, such as skills training, job development, workplace orientation and job counseling. American policymakers believe that it is crucial that employment be found soon after arrival, as employment leads not only to early economic self-sufficiency for the family, but adds greatly to the integrity of families who seek to establish themselves in a new country and provide for their own needs. Generally, the program implementation would encourage more than one member of the family becoming employed.

Obviously, the principles underlying these two policy objectives reflects economic reality and American value—returning back to normal life as quickly as possible, participating in the labor market to support family and children, self-sufficiency and independence. The impact of these policy objectives on refugee children is mixed. On one hand, the current U.S. refugee resettlement program and services can benefit refugee children by rebuilding their routine family life and strengthening their family functions quickly and effectively. Experience from other countries indicates that labor market participation is a key factor affecting the success of refugee resettlement.[19] Sustained provision of free services after the emergency phase would erode the refugee family's mechanisms. Sweden offers an example. While the Swedish government in 1985 shifted the focus of refugee resettlement from labor market integration to income support, and extended the initial stage of free services to 18 months, the overall effect of this reform was that refugees suffered substantial long-term earnings losses, and consequently, the poverty rate among refugees rose.[20] Therefore, there is nothing more important than a well-functioning, economically self-sufficient family unit; the U.S. resettlement program and services might be exactly the one to fulfill children's needs for psychological and physical well-being and development.

On the other hand, refugee children and their families need to access a wide range of key services to support their transition from arrival to eventual settlement, and their needs go far beyond basic economic self-sufficiency. The lack of key services would negatively affect refugee children's development and jeopardize their process of integrating into the community. Service providers and researchers have identified many refugee children's needs during their early years in the United States that must be addressed, such as cultural orientation, ethnic identity, family conflicts, and social adjustment at schools, to name a few. Refugee parents and families cannot easily, if not possibly, assess these needs, which centrally pertain to refugee children's development. Professional help for refugee children are of necessity. Meanwhile, more resources and long-term services are needed in order to provide and sustain ongoing emotional and psychological supports. Due to cultural misunderstandings, discrimination, identity disorientation, school adjustment problems, peer relationships, and many other factors, refugee children's daily struggles do not subside after the initial stage of resettlement. A study of refugee children from Chile and the Middle East in Sweden suggests that the poor mental health condition of refugee children persisted 13 months after resettlement.[21] And the process of assimilation of a group of people into mainstream society generally takes about three generations.[22] As such, the U.S. resettlement program fails to provide refugee children with comprehensive services, and does not support them and their families for development.

As refugee children are facing increasing risks and challenges during their resettlement, how to strengthen refugee families, increase family resources, empower parents, build parents' upward initiative and persistence, and provide adequate supports to refugee children on a long-term and consistent basis is what American resettlement programs need to address.[23] Here we present a Parenting Empowerment Program provided to Somali and Somali Bantu refugees in Colorado; the program evaluation then leads to further discussions on U.S. refugee resettlement programs and practice.

SNAPSHOT OF A PARENTING EMPOWERMENT PROGRAM IN COLORADO

Program Background

Colorado has resettled more than 32 thousand refugees since 1975, coming from countries around the globe. Between the years 1984 and 2004, more than two thousand African refugees arrived in Colorado.[24] In the summer of 2004, Colorado received more than a dozen Somali and Somali Bantu refugee families for resettlement. Before arrival, these refugees had been in a resettlement process for an unexpected 5 years, moved from one refugee camp to another, and endured many challenging events, in addition to traumatizing experiences in their own country.

The Somali and Somali Bantu families arrived in Denver in 2004; many included elementary-aged children, who were eventually enrolled at a community-based elementary school. However, not fully aware of the refugee children's imminent enrollment, the school was unable to adequately prepare to receive them. In addition to communication difficulties, as most of the children only had limited English ability, school teachers increasingly expressed concerns for the safety and well-being of the children. Observations indicated that refugee parents and families were either not fully aware of the changed environment for their children, or were too vulnerable to be able to cope with these changes, or both. For example, refugee parents dropped their children off early at school and picked them up late; refugee children walked or ran into the street without apparent caution; or children came to school unprepared for the day's work. When the elementary school recognized that it lacked the capacity to address these concerns, it reached out to the community for assistance. The effort resulted in collaboration between a local refugee resettlement agency and the community-based elementary school. A structured Parenting Empowerment Program was developed to mitigate presenting concerns over refugee children's well-being, and to empower refugee parents for their successful transition in the community.

Program Development and Implementation

The Parenting Empowerment Program was developed in 2004, and consisted of an 8-week program focusing on the following issues: (1) Parent—School Relations; (2) Discipline and Neglect; (3) Behavior Management; (4) Household Safety; and (5) Child Development. These issues were carefully chosen considering the huge difference in childcare, school system, and community environment between refugee children's original country and the United States. The program also took into account the knowledge and skills that pertain to refugee children's development and involvement in the new society. The content of the program included issues of parents' involvement in school and education; U.S. child-care policies and consequences for violating policies; appropriate and legal ways to discipline children and child abuse laws in America; and children's developmental needs at various stages of childhood.

The Parenting Empowerment Program was designed to orient refugee parents to the U.S. educational systems, familiarize them with appropriate child care in the United States, aid them in the resettlement process, promote self-efficacy, and empower parents to become effective parent advocates. The program was available to refugees living in Denver metropolitan area from Rwanda, Ethiopia, Sudan, Liberia, and Somali, and refugees entered the program through several Denver resettlement agencies. The first 8-week parenting program was held in the summer of 2004, with six Somali and Somali Bantu families participating in the program. The program was conducted at the elementary school by the agency's staff, in collaboration with staff from the school and with the assistance of translators.

Evaluation Approach

A preliminary evaluation of the initial program was conducted in the summer of 2005 in order to evaluate the perceived impact of the Empowerment Parenting Program on refugee parents. The program evaluation was designed primarily as a tool and methodology to enhance shared understanding and knowledge about various aspects of the Parenting Empowerment Program, and the residual needs and concerns of participants. The evaluation is built on the premise shared by researchers and practitioners that refugees are most intimate with their own experience, which necessitates a qualitative research approach. Considering complicated issues in the process of refugee resettlement, qualitative approaches also allow for a more participatory process that includes refugee families, resettlement agencies, school staff, and other program collaborators.

The evaluation involved a systematic collection of information from the resettlement agencies about the program activities, characteristics, and outcomes. In addition to the agency's documentation, agency personnel, program administrators, and school representatives were interviewed and consulted with throughout the project's duration. These interviews provided opportunities to further conceptualize the present problems, as well as additionally identify other concerns about refugee children's resettlement. Agency staff and other parenting program affiliates were involved in all steps of the evaluation process, also as a measure to further ensure accuracy of information and data collection. This collaborative and formative approach provided an opportunity to clarify issues and make any necessary refinements to the questioning or methodology.

Through narrative design strategies and also considering the nature of this preliminary program evaluation, open-ended in-depth interviews with refugee parents were conducted. Three refugee families participated in the evaluation; they are comprised of Somali and Somali Bantu families. Due to the absence of refugees' English proficiency, and considering the likelihood of refugees' minimum formal education and their unique culture characteristics, an interpreter, a Somali refugee, was identified and contracted with for interpretation and translation assistance. The same interpreter was used for all interviews and obtained informed consent in each case. The interview questions were designed to explore the perceived impact of the Parenting Empowerment Program. The interview script was derived from the program content. Because of the level of parents' education, English language proficiency, and other cultural factors, the degree of comprehension of the questions was uncertain in all cases. To mitigate miscommunication most questions were rephrased several times to facilitate accurate translation.

Perceived Needs of Refugee Parents

Program documentation records indicated that this group of Somali and Somali Bantu refugees participated in a 2-week cultural orientation session in a Kenyan refugee camp, in preparation for their resettlement in the United States. Their resettlement process in Colorado consists of two phases; the first phase lasted up to 1 year and was the period when refugees were received and resettled through local resettlement agencies. The second phase could last up to 5 years and is considered the service phase of resettlement. Upon arrival in the United States, case managers were assigned to each Somali and Somali Bantu family. Case managers are responsible for receiving refugees at the airport and then transporting them to housing, securing them food, and leaving them to rest and reflection. They are also responsible for orienting them to life in the United States.

Conversations with agency and school personnel revealed multiple concerns toward refugee children's well-being and their families' ability in caring for these children. Information gathered from interviews suggested several perceived needs of refugee parents. The first and most important of their needs is to acquire English language skills. Lack of English proficiency not only has blocked communications between school and refugee parents, but also caused difficulties for parents in helping their children with school work and school adjustment issues. High levels of stress have been observed for refugee parents. Refugee parents reported frustration to their case managers over the fact that they cannot read the letters sent home by school officials. It was also reported that refugee parents, without an understanding of American culture and social context, had a difficult time "taking in" all the necessary information at once. In addition to the challenges of language, refugee parents expressed unfamiliarity with the concept of "parent involvement in education," which is a well-grounded educational approach in the United States. As one refugee parent put it, in their country of Somalia, "teachers teach and parents parent—there is no interaction." Refugee parents' lack of knowledge about U.S. educational system and their lack of the interaction with schools could jeopardize refugee children's settlement and adjustment.

Therefore, it is perceived that refugee parents need support ranging from abilities in reading and speaking English in order to communicate with school teachers, to orientations of parent involvement in children's education and coping with American educational system, and knowledge of appropriate child care in the United States. In doing so, it is anticipated that refugee parents would be better prepared to help their children adjust to the new school, new community, and new country. The importance and necessity of continuing and further developing the Parenting Empowerment Program has been recognized by the school principal, resettlement agency staffs, and teachers.

Need Assessment

The Parenting Empowerment Program is empowering parents to begin taking greater control over issues related to their children's safety, care, discipline, and education. Although language barriers had a noticeable and adverse impact on the ability of some refugees to fully and actively participate in the program, despite the use of translators, all participants expressed value in participating in the program. However, interviews with refugee parents revealed a variety of compelling issues and themes; there are still remaining unmet needs that will impact further empowerment as part of the resettlement process.

From interviews with refugee parents, the Parenting Empowering Program effectively highlighted the differences and legal forms of childcare. Participants in this study articulated an understanding of what constitutes child care in America, and learned the importance of, such issues as dropping off and picking up their children on time from school, including the legal implications of not being in compliance. Nevertheless, cultural variances emerged during all interviews. One mother mentioned that she now understood she had to watch her children at all times. She connoted that "the child care in the U.S. is not the same at home in Somalia; kidnapping is not a problem—if children get lost in Somalia, they are eventually found by police and returned home." As a result of the parenting program, refugee parents were also made aware of other environmental issues and different standards of raising children in the United States. One mother stated that the program clarified expectations about nutrition, sleep/rest needs at different stages of development, and the importance of helping children with homework. The session on child safety particularly had a positive impact and had changed refugee parents' caregiving practice. Participants talked about placing knives safely out of the reach of children, having ready access to important telephone numbers, and bathing children and preparing food in hygienic ways; they also followed these practice at home.

Regardless of the awareness and knowledge refugee parents have gained about appropriate ways of child care in the United States, all parents in this study expressed difficulties related to fulfilling some parental responsibilities as suggested in the program. Again, not being able to speak English blocked their involvement in their children's education, and made it difficult to help their children with homework and effectively communicate with the school. Interviews revealed that refugee parents still needed help from the resettlement agency. In one case, a staff person from the agency visited refugee families' homes on a weekly basis to help their children with homework and to help parents with their English. In addition, the parenting program has also caused unpredicted consequences. For example, one mother asked to learn more about how to handle conflicts with her children. She felt unable to discipline them because she was informed during the program that in America she should never hit her children. She was worried because her child had threatened to "report her" if she used physical means for discipline. The mother felt her parenting authority was being restricted, and she was lacking full information about normative child discipline in the United States. While this confusion is normal for refugee parents especially during their resettlement and adjustment period of time, parents' responses to the program suggested unmet needs and implications for future program development.

Although the Parenting Empowerment Program aims to educate refugee parents for the good of their children, the issue of unemployment and family poverty emerged strongly in this study. For some refugee parents where English proficiency and any degree of formal education were lacking, frustrations over the need to learn skills and finding jobs were evident. They expressed dissatisfaction with the quality of their life in the United States, saying it was "a hard life." Most refugee parents in this study were either still unemployed or had difficulty keeping a job. Regardless of job training and searching efforts, limited English and lack of culturally appropriate work training hampered their ability to remain employed and self-sufficient. Accessing services was another expressed impediment to successful resettlement of refugee families. In particular, refugee parents expressed the need of monetary assistance for extended periods of time. One family in this study reported that the employment training, financial management, and resettlement services were helpful, but the reality was they lacked sufficient income for rent and were threatened with eviction.

Implications and Recommendations

The Parenting Empowerment Program was a response to problems jeopardizing the resettlement of Somali and Somali Bantu refugee families. Their problems were perceived to be the inability to care for their children in their new community appropriately, as well as in American society in general. Following the parenting program, positive changes in parent behavior were observed and anecdotally reported. These include such behaviors as getting children to school on time, paying close attention to traffic while taking children across streets, and being mindful of children's safety at home. Despite the positive impact of the parenting program, Somali and Somali Bantu refugees appear to need longer-term, population-specific intervention, if integration and sustained empowerment are expected. This evaluation suggests that refugee families have faced a multitude of difficulties during their resettlement, that consequently make refugee parents unaware of their children's needs, or insufficiently capable of supporting them. As such, refugee families might endanger their roles and functions in the process of refugee children's social and human development.

Learning from this Parenting Empowerment Program, we summarize following recommendations. First, the U.S. refugee resettlement policies should still emphasize job training and employment. Apart from the assumption that refugees receive adequate assistance that enables refugee families to be financially secure and to live properly in the United States, this evaluation reveals that unemployment and poverty are still clear and compelling issues. As employment remains a challenge to durable resettlement, it is recommended that the strengths of Somali and Somali Bantu people—their experience in agriculture, strong community orientation, social capital in family and religion—could be used as leverage to identify and develop employment opportunities and training priorities.

Meanwhile, as language is still a critical barrier for a successful and smooth refugee resettlement, it is recommended that funding for long-term language training should be provided to resettlement agencies. Taking into account the difficulties and time invested to overcome many identifiable employment barriers, long-term assistance, and efforts aimed at poverty relief are critical. While this Empowerment Parenting Program in Colorado focused on refugee children, the program evaluation reveals the necessity of reforming thoroughly U.S. resettlement policies and programs, which heavily focus on the early stages of settlement, and largely ignores the long-term needs of refugee families and children, greatly impacting those with unique situations and needs.

Also, as indicated in the Empowerment Parenting Program, collaborations between resettlement agencies and interstate social service agencies would contribute to positive impacts on refugee families. It is recommended that government funding should support collaborative approaches, including education, training, and service provisions. While resettlement and other social service agencies serve the same population at different stages of refugees' resettlement, adjustment and assimilation processes, interand intra-agency approaches would increase programming effectiveness and efficiency. Nevertheless, provision of services developed specifically for refugee children remains essential and lack of such services would lead to further concerns over refugee children's development. Experiences from this Empowerment Parenting Program suggest that educating, training, and empowering refugee parents are helpful. However, due to the barriers that refugee families have endured, the parenting program and other family strengthening programs fail to address the specific challenges that refugee children continue to face.

SUMMARY AND CONCLUSION

Overall, like many refugee groups from the world, Somali and Somali Bantu refugees studied face clear and distinct resettlement challenges. From the positive experience of the Parenting Empowerment Program, there is an opportunity for the resettlement agency to further impact empowerment growth with strategic planning and selective partnerships. This evaluation study indicates that long-term resettlement success is contingent on recognizing the distinct challenges that each refugee group is presenting, as refugees work to become responsible and supportive parents to their children, and contributing members of American society.

It is recognized that refugee children are living in a rapidly changing American society. The majority of post-9/11 refugees might be subjected to increased discrimination, while simultaneously living below the poverty level. Changes in American social and political dynamics have resulted in tightened funding for refugee resettlement services. For refugee children, there is no current policy that ensures refugee children's long-term development. This presents a mandate for policymakers to begin deliberations on the future of U.S. refugee resettlement programs, from the perspective of children as primary and compelling stakeholders.

ACKNOWLEDGMENT

The authors would like to thank Dr. John F. Jones at the University of Denver and the Western Union Foundation for their generous support.

NOTES

1. U.S. Bureau of Citizenship and Immigration Services, *Yearbook of Immigration Statistics: 2004* (Washington, DC: U.S. Bureau of Citizenship and Immigration Services, 2004).

2. United Nations High Commissioner for Refugees, *2002 UNHCR Statistical Yearbook* (United Nations High Commissioner for Refugees, 2002).

3. Which included 26% school-age children (age 5–19). The number of refugee children is calculated by the number of refugees who had been granted permanent resident status from 1989 to 2001. Immigration and Naturalization Services, *2001 Statistical Yearbook of Immigration and Naturalization Services* (Washington, DC: Immigration and Naturalization Services, 2001)

4. Bridging Refugee Youth and Children's Services, *Refugee Minors Arriving in the United States: Statistics from FY 1997–FY 2002* (Lutheran Immigration and Refugee Service and U.S. Conference of Catholic Bishops/Migration and Refugee Services, 2003). Available at http://www.brycs.org/documents/MINORS⁻1.PDF

5. Qingwen Xu, "In the Best Interest of Immigrant and Refugee Children: Deliberating on Their Unique Circumstances," *Child Welfare* 84(5) (2005): 747–770.

6. Anna Freud and Dorothy T. Burlingham, *Children and War* (New York: Medical War Books, 1943).

7. Marina Ajdukovic and Dean Ajdukovic, "Psychological Well-Being of Refugee Children," *Child Abuse & Neglect* 17(6) (1993): 843–854; Maryanne Loughry and Eirini Flouri, "The Behavioral and Emotional Problems of Former Unaccompanied Refugee Children 3–4 years after Their Return to Vietnam," *Child Abuse & Neglect* 25(2) (2001): 249–263.

8. Patricia G. Fox, Julia Muennich Cowell, and Andrew C. Montgomery, "The Effects of Violence on Health and Adjustment of Southeast Asian Refugee Children: An interview Review," *Public Health Nursing* 11(3) (1994): 195–201.

9. William H. Sack, Gregory N. Clarke, and John Seeley, "Post-Traumatic Stress Disorder across Two Generations of Cambodian Refugees," *Journal of the American Academy of Child & Adolescent Psychiatry* 34 (1995): 1160–1166; Stevan Weine, Daniel F. Becker, Thomas H. McGlashan, Delores Vojvoda, Stephen Hartman, and Judith P. Robbins "Adolescent Survivors of 'Ethnic Cleansing': Observations on the First Year in America," *Journal of the American Academy of Child & Adolescent Psychiatry* 34 (1995): 1153–1159; Dan Savin, William H. Sack, Gregory N. Clarke, Nee Meas, and I.M. Richart. "The Khmer Adolescent Project: III A study of Trauma from Thailand's Site II Refugee Camp," *Journal of the American Academy of Child & Adolescent Psychiatry* 35 (1996): 384–391.

10. Crispin Jones and Jill Rutter, eds., *Refugee Education: Mapping the Field.* (Staffordshire, England: Trentham Books, 1998); Toyin Okitikpi and Cathy Aymer, "Social Work with African Refugee Children and Their Families," *Child and Family Social Work* 8 (2003): 213– 222.

11. Ana Marie Fantino and Alice Colak, "Refugee Children in Canada: Searching for Identity," *Child Welfare* 80(5) (2001): 587–596.

12. Perry M. Nicassio, J.D. Labarbara, P. Coburn, and R. Finley. "The Psychosocial Adjustment of the Amerasian refugees: Findings from the Personality Inventory for Children," *Journal of Nervous and Mental Disease* 174, no. 9 (1986): 541–544.

13. Samuel Noh, Morton Beiser, Violet Kaspar, Feng Hou, and Joanna Rummens. "Perceived Racial Discrimination, Depression, and Coping: A Study of Southeast Asian Refugees in Canada," *Journal of Health and Science Behavior* 40(3) (1999): 193–207.

14. Kjerstin Almqvist and Anders G. Broberg, "Mental Health and Social Adjustment in Young Refugee Children $3^{1}/_{2}$ years after Their Arrival in Sweden," *Journal of the American Academy of Child & Adolescent Psychiatry* 38(6) (1999): 723–730.

15. For example, Barry N. Stein, Occupational adjustment of refugees: The Vietnamese in the United States. *International Migration Review: IMR* 13(1) (1979): 25–45; Adrienne Chambon, "Refugee Families' Experiences: Three Family Themes—Family Disruption, Violent Trauma, and Acculturation," *Journal of Strategic and Systemic Therapies* 8(2) (1989): 3–13; Morton Beiser, et al., "Poverty, Family Process, and the Mental Health of Immigrant Children in Canada," *American Journal of Public Health* 92(2) (2002): 220–227; Rashmita S. Mistry, Elizabeth A. Vandewater, Aletha C. Huston, and Vonnie C. McLoyd. "Economic Well-Being and Children's Social Adjustment: The Role of Family Process in An Ethnically Diverse Low-Income Sample," *Child Development* 73(3) (2002): 935–951.

16. Angel Hjern, "Organized Violence and Mental Health of Refugee Children in Exile: A Six-Year Follow-Up," *Acta Paediatrica* 89(6) (2000): 722–727.

17. Monica Laude, "Assessment of Nutritional Status, Cognitive Development, and Mother-Child Interaction in Central American Refugee Children," *Pan American Journal of Public Health* 6(3) (1999): 164–171; Almqvist and Broberg, "Mental Health and Social Adjustment in Young Refugee Children $3^{1}/_{2}$ years after Their Arrival in Sweden"; Ajdukovic and Ajdukovic, "Psychological Well-Being of Refugee Children."

18. David Woodhead, *The Health and Well-being of Asylum Seekers and Refugees* (London: Kings Fund, 2000).

19. Alice Bloch, "Refugee Settlement in Britain: The Impact of Policy on Participation," *Journal of Ethnic and Migration Studies* 26(1) (2000): 75–88; Per-Adners Edin, Peter Fredriksson, and Olof Aslund, "Settlement Policies and the Economic Success of Immigrants," *Journal of Population Economics* 17 (2004): 133–155.

20. Edin, Fredriksson, and Aslund, "Settlement Policies and the Economic Success of Immigrants."

21. Hjern, "Organized Violence and Mental Health of Refugee Children in Exile."

22. Liang Tien Redick and Beverly Wood, "Cross-Cultural Problems for Southeast Asian Refugee Minors," *Child Welfare* 61(6) (1982): 365–373.

23. Val Colic-Peisker and Farida Tilbury, "'Active' and 'Passive' Resettlement: The Influence of Support Services and Refugees' Own Resources on Resettlement Style," *International Migration* 41(5) (2003): 61–91; Barbara Franz, "Bosnian Refugees and Socio-Economic Realities: Changes in Refugee and Resettlement Policies in Austria and the United States," *Journal of Ethnic and Migration Studies* 29(1) (2003): 5–26; Bloch, "Refugee Settlement in Britain.

24. Colorado Department of Human Service, *Colorado Refugee Arrivals, Federal Fiscal Year 1975-2004* (Colorado Department of Human Service, 2005). Available at http://www.cdhs.state.co.us/oss/Refugee/colorado_refugee_arrivals.htm

INDEX

ABOUT THE EDITORS
AND CONTRIBUTORS

Barbara A. Arrighi is associate professor of sociology at Northern Kentucky University. Her research interests include work and family, as well as issues related to race, class, and sexism. Her books include: *America's Shame: Women and Children in Shelter and the Degradation of Family Roles* and *Understanding Inequality: The Intersection of Race/Ethnicity, Class, and Gender.* Professor Arrighi has published in the *Journal of Family Issues* and elsewhere.

David J. Maume is professor of sociology, and Director, Kunz Center for the Study of Work and Family, at the University of Cincinnati. His teaching and research interests are in labor market inequality and work-family issues, with recent publications appearing in the *Journal of Marriage and Family*, *Work and Occupations*, and *Social Problems*. He is currently researching gender differences in providing urgent child care in dual-earner families, gender differences in the effects of supervisor characteristics on subordinates' job attitudes, and the effects of shift work on the work and family lives of retail food workers (funded by the *National Science Foundation*).

Ronald J. Angel, PhD, is professor of sociology at the University of Texas, Austin. His research and writing deal with social welfare, health policy, and the health risks faced by Hispanic and other minority populations, as well as the role of nongovernmental organizations in providing health and social services in Latin America. With Laura Lein and Jane Henrici he is author of *Poor Families in America's Health Care Crisis*, and with his wife, Jacqueline Angel, he is author of *Painful Inheritance: Health and the New Generation of Fatherless Families* (University of Wisconsin Press, 1993) and *Who will care for us? Aging and Long-term Care in Multicultural America*, (New York University Press, 1997). Professor Angel served as Editor of the *Journal of Health* *and Social Behavior* from 1994 to 1997, and he has served on the editorial boards of numerous other journals. He has administered several large grants from NIA, NIMH, NICHD, and several private foundations. He is currently involved in a large multimethod national study of the impact of welfare reform on poor families. For more information see: http://www.jhu.edu/˜welfare/.

William T. Armaline will be an assistant professor in the Justice Studies Department at San Jose State University fall of 2007. His scholarship is best described as multi-disciplinary and unflinchingly driven by and dedicated to public intellectualism and social justice. It reaches across the areas of Sociology, and Criminology. Education, and Human Rights. Generally, his teaching and research interests lie in the following areas: Racism Theory, Inequality and Social Control, Political Sociology, Social Problems, Human Rights, Inequality and Youth, Qualitative/Ethnographic Research, Participatory Action Research ("PAR"), Educational Policy, and Critical Pedagogies. He is currently finishing (dissertation) research on "Racism, Human Rights, and Juvenile Justice."

Alexandra M. Curley holds a PhD in Sociology from Boston University and is a research associate at the Center for Urban and Regional Policy at Northeastern University. Her research interests include urban poverty, social policy, and housing mobility. She has authored numerous reports on urban housing programs and several scholarly articles, including: "Theories of urban poverty and implications for public housing policy" (2005). *Journal of Sociology and Social Welfare*, 32(2), 97–119.

Garrett Albert Duncan is associate professor in arts and sciences at Washington University in St. Louis. He holds appointments in education, African and African American studies, American culture studies, and urban studies. His research focuses broadly on race, culture, education, and society.

Roseanne L. Flores is currently an assistant professor in the Department of Psychology at Hunter College of the City University of New York. She is currently interested in the effects of poverty on young children's cognitive and linguistic development. More specifically, she is interested in how environments of poverty influence children's understanding and use of time concepts, and the link between temporal language and literacy practices within the preschool population. Some of her current research examines the relationship between teacher's reading practices and children's use of temporal language during story-book reading. More recently Professor Flores has begun to examine the relationship between multiple environmental risk factors, such as poverty, violence and parental education and children's literacy skills.

Jane Gilbert-Mauldon is associate professor in the Goldman School of Public Policy and associate director of the Survey Research Center at the University of California, Berkeley. She is coprincipal Investigator on the evaluation of the welfare time limits in California. Her other research interests include foster care, reproductive health, and transitions to adulthood among disadvantaged youth.

Jane Henrici, PhD, is an anthropologist with an interest in gender and ethnicity in their relationship to poverty and development. She conducts research on policy change and social programs and their effects on poorer women in the U.S., and on tourism and export development and their interaction with ethnicity and gender in Peru. Henrici is coauthor with Ronald Angel and Laura Lein of *Poor Families in America's Health Care Crisis: How the Other Half Pays*, (Cambridge University Press 2006) and editor of *Doing Without: Women and Work after Welfare Reform* (University of Arizona Press 2006). She is assistant professor in the Department of Anthropology, and affiliate of the Center for Research on Women and the Hooks Institute for Social Change, at the University of Memphis.

Laura Lein, PhD, is professor in the School of Social Work and the Department of Anthropology at the University of Texas at Austin. She is a social anthropologist whose work has concentrated on the interface between families in poverty and the institutions that serve them. She received her doctorate in social anthropology from Harvard University in 1973. Her research on families in poverty has extended over two decades. She recently coauthored (with Ronald Angel and Jane Henrici) *Poor Families in America's Health Care Crisis* (Cambridge University Press, 2006). She is the author, with Kathryn Edin, of *Making Ends Meet: How Single Mothers Survive Welfare and Low-Wage Work* (New York: Russell Sage Foundation, 1997). She is also continuing work on the experience of welfare reform among groups in Texas and on the experience of poverty among families living in the Monterrey/San Antonio corridor.

Rebecca A. London is Associate Director of Research at the John W. Gardner Center for Youth and Their Communities at Stanford University. Her research concentrates on low-income families and high-risk youth, examining programs and policies aimed at improving their well-being.

Denise Pearson, PhD, is the assistant dean of academics and director of the Alternative Dispute Resolution Program at the University of Denver's University College (UCOL). Her research interests evolve around leadership and organizational development at the nexus of conflict analysis and resolution. She has worked directly with Somali-Bantu refugees in Colorado and collaborated with the NGOs and other agencies that work on behalf of resettling this population. The work includes examination and analysis of intervention efforts at the community and family level.

Heidi Sommer, M.P.P. is a PhD candidate at the Goldman School of Public Policy, Univeristy of California, Berkeley. She has written on the policy response to homelessness in the United States and the impact of time limits on family formation and well-being. Current research focus also includes the provision and evaluation of independent living services for emancipating foster care youth.

Hassan Tajalli is an associate professor of political science at Texas State University. He received his PhD from the University of Texas at Austin, his MA and MBA from University of North Texas, and his BBA. from the Iranian Institute of Accounting. Dr. Tajalli teaches graduate courses in statistics, methodology, and public policy. He has published numerous articles on various American public policies.

Kathleen Wells is a professor of social work at the Mandel School of Applied Social Sciences at Case Western Reserve University, Cleveland, Ohio. Her research interests include substantive issues in child mental health and child welfare and methodological issues in research syntheses and qualitative methods. She received the 2005 Humanitatae Literary Award-Herbert A. Raskin Child Welfare Article Award from the North American Resource Center for Child Welfare for part of the work reported in the chapter in this volume.

Gail E. Wolfe is a doctoral student in the Department of Education at Washington University in St. Louis. Her areas of scholarly interest include educational history and urban education, with a focus on issues of gender and race.

Qingwen Xu, PhD, is an assistant professor of Boston College Graduate School of Social Work. Professor Xu's major research focuses on immigrant and refugee children and their families, law and social work, and social development and community service.